International

Spa Management

Principles and practice

Sarah Rawlinson and Tim Heap

(G) **Goodfellow Publishers Ltd**

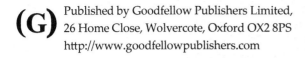 Published by Goodfellow Publishers Limited,
26 Home Close, Wolvercote, Oxford OX2 8PS
http://www.goodfellowpublishers.com

British Library Cataloguing in Publication Data: a catalogue record for this title is available from the British Library.

Library of Congress Catalog Card Number: on file.

ISBN: 978-1-910158-69-2

 Design and typesetting by P.K. McBride, www.macbride.org.uk

Cover design by Cylinder

Printed by Baker & Taylor, www.baker-taylor.com

Contents

Preface   v

About the editors   vii

Contributors   viii

1   **The Evolution of Spa**   1
Sarah Rawlinson

2   **The Spa Industry Today**   14
Angela Anthonisz and Isobel Stockdale

3   **Thermal and Mineral Springs**   23
Louise Buxton

4   **Eco-spa: Sustainability Agenda in the Spa Industry**   36
Gaurav Chawla

5   **The Wellness Industry: From Therapy to Hedonism**   49
Pascal Mandelartz and Isobel Stockdale

6   **Principles and Practices of Spa Consumer Behaviour**   60
Iride Azara

7   **Guest Service and the Guest Journey**   73
Angela Anthonisz, Tim Heap and Lorraine Baker

8   **Spa Operations Management**   83
Faith Samkange, Amon Simba and Lorraine Baker

9   **Selling the Total Spa Product**   99
Louise Buxton

10   **Marketing for the Spa Industry**   114
Eleni Michopoulou

11 Developing an Effective Human Resources Strategy   130
Angela Anthonisz, Tim Heap and Olivia Ramsbottom

12 Finance for the Spa Industry   146
Tony Loynes and Victoria Rosamond

13 Training and Development in the Spa Industry   156
Sarah Rawlinson

14 Strategic Management in the Spa Industry   175
Tim Heap and Angela Anthonisz

15 Future Directions   185
Tim Heap

Index   193

Preface

This book been produced by the academic team at the University of Derby, with contributions from Angela Anthonitsz from the University of Northampton, and Gaurav Chawla from University of South Wales. The book is long overdue and is driven both by the demand from the industry for graduate level employees, and from the increasing number of universities and colleges that are offering undergraduate and postgraduate degrees within spa and wellness related studies. It is further proof of the development of spa and wellness as a legitimate academic subject area for study, and fills the gap in the academic literature for a management text.

The chapters use current situational analysis of the industry, validated by research undertaken by the industry and the academic team. The approach is to test each of the current paradigms that form the basis for management in spas, and that in turn has exposed new areas for further research and identified and/or confirmed many of the challenges that are facing the industry. We look at the characteristics of the business to create typologies, rather than the traditional method of identifying type of facility and treatment. By defining the characteristics we are then able to explore each area (e.g. finance, marketing, HRM) in relation to the spa business and not in generic service sector terms.

The industry is experiencing sustained exponential growth, fueled by continuous product development, re-branding and training of a workforce for the future. To sustain growth and maximize profits spas need to be learning organisations that demonstrate how training and development improve organisational performance and support business decision making, and put to an end the unacceptable levels of staff turnover. We introduce the employee experience journey, which through the use of HRM strategy can mitigate the negative impacts of those high turnover figures. As wellness can be a hedonistic indulgence, as well as a therapeutic endeavour, we explore the customer service journey from both sides of the service encounter. We conclude that the industry needs to continually focus on the individual emotional responses to the spa/wellness journey.

The book is by necessity a snapshot of the industry, but we conclude that competition has led to a forward thinking, innovative industry which continuously drives customer satisfaction levels upwards and unlike many other service sector industries it never stands still.

Sarah Rawlinson

Tim Heap

Acknowledgements

The editors gratefully acknowledge the contributors and industry partners for their chapters and case study material that we hope will provide interesting and stimulating discussions and help prepare students for graduate positions in one of the world's fastest growing sectors. We would like to acknowledge the work of the Global Spa Summit in their contribution to the research that underpins many of the chapters in this book. Our thanks also go to the staff at Goodfellows for their patience and support.

About the editors

Sarah Rawlinson is the Head of Department of Hotel, Resort and Spa Management, University of Derby. She has led the development of spa management as a subject area in higher education in the UK. The University of Derby is currently the world leader in spa management degrees and provides graduates to some of the most prestigious spas in the world. She has worked in education for over 20 years, including teaching, management and research, and has published several journal articles and book chapters. Sarah has been invited to speak at international conferences, and has undertaken research on the impact of spa graduates on spa businesses, and the development of curriculum, work-based learning and the different use of knowledge in the workplace. Her most recent teaching and research focus has been on reconfiguring tourism destinations.

Tim Heap is a University Principal Tutor and Research Manager at the University of Derby, and has developed an extensive research profile in the field of tourism and destination management. He currently teaches at undergraduate, postgraduate and PhD level in the UK, and has international teaching experience in a number of countries including Switzerland, Zimbabwe, Israel and Malawi.

Contributors

Angela Anthonisz is a Senior Lecturer in Tourism and Events at Northampton University, and has recently relocated back to the UK after 5 years working in hospitality education in Dubai. With an international academic career, she has also worked in Switzerland, Israel and Hong Kong. Before moving into academia 18 years ago, Angela spent a number of years in the hospitality, tourism and events industry in the UK and has run her own business. She is currently in the final stages of a PhD at the University of Derby, specialising in Strategy and Human Capital.

Iride Azara is a Senior Lecturer in Tourism at the University of Derby and the Masters Scheme Leader for the Postgraduate taught courses in tourism, hospitality, events and international spa management. Her research is on host and guest relationships, cultural change and tourism performance within socially and spatially regulated spaces of encounter. She is particularly interested in changing dynamics of cultural practices such as heritage, festivals and cultural tourism within sensitive environments. She has led the development of the *International Spa and Wellness Journal* and now serves as a European editor.

Lorraine Baker is a Programme Leader of the Foundation Degree in International Spa Management and teaches both on the FDSc and BSc programmes at the University of Derby. She is a graduate of the University's spa management programme and has a background in hospitality, spa and sports massage. She has a passion and interest in spa treatments and the guest journey. Lorraine enjoys using her experiences to develop students in their practical skills and knowledge, and is part of the team that helped the University's commercial day spa win 'Day Spa of the Year' 2016.

Louise Buxton is a Senior Lecturer in the Department of Hotel, Resort and Spa Management at the University of Derby. Louise is passionate about professionalization of the spa industry and widening participation in higher education. Her research interests include consumer behaviour and the evolution of spa and wellness.

Gaurav Chawla is currently working as Course Leader for BA (Hons) Hotel and Hospitality Management at the University of South Wales. He is also pursuing his PhD, focusing on food waste prevention in the hospitality sector. Gaurav's research interests include sustainability, food waste management and pro-environmental behaviours.

Tony Loynes is the Deputy Head of Department with responsibility for the Events Management subject area at the University of Derby. He draws on his extensive industry experience to ensure that students graduate with the relevant skills and subject expertise to enter the world of work immediately on completion of their studies.

Pascal Mandelartz is a lecturer in Tourism and Event Management at the School of Hotel, Resort and Spa Management at the University of Derby. His research interests include subcultures in tourism, the tourist bubble, tourism within the risk society and wellness attractions in touristscapes. His work examines tourist behaviour in terms of attitudes, perceptions and response mechanisms as well as providing insight into destination and attraction development.

Eleni Michopoulou is a Senior Lecturer in Business Management at the University of Derby. Her research interests include technology and e-tourism, and accessible and wellness tourism. She is the author of a number of journal articles and book chapters on these subjects. Additionally, she is a founding member of the Global Wellness Institute's Wellness Tourism Initiative and the European editor of the *International Journal of Spa and Wellness*.

Olivia Ramsbottom is a Senior Lecturer, Programme Leader and Management Trainer and Consultant. Her expertise is built on management and teaching and training qualifications, as well as years of experience as a service sector manager in organisations as varied as an internet training provider, a membership organisation for accountants, a funding bod,y and universities.

Victoria Rosamond joined the University of Derby in 2012 as Programme Leader for the BSc (Hons) International Spa Management. After graduaing from the University of Derby's spa management programme she travelled to Hong Kong to work with the prestigious Mandarin Oriental Hotel Group. She returned to the UK to become the first graduate of the University's MA International Spa Management programme. Prior to Victoria's current role she held the position of Regional Business Manager and Retail Operations Executive with British spa brand *Elemis*. Victoria is currently engaging in further research into possible new programmes within the subject areas and aims to develop her academic and published profile within the spa industry.

Faith Samkange's research interests lie in Technology, Management and Pedagogics, Development Economics and Gender issues in management. Her speciality is Hospitality Management. Her research activities with the Rockefeller foundation on community development included work across several African countries. Currently she is working on digital pedagogical transformation research with the Swiss Hotel Management school. Her experience in the industry spans over two decades, having worked in Canada, Switzerland, Africa and United Kingdom

Isobel Stockdale is the Deputy Head of Department for Spa, Tourism and Wellness at the University of Derby. She has taught at the university for 20 years. Isobel has extensive industry experience in spa and beauty, and regularly collaborates with industry. She was part of the team to develop the world's first spa degree, and was instrumental in the design and development of the University's commercial day spa. Isobel is a regular contributor to trade press and her research interests are vocational degrees, spa design and development.

1 The Evolution of Spa

Sarah Rawlinson

Introduction

Much has already been written about the evolution of spa beginning with ancient civilisations through to the Victorian era and the fashion for taking the waters. This simple time series view of evolution tends to miss the key factors that were involved in the development of those spas, and most importantly those products, over time and space. The current industry product portfolio in broad terms includes tourism, health, sustainability and wellness, with organic change often adapting from historic products into consumer driven demand for new products that are often global. This has led to a curious mix of brands and sub brands that can all trace their roots to other traditional products that were built upon history and culture. Current demands are, in essence, dichotomous as they are both unique and global.

This chapter explains how the spa product has evolved from the historic definitions of spa and its products to a globalised industry built upon that history and culture. We explore the evolution of spa from the natural thermal spring waters discovered by the Romans to the establishment of treatments for the wealthy in beautiful spa resorts. We trace the development of the hospital system, from the medicinal properties of the waters and access to medical treatments, and how this has led to the globalisation of the health care system and a billion dollar global health tourism industry. We see how the fashionable leisure activity of the Victorians to 'take the waters' has grown into a wellness tourism industry worth billions, and finally we discover well known organisations that have their origins in spa.

From natural thermal springs to global spa treatments

The benefits of therapies and treatments have been packaged and sold by a spa industry that has grown rapidly in recent years. These therapies and treatments have their origins in the nineteenth century and use thermal waters in hydrotherapy treatments; espouse the benefits of fresh air and exercise in beautiful locations based on the philosophy of the sanatorium movement; use naturopathy and alternative medicine such as homeopathy, herbalism, and acupuncture; and have developed manipulative therapies from around the world into massage therapies such as Tui na massage, Swedish massage and Indian head massage.

■ Hydrotherapy

Hydrotherapy is the use of water in the treatment of different conditions such as arthritis and rheumatic complaints. The treatment often takes place in spa water as it is believed by many that the mineral content of spa water has special health-giving properties.

The first hydrotherapy spa was established in Grafenburg in Germany (formally in Czechoslovakia) in 1829 by Vincent Priessnitz. The spa offered a range of treatments including diet, exercise, bathing, fresh air and health. The 'Priessnitz cure' included various cold water treatments that are still in use today.

Fr. Sebastian Kneipp continued Priessnitz's work and popularised it in 1880. The 'Kneipp cure' is a form of hydrotherapy involving the application of water through various methods, temperatures and pressures. Kneipp advocated a comprehensive natural healing treatment that covers human physical, mental and spiritual wholeness and is used today in a variety of ways in many spas to help relax tired muscles and relieve stress. (Crebbin-Bailey *et al.*, 2005; van Tubergen and van der Linden, 2002)

■ Sanatorium movement

The first sanatorium, dedicated to the treatment of tuberculosis, was established by Hermann Brehmer in 1854 in Görbersdorf, Silesia (now Poland). Sanatoriums provided rest, a healthy diet, gentle exercise and fresh air which, although they did not cure tuberculosis, provided some relief and helped to strengthen immune systems. In Switzerland, many sanatoriums provided entertainment for patients, and are an early example of spa resorts. They were located in mountain villages such as Davos where the air was deemed to be particularly pure.

■ Naturopathy

Naturopathy is a form of alternative medicine using a variety of 'natural' modalities, including homeopathy, herbalism, and acupuncture, as well as diet and lifestyle counselling, and was first used by Dr John Scheel in 1895. Johann Schroth, was the first modern naturopath to use clinical nutrition, or the use of diet as a therapy. According to the General Council and Register of Naturopaths (n.d.) his original treatment, the *Schrothkur*, or dry diet, is still used in central Europe. Naturopaths continue to prescribe nutrition, food rotation, wholefood diets, dietary support or restrictions as part of naturopathic treatment.

Manipulative therapies

Physiology was a rapidly growing science championed by a Swedish physiologist Peter Henry Ling who was an advocate of the beneficial therapeutic effects of physical exercise. He is credited with starting the Swedish Gymnastic Movement System. The Swedish massage system, a popular therapy, is often accredited to Ling but it was developed by Johan Mezger, who adopted the French terms of *effleurage, petrissage, tapotement,* and *friction* that are associated with the classic massage of today. It involves the application of pressure to relax muscles to increase the oxygen flow in the blood and release toxins from the muscle. It is one of the most common and best known massage techniques used today. Ling gave scientific credibility to the massage stokes. He learnt the benefits of hands-on body treatment as a therapy from Ming, a Chinese martial artist and expert in Tui na. Massage and remedial exercise grew in popularity with English nurses providing musculoskeletal rehabilitation on injured British soldiers during the First World War. Demand for massage therapy grew in other areas of medicine and is commonly used in hospitals, nursing homes and birthing centres. It is also used in physical therapy and in chiropractic clinics to treat pain, increase circulation and accelerate the healing of injured muscles. Massage is also used as a preventative measure to maintain health and promote wellbeing.

Thalassotherapy

Thalassotherapy was developed by Dr. La Bonardhiere in 1867. Thalassotherapy is the use of seawater, sea products and shore climate as a form of therapy believed to have beneficial effects on the skin. The International Thalassotherapy Federation (Fédération International de Thalassothérapie Mer & Santé) was founded in France, in 1986. France continues to be the centre for thalassotherapy and has nearly fifty thalassotherapy centres. The best-known thalassotherapy centres are in Biarritz, Saint-Jean-de-Luz and resorts in Brittany.

Growth of global spa therapies

The globalisation of the spa industry has inevitably led to a growth in spa therapies from around the world. It is possible to experience spa therapies that have their roots in ancient civilisations, and are increasingly focused on holistic health and wellbeing, and not just pampering and relaxation. For example, Temazcal is an ancient Mexican practice dating back to Mayan and Aztec cultures. The treatment, by a trained healer known as a Temazcalera, takes the guest through a process that seeks to cleanse their body, mind and spirit and leave them revitalised and reinvigorated. A further example is Ayurveda, a traditional healing modality from India, based on the belief that health and wellness depend on the balance between the mind, body, and spirit.

From 'cure' to medical and health tourism

The curative properties of mineral waters have been known since Roman times, although records of the treatments and uses can only be traced from the 16th century when mineral springs, rich in iron and thermal waters, began to be used for medicinal purposes. The identification of the relationship between properties, outcomes (in terms of effects), products (in terms of medicines first and therapies second) and places were established as the basis for spas as we know them today. To ensure access to these cures, charities were established as early as 1570 to provide the poor with access to bathing in the medicinal waters. These charities established charity hospitals and were the pioneers of the hospital system we have today. Many European spa towns continue to provide health related treatments supported by national health care systems. (Langham and Wells, 2003; Riva and Cesana, 2013; Skinner, 2015; Starr, 1982; Waddington, 2000; Wilson, 1996) The health services provided throughout Europe continue to include special diets, vitamin-complex treatments, herbal remedies, hydrotherapy, thalassotherapy and other treatments that have their origins in spa. (Gilbert and Van De Weerdt, 1991).

The Devonshire Royal Hospital in Buxton, Derbyshire was established by the Buxton Bath Charity in 1779 and was the last hydropathic center to close in the UK in 2000. It continued to provide treatments using its thermal waters when it became part of the National Health Service in 1948, and the hospital developed links with teaching hospitals specialising in rheumatology, rehabilitation and orthopedics (Copp, 2004). By 1978 Leamington Spa was the last remaining spa in the UK. (Smith and Puczkó 2010)

Rheumatologists were mainly responsible for the decline of the spa culture in the UK. They found spa treatment unscientific, but did not produce any scientific evidence to prove the ineffectiveness and ignored the millions of patients over the years that had benefited from spa treatment in many countries throughout Europe. (Gilbert and Van De Weerdt, 1991). The advent of modern medicine, as we know it, meant that the whole person, system-based approach of natural medicine was no longer popular. (Duffy, 2011; Strohecker, 2006). These specific uses were now emerging from a scientifically based approach to fit products to specific illnesses or traumas. The consumer was, and still is, sold on benefits that are research based and can be explained in terms of natural science.

In Germany the reform of the health care system did not only consider increased efficiency, quality and higher individual financial contributions to the system, but it also placed a greater emphasis on prevention and the personal responsibility of the individual. This has led to considerable growth in what is known as the 'second healthcare market' (Pforr and Locher, 2014). This includes wellness products and services such as spas. It is still possible to be prescribed a medical 'cure' at a registered spa town through German medical insurance companies. It must be prescribed by a doctor and the treatment should minimise or delay the development of a potential condition or treat a chronic condition. Once approved the patient is sent to a certified spa for a holistic experience of exercise, nutrition, relaxation and motivation designed by the medical team. The focus is to provide a natural and relaxing environment to prevent the further development of the illness.

In the Czech Republic, Danubius Health Spas specialise in medical and rehabilitation and provide medically regulated treatments prescribed by a team of expert physicians and specialists experienced in the fields of natural and spa medicine. They provide treatments for conditions related to rheumatism, arthritis, kidney infection, chronic inflammatory degenerative diseases, posture issues, digestive issues, blood pressure and respiratory conditions. (HealthCzech 2016).

Medical and health tourism is an area of significant growth involving travel for medical and health purposes. Whilst the terms are often used interchangeably, they are distinctly different. Medical tourism involves tourists travelling to another country other than where they reside for the purpose of receiving medical care. The most common procedures include cosmetic and dental surgery, hip replacements, transplants and infertility treatment. According to Hall (2013) countries including China, Cuba, Hungary, India, Thailand, Malaysia and Singapore actively promote and compete for medical tourism. Health tourism can be defined as "those forms of tourism which are centrally focused on physical health, but which also improve mental and spiritual well-being and increase the capacity of individuals to satisfy their own needs and function better in their environment and society". (Smith and Puczko, 2015:206). The growing interest in wellbeing has led to significant developments in products and services in the tourism and leisure sector to meet this consumer demand.

Many companies are realising that the health and wellness of their workforce is an important issue. The reason for a growing emphasis on employee wellbeing can vary from reducing absenteeism, and improving health and wellbeing to the cost of providing health care and the need to compete for the best employees. In 2008, at the World Economic Forum in Davos, Switzerland, CEOs from 13 multinationals called on business leaders to take action on workplace wellness around the globe (Vesey 2012). Towers Watson (2011), a leading global professional service company, conducted a multinational workforce health survey in 2011 including 149 participants representing 5.2 million employees in 37 countries. They found that around a third (32%) of all respondents have a workforce health strategy and nearly half (47%) are planning to have one. These strategies include corporate wellness programmes that typically involve activities as wide ranging as yoga classes, fitness programmes and challenges, lunchtime stress management and work life balance seminars, advice on financial management, healthy recipe exchanges, cooking classes and weight loss challenges. Towers Watson identified that the top five wellness programmes offered health screenings, vaccinations, mental health/stress management, subsidised fitness clubs and healthy eating.

The health outcomes of corporate wellness programmes can include smoking cessation; weight loss; the management of diabetes, cholesterol, blood pressure and stress; and advice on diet and nutrition, sleep, anxiety and personal health. The strategic advantage of a happy, healthy workforce provides a number of benefits for employers including lower levels of absenteeism, higher job satisfaction and work productivity and better employee retention. Employees are the most valuable asset to many companies and the welfare of employees can have a direct impact on the success of a company. Employee wellness programmes can help companies reduce costs and improve employee wellbeing.

From the fashion to 'take the waters' to wellness tourism

The evolution of spa can be traced from the natural thermal spring waters discovered by the Romans to the establishment of treatments for the wealthy in beautiful spa resorts such as Fusion Maia Da Nang, Vietnam or Lefay Resort & Spa, Gagnano, Italy. The interest in wellness tourism today, for example, still has its origins in the Victorian spa towns of Bath, Buxton, and Leamington Spa and coastal resorts that developed from centres of medical treatment to fashionable leisure and tourism destinations, such as Teignmouth or Biarritz. Large hotels were constructed to meet the demand, fashionable town houses sprang up, and leisure and entertainment facilities were built that formed the classic model of seaside resort development.

Spa towns were quick to respond to advances in medicine which led to them losing their original purpose of 'cure' and becoming leisure destinations. Changing demands and expectations of their new pleasure seeking visitors, centered on social occasions, receptions, balls, horse races, adventures and gambling. Victorian spa town planners recognised the value of green spaces and the need for visitors to enjoy the scenery. They developed parks and green spaces to enhance the visitor experience and spa towns developed as tourist centres that provided access to a rural experience (Borsay, 2012). Spa towns became a base to explore the countryside and visitors were encouraged to take walks and drives for the benefit of their health. According to UNESCO (n.d.):

> *"spa towns enjoy a special relationship between their urban fabric and surrounding landscape. This landscape setting was promoted and managed as an essential part of the 'spa offer' and contributed to the cure. Accordingly, there are complex*

cultural values associated with landscape in and around spa towns. The landscape setting of the spas was an essential part of the prescribed spa cure and so the area surrounding the spa town with the spa buildings is held to be a 'Therapeutic Landscape'. There the spa life entered thanks to the promenades for activities and social gatherings of spa guests in an aesthetically extraordinary ambience".

Visitors travelled not only to experience wellbeing activities and health treatments, but also to engage in cultural heritage and entertainment. Spa towns are a testimony to a successful social, scientific and cultural movement that provided a stage for international events, fairs, exhibitions and audiences for composers, musician and artists. Theatres, concert halls, assembly rooms, colonnades with shops and open air bandstands were erected to entertain visitors.

The development of the railways provided easy access to spa towns, bringing increasing numbers of visitors. The growing popularity of spa towns with the middle classes was balanced by the departure of the aristocracy and competition from seaside towns. Seaside resorts became the alternative to spa towns along with the belief that sea water had medicinal properties. Sea bathing became a respectable middle-class pursuit in the Victorian era with the expansion of the railways to the coast. Many of the traditional seaside activities, such as Punch and Judy shows, donkey rides, roundabouts and boat trips, stem from Victorian traditions.

These are early examples of tourist destinations, and their management led to the development of an emerging tourist industry. What was evident at the time, and remains important today, is that a successful wellness tourism offer needs to focus on its natural assets, the natural environment of the destination and to draw on local traditions to create wellness experiences (Pesonen *et al.*, 2011; Georgiev and Vasileva, 2010; Quintela *et al.*, 2011; hun Kim and Batra, 2009; Magdalini and Paris, 2009; Laing and Weiler, 2008; Mair, 2005; Messerli and Oyama, 2004). The success of any tourism destination is where its competitiveness is built on markets that best match its resources (Sheldon and Park, 2009; Prideaux *et al.*, 2013). Voigt *et al.* (2011) suggest that the wellness tourism offer is the sum of a destination's physical, psychological, spiritual and social wellbeing resources. An early example of how Victorian resorts branded and promoted the destinations' attributes is still evident today in the "Skegness is so bracing" poster selling the physical, psychological and social benefits of the sea air and visiting the seaside. (Figure 1.1)

Figure 1.1.

These early examples are mirrored in the exponential growth of wellness tourism destinations worldwide, now reaching a global phenomenon. The model for success depends on a mix of health and wellness assets that help to create a unique selling proposition and distinctive brands to attract the new wellness tourists, who are self-aware, and seek enhanced well-being, health and happiness (Rawlinson and Wiltshier, 2017). The characteristic of the wellness tourist then leads to the niche tourism offer or brand; this then signifies that the location has a wellness tourism 'niche product' tag.

Wellness tourists appear to have similar characteristics to eco-tourists, cultural tourists and sports tourists, and this provides a destination with numerous opportunities to cross-market niche tourism products. They may contribute more to the economy of the destination than other types of tourists because wellness tourists are more likely to be wealthier, better educated and spend more in the destination (Yeung, 2013). Wellness tourists are also seen to be more likely to contribute to the sustainability of cultural assets and events such as local festivals, and to engage in sports and sporting activities, adventure and other activities (Clapham, 2015). The historic changes, noted above, in the Victorian seaside resorts, with changing tourist typologies leading to new emergent products and consumers may, however, be repeated within the 'new' wellness destinations. Clapham's links to sustainability may therefore be tenuous, as the Victorian Punch and Judy and Donkey rides are replaced by modern day aqua parks and 'off-roading' adventures.

The destinations are putting up more barriers than the Victorians, as they suggest wellness tourists are more self-aware; they seek enhanced well-being, health and happiness. Destinations are therefore reinforcing the nature of the leisure and recreation offers, or brands, to continue to meet the needs of the wellness tourist. Where once the spa town would encourage walking and drives in the countryside, wellness resorts are investing in recreation and sports projects, including hiking and cycling (Hadzik and Grabara, 2014). This is where the comparison ends. Instead of offering the traditional cultural activities, horseracing and gambling, wellness resorts take a more holistic approach to wellbeing including physical, psychological, spiritual and social wellbeing

From spa to multi-national business

Sustainability of the wellness tourism offer depends upon the economic contribution of those tourists, as we cannot have the other pillars of sustainability without finance. The companies outlined below, many of which we are familiar with today, secured their future and their economic sustainability by building a strong brand around naturopathic medicine, healing remedies, cosmetics, food products and water.

■ Kellogg's

John Harvey Kellogg, a natural health pioneer, founded a sanatorium at Battle Creek, Michigan, helping people to maintain good health through diet, exercise and other lifestyle measures. He developed the well-known corn flakes with his brother, for his patients at Battle Creek Sanitarium during the 1880s. W.K. Kellogg opened the Battle Creek Toasted Corn Flake Company in 1906 and Kellogg's became the largest cereal maker in the world. (Strohecker, 2006) The Kellogg brothers were influenced by William James who emphasised the relationship between spirituality and health in his 'mind-cure movement', more generally known as New Thought and Christian Science.

■ Kneipp

Kneipp is more commonly known for naturopathy than hydrotherapy. Kneipbrød (Kneipp Bread), his bread recipe based on whole wheat, is the most commonly eaten bread in Norway. Kneipp went on to form a partnership with a Würzburg pharmacist to produce naturopathic medicine and healing remedies using only natural plant essences and pure ingredients. They created the formulas and developed products that form the basis of an internationally operating company with headquarters in Würzburg (Bavaria, Germany), who continue to export medicinal products, nutritional supplements, body care and bath products to many countries throughout the world. (Kneipp, 2016).

■ Buxton water

According to Gordon (2012: 53) bottled water is 'the real fortune of the spa business'. The UK bottled water industry is worth over £2bn p.a., and natural mineral water accounts for 60% of the UK bottled water market. The spa town of Buxton in Derbyshire began selling its water as early as1912, and by 1987 Perrier UK was selling 600,000 bottles of Buxton water a year. Today, Buxton Water has grown to be the Number 1 mineral water brand in the UK and is owned by Nestle Water. In 2010, 180 million litres of Buxton bottled water were sold in the UK, generating £50.5m of turnover at the Buxton plant and supporting approximately100 jobs.

■ Vichy

The spa town of Vichy in France bottled its water as early as 1684 (Gordon, 2012). In 2012, 40 million bottles were produced, of which 20% were exported overseas. Vichy has taken its economic security a step further and established a partnership with L'Oreal in the production of cosmetics derived from Vichy water. Vichy also produces sweets known as Bassin de Vichy or Vichy pastilles, renowned as a course of treatment in the 19th century spa town to aid digestion. Some of today's largest food companies can be traced back to the healthy diets and advice provided in spa resorts.

Conclusion

Interest in spa and wellness continues, not only amongst the ageing baby boomer population who helped revitalise an interest in spa in the 1970s, but also with a younger generation well informed on the benefits of fitness and wellbeing in their busy stressful lives. The resurgence of spa has led to a departure from the original concept of spas as a place to recover from illness or injury, to a focus on prevention of illness and maintenance of good health and wellbeing. According to Smith and Puczkó (2010) Central and Eastern Europeans continue to focus on traditional medical tourism in thermal baths, whereas Western Europeans are developing wellness and holistic tourism in spas, hotels and retreats. Northern Europeans are developing wellness products based on landscape and lifestyle, whereas Southern Europeans are still promoting thermal baths in addition to thalassotherapy, but many of these have been regenerated and now include elements of wellness tourism. Spas are combining the therapeutic properties of mineral and thermal waters with wellness treatments and therapies and an enjoyable holiday experience.

The following chapter explores how this diverse set of products and brands fits within the emergent service sector economy. The ownership of the brand, the operations management, the location of the destination being part of the globalisation of a product that is now worth billions of dollars to the global economy.

Case study: Champneys

One of the first spa resorts in the UK was Champneys Health Spa. It is an example of how spa has evolved from a nature cure resort to a multi- faceted spa business.

In 1925, Stanley Lief, a pioneer in the field of naturopathy, purchased the stately home of Champneys, converting it into a Nature Cure resort. Champneys Health Spa was the first health resort in the UK and a forerunner in re-establishing an interest in holistic health and wellbeing (Champneys, 2016). Champneys continued as a health resort under various ownerships and with varying degrees of success during the mid-20th century. It became the first UK health spa chain under the patronage of the Purdrew family in the late 1990s.

In 2004, Champneys launched a range of spa products called the Champneys Collection, and in 2006 Champneys opened a high street day spa in Chichester. Champneys Day Spas now operate in six locations. In April 2011, Champneys re-launched its spa product range in the UK with Boots the Chemist, and is now available internationally. In 2012, Champneys teamed up with controversial doctor Professor Mohamed Taranissi to offer IVF treatments at the spa.

Today, Champneys is synonymous with beauty, health and wellbeing in luxury surroundings. Its philosophy is "to help people who visit Champneys to detoxify their mind and body. Whether you want to change the way you feel, the way you look or the way you live, we have the know-how, to help you improve your lifestyle and wellbeing, through pampering treatments, healthy food and fitness".

Image 2: Lief's Nature Cure Resort, Champneys, Tring, Herts. Possibly one of the earliest cards illustrating the resort

References

Borsay, P. (2012). Town or country? British spas and the urban-rural interface. *Journal of Tourism History*, **4**(2), 155-169.

Champneys (2016). Champneys' Philosophy. http://www.champneys.com/about-champneys/philosophy/. Accessed 09 July 2016.

Clapham, M. (2015). BRDC Continental. http://bdrc-coninental.com/opinions/wellness/. Accessed 15 October 2015.

Copp, E.P (2004). The Devonshire Royal Hospital Buxton, *British Society for Rheumatology* **43**(5), 385-386 doi:10.1093/rheumatology/keg008. Accessed 09 July 2016

Crebbin-Bailey, J., Harcup, J. and Harrington, J. (2005). *The Spa Book: The Official Guide to Spa Therapy*, Thomson.

Duffy, T. P. (2011). The Flexner Report 100 years later. *The Yale Journal of Biology and Medicine*, **84**(3), 269–276.

Eylers, E. (2014). Planning the Nation: The sanatorium movement in Germany, *The Journal of Architecture*, **19**(5), 667-692.

Georgiev, G. and Vasileva, M (2010). Some problems related to the definitions of Baleno, Spa and Wellness Tourism. *Tourism & Hospitality Management* Conference Proceedings.

General Council and Register of Naturopaths (n.d.). http://gcrn.org.uk/introduction/early-history-of-naturopathy./ Accessed 09 July 2016.

Gilbert, D. and Van De Weerdt, M. (1991). The health care tourism product in Western Europe, *The Tourist Review*, **46**(2), 5-10.

Gordon, B. (2012). Reinventions of a spa town: the unique case of Vichy, *Journal of Tourism History*, **4**(1), 35-55.

hun Kim, B. and Batra, A. (2009). Healthy-living behavior status and motivational characteristics of foreign tourists to visit wellness facilities in Bangkok. In *The 2nd Annual PSU Phuket Research Conference, Proceedings, Prince of Songkla University* (pp. 1-8).

Hadzik, A. and Grabara, M. (2014). Investments in recreational and sports infrastructure as a basis for the development of sports tourism on the example of spa municipalities, *Polish Journal of Sport and Tourism*, **21**(2).

Hall, C. M. (2013). *Medical Tourism: The ethics, regulation, and marketing of health mobility.* Routledge.

HealthCzech (2016). http://www.healthczech.com/treatments/medical-spas-and-rehabilitation/featured-clinics-and-hospitals/danubius/. Accessed 09 July 2016.

Kneipp (2016). http://www.kneippus.com/the-kneipp-story/. Accessed 09 July 2016.

Laing, J. and Weiler, B. (2008). Mind, body and spirit: Health and wellness tourism in Asia. in J Cochrane (ed.), *Asian Tourism: Growth and Change*, Oxford: Elsevier, 379-389.

Langham, M. and Wells, C. (2003). *A history of the Devonshire Royal Hospital at Buxton and the Buxton Bath Charity.* Leek : Churnet Valley Books.

Magdalini, V. and Paris, T. (2009). The wellness tourism market in Greece: An inter-disciplinary methodology approach. *Tourismos*, **4**(4), 127-144.

Mair, H. (2005). Tourism, health and the pharmacy: towards a critical understanding of health and wellness tourism. *Tourism (Zagreb)*, **53**(4), 335-346.

Messerli, H. R. and Oyama, Y. (2004). Health and wellness tourism-global. *Travel & Tourism Analyst*, (August), 1-54.

Pesonen, J., Laukkanen, T. and Komppula, R. (2011). Benefit segmentation of potential wellbeing tourists. *Journal of Vacation Marketing*, **17**(4), 303-314.

Pforr, C. and Locher, C. (2012) The German spa and health resort industry in the light of health care system reforms, *Journal of Travel & Tourism Marketing*, **29**(3), 298-312.

Prideaux, B., Berbigier, D. and Thompson, M. (2013). Wellness tourism and destination competitiveness, in Voigt, C. and Pforr, C. *Wellness Tourism: A Destination Perspective*, pp. 45-60.

Quintela, J. A., Correia, A. G. and Antunes, J. G. (2011). Service quality in health and wellness tourism–trends in Portugal. *International Journal of Business, Management and Social Sciences*, **2**(3), 1-8.

Rawlinson, S. and Wiltshier, P. (2017). Developing a wellness destination: a case study of the Peak District. In Smith M. K. and Puczko, L. (eds) *The Routledge Handbook of Health Tourism*.

Riva, M. A. and Cesana, G. (2013). Special article: The charity and the care: the origin and the evolution of hospitals. *European Journal of Internal Medicine*, **24**(1), 1-4. doi:10.1016/j.ejim.2012.11.002

Sheldon, P. and Park, S.-Y. (2009). Development of a sustainable tourism destination. In Bushell, R. and Sheldon, P.J. (Eds.) *Wellness and Tourism. Mind, Body, Spirit, Place,* 99–113. Cognizant Communication, New York.

Skinner, A (2015) 'Voice of the Visitors': An exploration of the work of the Charity Organisation Society in Oxford, 1878–1880, *Midland History*, **40**(1), 74-94.

Smith, M. and Puczkó, L. (2010). Taking your life into your own hands? New trends in European health tourism, *Tourism Recreation Research,* **35**(2), 161-172.

Smith, M. and Puczkó, L. (2015). More than a special interest: Defining and determining the demand for health tourism, *Tourism Recreation Research*, **40**(2), 205-219.

Starr, P. (1982). *The Social Transformation of American Medicine*. New York Basic Books.

Strohecker, J. (2006). A Brief History of Wellness, HealthWorld Online, www.mywellnesstest.com/certResFile/BriefHistoryofWellness.pdf. Accessed 09 July 2016.

UNESCO (n.d.) http://whc.unesco.org/en/tentativelists/5928/. Accessed 09 July 2016

Van Tubergen, A. and Van der Linden, S. (2002) A brief history of spa therapy, *Annals of Rheumatic Diseases*, **61**, 273-275 doi:10.1136/ard.61.3.273. Accessed from http://ard.bmj.com on 26th June 2016

Vesey, R (2012) Special Report: International companies starting to take wellness to heart. Workforce http://www.workforce.com/articles/print/special-report-international-companies-starting-to-take-wellness-to-heart. Accessed 09 July 2016

Voigt, C., Brown, G. and Howat, G. (2011). Wellness tourists: in search of transformation. *Tourism Review*, **66**(1/2), 16-30.

Waddington, K. (2000). *Charity and the London hospitals, 1850-1898*. London: Royal Historical Society/Boydell Press

Willis Towers Watson (2011). Multinational workforce health: Building a sustainable global strategy. www.towerswatson.com.

Wilson, A. (1996). Conflict, consensus and charity: politics and the provincial voluntary hospitals in the eighteenth century. *The English Historical Review*, **CXI** (442), 599-519.

2 The Spa Industry Today

Angela Anthonisz and Isobel Stockdale

Introduction

The world spa market has over 120,000 operators with new additions and offshoots of the spa product being developed every day (Global Wellness Institute, 2015). The availability of funding for new spas and the change in ownership of hotels are key trends driving growth in the spa industry. Smaller boutique hotel operations now look to add spas as a means of adding value to the consumer and driving hotel room occupancy. A number of the larger mainstream hotel operators such as Fairmont, MGM, Sofitel and ICHG are looking to develop the 'healthy hotel', focussing on wellness as a new approach to marketing and packaging the guest experience (Spa Creators, 2014). Spa towns and destinations are reinventing themselves to appeal to the ever-increasing number of wellness tourists, while resorts use spas as an integral part of a wider experience that might include golfing, skiing or walking.

As the medical and wellness tourism industry grows, both businesses and governments are grappling with how to define, organise and promote these sectors (Global Spa Summit, 2011). This is especially challenging for the spa industry because spas offer products and services that cut across both wellness and medical related tourism, and the integration of spas into these markets varies widely across different countries and regions. Over the years, the definition of spa has evolved and transformed, but an agreed position has never been accepted as the organic changes and pace of growth within the industry has meant that the spa offering has often changed before a definition can be accepted. Foley (2003:8) stated that 'spa' is an international word with the same meaning in any language, but it provides different experiences depending where you go in the world. Berge, even earlier (1999:9) described spa as *"the millennium buzzword for health, beauty and relaxation".* The academic debate seems to have moved forward into the consumption of the products continually driving the development of new products. The reality is that spa has become part of society and everyday life, and is a common word that is used daily within a range of contexts (Pytell, 2012). In recent years the popularity of the spa industry has seen the term spa linked to anything from shower gels, dog groomers and beauty salons, with the possibility of a spa experience being delivered by walking through certain aisles of the supermarket. The association for the consumer could be that if a product was called 'spa' or the word 'spa' was included in the title, then it was pampering/indulgent.

This lack of clarity when it comes to developing our understanding of spa is addressed in this chapter, as it considers the current size and shape of the spa industry, the diversification of the spa product and some recent attempts at classifying what is meant when we talk about spas. It could be argued that the complexity of the spa offering makes it impossible to classify and subsequently makes it difficult for managers to identify how to position themselves within the business environment. Chapter 1 of this book has made some inroads into being able to categorise spa operations by creating the distinctions between therapies and treatments, leisure and tourism offerings, and businesses and products. This chapter attempts to build on these concepts by considering the size and structure of the spa industry internationally and looking at the extent to which the scope of the business operation may impact on operational, business and corporate level strategy, and then on operations. On that basis we consider the creation of a typology of spa by looking at the characteristics of the business rather than the type of facility and treatment.

Size and shape of the spa industry

The global wellness economy, as seen in Figure 2.1, was valued at US$3.7 trillion in 2015 (Global Wellness Institute, 2014). Within that global economy the spa industry was valued at just under US$100 billion. The growth in spa is fuelled by a number of trends which include: the increasing numbers of wellness tourists, who made 691 million trips in 2015; the increase in associated locations, such as thermal and mineral springs with 27,507 locations, and the increasing demand for beauty and anti-aging products. These sectors have contributed to an average growth of 8% every year, with the number of spa locations rising from 105,591 in 2013 to 121,595 in 2015 (Global Wellness Institute, 2014). As this growth was achieved in and post the economic crisis, it could be assumed that the projections are set to follow this trend.

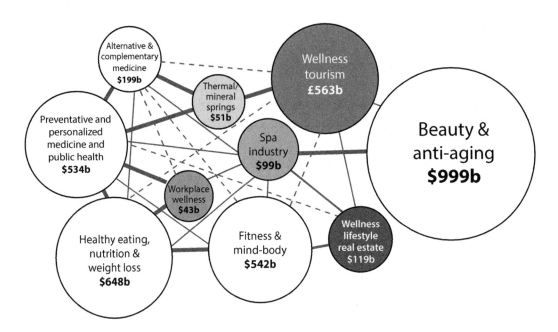

Figure 2.1: The Global Wellness Economy in 2015.

Source: www.the globalwellnessinstitute.org [Accessed 22/11/2016]

Within this context, the top ten key spa markets in terms of revenue continue to perform to these targets. (See Figure 2.2). While the U.S., Germany and Japan have ranked as the top three spa markets in terms of revenue over the last six years, there has been some interesting movement on the "top ten list" with China entering the top five for the first time, and Russia entering the top ten. The top five spa nations currently account for almost half of the worldwide industry revenues. While the majority of spa business is dominated by these markets there is significant growth being created by changes in tourism flows, and includes the economic growth and maturity of many developing countries. Sub-Saharan Africa and the MENA regions, as well as Eastern European locations have all generated increased revenues in the spa industry since 2007 (Global Wellness Institute, 2014).

While there are a number of general trends associated with the international growth of the spa market, making it one of the few industries that has been resilient to fluctuations in the economy (Frewin, 2014), each market will present the spa manager with a unique set of challenges in which to determine how best to compete. Again, the complexity of the spa industry is such that there is a need to find a way to create a typology that may help in positioning the spa from a management perspective.

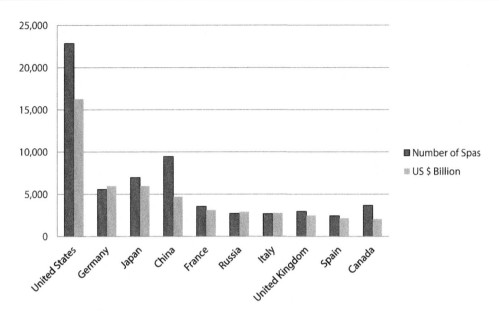

Figure 2.2: Top ten spa markets

Diversification of the spa product

The spa industry has, in recent years, diversified at a considerable pace and subsequently the range of services offered as part of the spa experience has also expanded. This is helped by businesses competing in an industry where there are relatively few barriers to entry. As the modern consumer now increasingly finds a way to include fitness, relaxation, beauty therapy and wellness treatments into their daily life, spa offerings now have adapted to cater to everyone from the millennial to the baby boomer. The spa industry has responded to this demand via constant innovation that includes the expansion of service lines, the inclusion of spa retail outlets, the introduction of budget spas, the creation of spa cruise ships, and most recently the *uberisation* of spa facilities, with companies such as Zeel, Soothe and Unwind Me that are growing their business via web and app booking services (Spa Business, 2015). A recent report on the Global Spa Services Market has identified several major companies leading the field between 2014 and 2022. These include Four Seasons, Emirates Palace, Six Senses Hotel Resorts and Spas, Gaia Retreat and Spa, Clarins Group and Massage Envy Franchising LLC.

As with so many other service sector industries, the larger companies tend to compete on the basis of competitive strength and geographic presence. The economies of scale afforded by size allow for the development of the spa product portfolio, greater customisation and increasing development of brand loyalty. The introductions of new products, on an almost continuous basis, that are offered under the commercial brand means that consumers are more willing to accept change. The smaller businesses compete via the development of a unique value proposition that can include some form of specialisation in terms of treatment, the ownership of a recognised franchise unit or proximity (location) within easy reach of the consumer.

Typologies of products

As identified at the start of this chapter there are advantages to be gained from being able to categorise spas in a way that can benefit both business and the consumer, however, the complexity of the spa industry and the range of services that may be available within an operation create significant problems in terms of creating a typology. An initial approach to categorising spas was made in 2011 when the Global Spa Summit produced a report that considered the placement of spas within the context of wellness and medical tourism. The categorisation of spas shown in Figure 2.3 was based on two axes. The first was the extent to which the business reflected a medical treatment as opposed to a wellness treatment. This was a simple dichotomy, but we wonder where medical becomes (or already is) wellness or vice versa, both in product and treatment. It does perhaps question yet again whether there is any value in creating typologies based upon product.

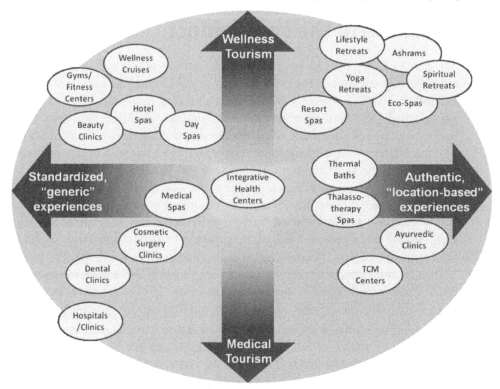

Figure 2.3: The wellness tourism and medical tourism market spectrum
Source: Global Spa Summit LLC (2011)

The second axis considered the nature of the experience in terms of the extent to which it was standardised or authentic/location-based. While this is a useful starting point from which to categorise spas, and clearly concepts such as eco spas and forest spas can be clearly defined, there are a number of blurred lines. For example, hotel spas are categorised as standardised, generic experiences, which is increasingly not the case as hotels recognise the value of offering a 'glocal' experience to the consumer. Destinations such as Dubai are creating centres which combine hotels with health and wellness facilities, offering some of the latest treatments; while medical treatments in Bangkok are provided in what can only be described as a *'hospitel'* where the patient is provided with high levels of personal attention in a 5 star hotel atmosphere.

A more recent approach to categorising spas has been produced by Allied Market research which produced a global opportunity analysis and industry forecast for 2014-2022. The report segments the market geographically, but more interestingly categorises the market in terms of six segments; salon spa, hotel spa, medical spa, destination spa, mineral spa and other (e.g. cruise ship spas). This approach has limitations in that there are once again overlaps in the spa offering, and classifying spas on the basis of only six categories does not allow for clarity in terms of differentiating the spa product in a way that facilitates clear positioning.

Being able to categorise spas more effectively may help operators to understand how to position themselves within their respective markets and may also provide consumers with a better understanding of what is being marketed to them. The basis for the consideration is the levels of organisational strategy presented by Johnson *et al.* (2007) as discussed in Chapter 14 of this book. This has been adapted and presented in relation to the spa industry in Figure 2.4.

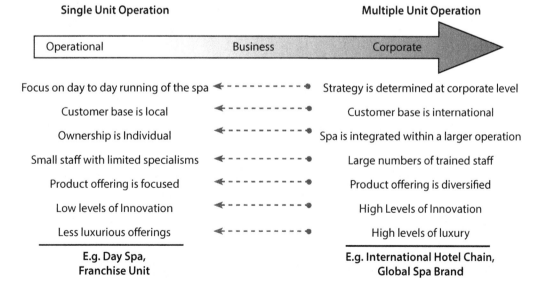

Figure 2.4: Characteristics of the spa business

The model in Figure 2.4 presents a range of possible business characteristics that may link to the size and scale of the operation. The day spa operation at one end of the continuum highlights the fact that the single unit operation is likely to be run by an individual owner with minimal staff. There is likely to be a specific focus to the operation as the customer base will be local and the approach to managing the business will be very much focused on the day to day running of the spa. Also included at this end of the continuum is the franchise operation. For example, the *Massage Envy* franchise has been operating since 2002 and now has over 1,100 units worldwide. Within this operation there are 113 units that are run by the company. These units are managed as part of the corporate strategy for the parent company, and the parent company sets the standards for how the franchisees run and manage their operations across the globe. However, the individual owner operators of the franchise units will be very much focused on the day-to- day operations as they have bought into a product where everything is provided, and the need to think about the business in more strategic terms has been removed. Franchisees buy into a system that includes profit coaching and a reporting structure that focuses on unit level economics (www.massageenvy.com, n.d.).

The other end of the continuum highlights the much larger international operations that now tend to characterise the industry, as hotels include a spa experience in order to increase room bookings and revenue per available customer. Within this context the spa is likely to be part of the brand, or may be developed as a separate hotel spa brand that can be rolled out across the hotels operations. For example, Jumeirah Hotels and Resorts developed the Talise Spa concept as a separate brand within the hotel portfolio. Operating in more tourist driven locations, these spas are likely to be highly diversified and their development and competitive position is likely to fall within the remit of the corporate strategy for the business.

The mid-point of the continuum may include larger individual units such as unique spa resorts or destination spas that act as a draw for the tourist and potentially offer a range of treatments specific to the location. Within this context there may be a combination of business characteristics that come from both sides of the continuum, and subsequently the spa manager will be able to delegate the day to day running aspects of the business to such an extent that he/she can start to focus on more long term decisions. For example, the *Golden Door Spa and Resort* in California, made famous by Elizabeth Taylor and Tza Tza Gabor, provides a unique spa experience that combines traditional spa treatments with a range of other options linked to fitness, nutrition and wellbeing. The business is not large enough to need to consider corporate level thinking and strategy, but its unique appeal does allow it to attract international tourists, and the size of the operation allows for a range of specialised treatments to be provided. This is not a hotel with a spa attached. It is a spa with the option of rooms provided to the customer who wants to do more than stay for a day.

One area that stands out in the context of the spa industry is that of innovation, and this is a key determinant of how the industry has evolved. While demand for innovation is a characteristic of all industries, within the context of spa it is one of the key elements that links to pace of growth and the diversification of a product that, at present, appears to have no clearly defined boundaries that act as constraints to market entry. New procedures in medical treatments, advances in technology, marketing innovations such as the creation of themed packages, research into complimentary therapies and demand for the 'wow' factor when it comes to the design of spa facilities are just some of the elements that have contributed to innovation in the industry. As commented by Navaro (2014) the kind of innovation present in the spa industry is clearly highlighted as the reason for its competitive intensity and the industry's partial nonconformity to the product lifecycle theory that can be applied to other industries.

The ease with which new products and services can now be imitated tends to shape the industry and subsequently enhances the level of competition. However, developing new innovations in terms of product, process and position (Bessant and Tidd, 2015) is often costly so the single unit operator is less likely to be responsible for developing new products and services, but more likely to take advantage of offering those products post development, process and positioning. We suggest that it is the new entrants into the market that are likely to be more innovative than existing players, but the cost of setting up a spa would indicate that it might only be the larger operations that are able to develop new offerings. The implication is that size and scale of operation, and the economies of scale associated with this provide the financial resources needed to develop new options in spa and new approaches to how products are bundled. The innovations developed at this end of the spectrum are likely to be more radical and these will then filter down to the smaller operations as they are imitated and developed in terms of providing lower cost and lower luxury models. Smaller operations will therefore survive by adopting more incremental innovations.

Conclusion

The concepts discussed in this chapter are seen as essential in terms of setting the parameters for operations and people management within the sector. They indicate strategic directions for an industry whose growth projections will need to be fueled by continuous product development, re-branding and training of a future workforce. It suggests that there is a future for the broad spectrum of the industry in terms of size and shape, and that the previous attempts to categorise the industry by product or type of spa are unnecessary; what is important is to look at the strategic level of decision making linked to size and shape. The requirement for the industry is for managers who are more receptive to change and have the ability to manage that change.

The following chapters will introduce types of spas as defined by product, and the demographics (typologies) of those consuming the products, and each chapter should be assessed within the continuum of Figure 2.4. The ability for the eco-spa to remain sustainable, for example, will depend upon many stakeholders who may have differing agendas and strategic imperatives.

The chapters on management, marketing, operations and finance should also be reviewed within the same context. For example the advent of new marketing techniques based upon e-technology requires each spa, whether within an international group or private ownership, to be able to exploit the medium.

The concept of the continuum (Figure 2.4) is further explored in the strategic directions chapter which looks at the levels of strategy and forms the basis of our ideas on the future of the industry.

References

Berge, S. (1999) *The Tropical Spa Asian Secrets of Health, Beauty and Relaxation*, Tuttle Publishing

Bessant, J. and Tidd, J. (2015). *Innovation and Entrepreneurship*, 3rd Edition. New York: Wiley.

Foley, J. (2003). Great Spa Escapes. 2nd Edition. London: Dakini.

Global Spa Summit (2011). Research Report. *Wellness Tourism and Medical Tourism, Where Do Spas Fit?*

Global Wellness Institute (2014). *Global Spa & Wellness Economy Monitor*, prepared by SRI International.

Global Wellness Institute (2015) Global Wellness Economy. Available at: www.theglobalwellnessinstitute.org [22/11/2016]

Johnson, G., Scholes, K. and Whittington, R. (2007). *Exploring Corporate Strategy*. 8th Edition. Prentice Hall.

Navaro, J. V. (2014). How innovation shapes the spa industry and determines its evolution. *Global Journal of Management and Business Research*. 14 (2), 7-23

Pytell, R. (2012). Greening Spas. Available at: http://www.lohas.com/greening-spas.

Spa Business (2015). Issue 3. Available at www.spabusiness.com [22/11/2016]

Spa Creators (2014.) *UK Spa Market Analysis*. Prepared by Alistair Johnson.

www.massageenvy.com (n.d.) Own a franchise. https://www.massageenvy.com/own-a-franchise [22/11/2016].

3 Thermal and Mineral Springs

Louise Buxton

Introduction

Water and spa are ubiquitous geographically and culturally, but the relationship between that water and bathing rituals has led directly and indirectly to the organic growth of many of today's spa products. The aim of this chapter is to explore the use of thermal and mineral waters for bathing, and it begins with a review of the origins, cultural and religious associations of bathing rituals. The current industry suggests that the approaches to hot spring bathing are broadly defined by three main categories:

■ Relaxation and connection with the environment, as seen in Asian cultures;

■ Health based and spiritual treatments, largely seen in European cultures;

■ Religious connections, evident in Indian and indigenous cultures.

This categorisation creates a debate within the industry as to whether globalisation fosters a blurring of these distinctions. Questions that result from this are:

■ Is connection to the environment evident in cultures other than Asia?

■ Where else are spiritual treatments seen other than in Europe?

■ Do religious connections exist outside of indigenous cultures?

The chapter also provides a historical illustration, drawing on examples of thermal and mineral spas from different continents, from the ancient Greek and Roman baths, the glamorous European spa resorts, to the onsen of Japan and hot springs of North America. The context is exampled in size and shape where Davidson (cited in Global Spa and Wellness Summit, 2013) and the Global Wellness Institute (GWI) (2014) concur in estimating that the global market is now worth over fifty billion US dollars. Furthermore, this market growth is driven by new manifestations, such as the rejuvenation of the Eastern European industry based around emerging tourism destinations. For example the Hungarian resort of Heviz, developments such as the Crescent Hotel in Buxton, England and in North and Sub-Saharan Africa. The efficacy of bathing in thermal and mineral waters is then discussed as is the relationship to the notion of 'existential authenticity'.

Nomenclature

Opinion varies on where the word 'spa' originates from. Interpretations include: that it may be derived from the Walloon word 'espa' meaning fountain, that it comes from the Belgian town named Spa where a thermal spring was discovered in the 14th century, from the Latin word 'spagere' meaning to scatter or sprinkle or that it is an acronym of the Latin phrase 'sanitas per aquas' healing through water (van Tubergen and van der Linden, 2002; Uherek-Bradecka and Bradeki, 2012). These myths and legends of spa feed the industry's mystification and allude that its longevity is a reason to trust its brands and products.

Lack of clarity also emanates from the many terms used to describe bathing in water and associated modalities; complicated further by the engagement of different fields in their use, namely the spa and wellness sector and the medical profession. For over a decade proposals have been made which call for a consensus on worldwide definitions of terms such as health resort medicine, balneology and climatology. A consensus statement confirming a common understanding had been achieved, for the requirement to develop definitions of terms was put forward in 2005 by the International Society of Medical Hydrology and Climatology (ISMH), Physical Medicine and Rehabilitation Board of Medical Specialists European Union (UEMS), World Organization of Thermalism (OMTH), World Federation of Hydrotherapy and Climatotherapy (FEMTEC), International Society of Hydrothermal Techniques (SITH) and Medical Committee of European Spa Association (ESPA) (European Spa Association, 2016a). Subsequently, Gutenbrunner *et al.* (2010), representing the medical profession, called for an agreement on worldwide definitions of: health resort medicine, balneology, medical hydrology and climatology. The rationale provided for the need for this agreement stems from the lack of international recognition for these modalities as independent medical specialities. Concurring, with Gutenbrunner *et al.* (2010), Varga (2010) emphasises the urgency of the task, noting that the lack of universally recognised terms inhibits the preparation of systematic reviews and meta-analyses. More complexity is added to this debate as, interestingly for the spa and wellness sector, one barrier Gutenbrunner *et al.* (2010) note to establishing worldwide recognition, is the trend to use balneotherapy interventions for wellness concepts, in hotels, health clubs and spas, suggesting that this type of promotion draws attention away from the medical use of such treatments.

The use of different terms is likewise complicated by the emergence of English as the principal scientific language, juxtaposed to the main development of areas such as balneotherapy in Roman, German speaking or Eastern European countries. Furthermore, Latin speaking countries often use the term crenotherapy instead of balneotherapy (Varga, 2010). This plethora of terms suggest the complex nature of bathing in thermal or mineral waters. An attempt to confirm basic definitions of these terms is provided below in Table 3.1.

3

Term	Definition
Taking the waters	Bathing in water for therapeutic purposes
Balneotherapy	Treatment employing bathing in thermal or minerals waters, gases or peloids, drinking water or inhaling gases or water
Balneology	The scientific field dealing with balneotherapy
Thalassotherapy	Treatment employing bathing in sea water or sea products
Hydrotherapy	Treatment immersing a part of or the whole body in plain water, often employing exercises, or the application of water jets
Pelotherapy	Application of peloids (mud or clay) for therapeutic purposes
Climatotherapy	Application of climatic factors for the prevention or treatment of disease or for rehabilitation

Table 3.1: Terms related to the use of thermal and mineral water and associated modalities (Adapted from Gutenbrunner *et al.*, 2010; Routh *et al.*, 1996; van Tubergen and van der Linden, 2002)

Origins, religion and culture

Water is fundamental to preserving and promoting health and wellbeing, and as such is the most valuable resource for life (FEMTEC, 2015). People have been bathing in mineral and thermal waters for millennia and its popularity continues today. Nevertheless, as an essential part of human existence, much of the knowledge of the cultural, historical and religious use of water has been integrated into everyday routine; as such, it has become tacit and little is formally documented.

Water forms part of purification rituals in many of the major religions (Routh *et al.*, 1996). The river Ganges is the Mother Goddess of Hinduism and the water with its life-giving capacities is worshiped as a divinity (Darian, 1978; Eck, 1983; Feldhaus, 1995). In Hinduism, bathing in the river Ganges and the natural springs of Vishnu, Ujjyan, Sitakundu, Puskar, Kumbha and Gangasagar frees a Hindu of their sins and brings wellness and peace, furthermore, immersing a dying person in water with the aim of curing their disease is well known (Routh *et al.*, 1996). In Judaism, Talmudic law emphasises the importance of using water to achieve cleanliness, and the healing aspects of the Dead Sea were well known (Routh *et al.*,

1996). Furthermore, water is employed in a number of Christian rituals including ablutions and baptisms. In Islam, water from the Well of Zamzam is considered holy, with many believers using it to cure various diseases; moreover, Muslims are required to wash five times a day, before each of the daily prayers (Routh *et al.*, 1996).

Bathing was a popular treatment for a range of diseases in the Greco-Roman era. Athenians first had private baths before their public baths were established by the Lacedaemonians (Routh *et al.*, 1996), however, in general the Greeks' preference was for fresh water bathing and thalassotherapy was widely undertaken (van Tubergen and van der Linden, 2002). In the private baths of classical Greece, bathing was confined to the wealthy, nonetheless, the arrival of public baths made bathing available to the masses. Homer extolled the merits of bathing in treating disease, and Hippocrates, in determining health and sickness, included water as one of the four humors to be used in balancing bodily fluids. Later Asclepiades introduced hydrotherapy and the drinking of water as part of the therapeutic regime for his patients (Routh *et al.*, 1996, van Tubergen and van der Linden, 2002).

The Romans, fascinated by the Grecian use of water, began to adopt many of their ideas, Uherek-Bradecka and Bradeki (2012) see the ancient Roman baths as the first spa spaces, initially using cold water (frigidaria), then hot (tepidaria and calidaria). The number of baths increased rapidly during the reigns of the Caesars (Routh *et al.*, 1996). In Rome three different types of baths were developed: home baths known as *balnea*, private baths known as *balnea privata* and public baths called *balnea publica* (van Tubergen and van der Linden, 2002). A military presence was often the impetus for the development of a spa resort at the site of mineral and thermal springs. Roman spas were used as recreation centres for healthy soldiers as well as to aid the recuperation of injured soldiers (van Tubergen and van der Linden, 2002). The oldest Roman baths known as *thermae*, found in Pompeii date back to the 2nd century B.C. (Uherek-Bradecka and Bradeki, 2012).

Influenced by the Roman Empire, bathing became part of European civilisation. Public baths were built in Buxton and Bath in England, and in Eastern Europe vapour baths were adopted in Russia and Turkey (Routh *et al.*, 1996). Under the Romans, bathing culture gradually changed, moving away from the treatment of disease, although this was always included, towards relaxation and pleasure; baths also became centres for various sexual activities (van Tubergen and van der Linden, 2002). The fall of the Roman Empire in 476 saw bathing decline; with the rise of Christianity, bathing fell into disrepute and was eventually prohibited (Routh *et al.*, 1996; van Tubergen and van der Linden, 2002). Many baths were abandoned and fell into disrepair, while others were converted to churches. This period lasted for centuries, with bathing only beginning to increase in popularity again from the 13th century onwards with the influence of the Moors in southern Europe (van Tubergen and van der Linden, 2002). Numerous baths were constructed during the Ottoman Empire; public Turkish baths (*hammam*) were popular in Islamic countries and many were also built in Ottoman conquered territories such as the Rudas Turkish bath in Budapest (Uherek-Bradecka and Bradeki, 2012). Having a bathing culture reputed to date back to pre-Roman Celtic times, Hungary is one of the richest countries of thermal waters in the world (Bender *et al.*, 2002).

During the medieval period, little attention was paid to water in England (Routh *et al.*, 1996), this era saw people abstain from bathing for long periods, often years (van Tubergen and van der Linden, 2002). Public baths were rebuilt as bathing regained its popularity from the 13th century onwards. In many cases entrance was free, however, baths were often overcrowded and in some, people bathed for days in the same water (van Tubergen and van der Linden, 2002). However, in Japan at this time, popular hot spring areas were well known in Kanto, Tokai, Tohoku and Koushinetsu regions; furthermore, their popularity for healing was fuelled by their use in the treatment of soldiers wounded in war, similarly to their use by the Romans (Serbulea and Payyappallimana, 2012).

The Renaissance period experienced several fluctuations in the perception of bathing. The 16th century saw the image of public baths decline again in many countries, however, during this time Bacci produced the first directory of spas in Europe (Routh *et al.*, 1996). There were several reasons for the decline; public baths were considered to be a source of contagious diseases such as leprosy and syphilis, furthermore, they became expensive due to a shortage of firewood (van Tubergen and van der Linden, 2002). However, during the Renaissance the therapeutic value of balneotherapy was reconsidered and taking the waters was increasingly prescribed under medical direction. This was driven in Italy by the discovery by Italian doctors of lost texts from the ancient world that extolled the virtues of balneotherapy. The new bathing culture resurrected in Italy spread across other parts of Europe with the development of spas in the Alps and redis-covered spas in France (van Tubergen and van der Linden, 2002). In Russia vast sums of money were invested is spa resorts, with a large proportion of medical personnel committed to spa therapy (Benedetto and Millikan, 1996). Interest in water also resumed in England where notable physicians recognised the value of mineral water for the treatment of diseases such as gonorrhoea, rheumatism and nervous conditions (Routh *et al.*, 1996). During this time, attempts were made to analyse the waters for their mineral content, recognising each mineral for its effect on the body in order to know which parts may be influenced by taking the waters (van Tubergen and van der Linden, 2002). Two types of spa evolved: hot springs for bathing and drinking, and cold springs for drinking only (van Tubergen and van der Linden, 2002). Japan was experiencing a rapid transition at this time; westernisation was evident, with western medicine being adopted from Europe. Economic prosperity meant *onsen* resorts were booming and becoming favourite destinations for short holidays. Although bathing was popular, drinking mineral water was not as popular in Japan as in Europe (Benedetto and Millikan, 1996).

The 18th and 19th centuries saw the development of hotels at the site of springs in Europe and in North America, where the transplanted Europeans learned of the virtues of the waters from the indigenous Native Americans (Routh *et al.*, 1996). The indigenous Native Americans revered their springs; so sacred were some of them considered to be that warring tribes would congregate peacefully around them to participate in ceremonial bathing, putting aside their differences (Benedetto and Millikan, 1996). Grand hotels arose in Europe and spa resorts had their own casinos and promenades; much importance was placed on ostentation in England, Austria, Belgium and in Germany, where Baden Baden became the most glamourous of spa resorts (van Tubergen and van der Linden, 2002). Spa resorts were places to be seen, meeting places for the elite and places of creativity for writers and painters (van Tubergen and van der Linden, 2002). In Saki, Russia the first ever mud resort was opened in 1828, as mud cure in Crimea became a basis of the Russian School of Peloidotherapy (Badalov and Krikorova, 2012). Research also began in the 19th century in Hungary with the foundation of The Hungarian Balneological Society in 1891 (Bender *et al.*, 2014). Australia saw its first wave of thermal and mineral spring developments at this time, with much of its spa culture borrowed from Swiss-Italian gold diggers. The first Australian springs to be documented were done so in the 19th century by Europeans, brought to the country by the gold rush, however, they were likely to have been shown to the springs by Aborigines (White, 2012). This introduction to thermal and mineral springs by indigenous people replicated the discoveries in North America. Australian spas of this era had less of an elite focus than their European counterparts, due to Australia's egalitarian culture and this democratic character of spas was sustained by so-called colonial socialism (White, 2012). With the aim of improving the use of mineral water in medicine, further attempts were made to analyse its content with the aim of matching each disease to a medicinal spring (van Tubergen and van der Linden, 2002). The principles of balneotherapy and hydrotherapy were further developed by Priessnitz, a Silesian peasant who attributed his recovery from broken ribs to the use of cold water and Kneipp, a Bavarian priest who advocated the use of hot and cold water as part of a holistic approach to the treatment of disease (Routh *et al.*, 1996; van Tubergen and van der Linden, 2002).

In the 20th century English spa resorts declined; competition from foreign resorts and an economic depression were the key factors, furthermore, spa therapy was excluded from the National Health Service, and in turn many UK spa resorts closed down (van Tubergen and van der Linden, 2002). In contrast, many other European countries saw spa treatments become available to the masses owing to reimbursement by state medical systems; in continental Europe the medical significance of bathing was recognised by rheumatologists and dermatologists and this aspect was viewed as more important for some resorts than prestige and leisure (van Tubergen and van der Linden, 2002). Furthermore, the 20th century saw a cultural shift in the meaning and function of bathing, from a focus on health and wellbeing to a more social – even decadent – identity (Breathnach, 2004; Shifrin, 2013 cited in Foley, 2014). This cultural shift saw the focus move from medical treatment toward relaxation and pleasure (van Tubergen and van der Linden, 2002). Baths and hydros were adopted social bodies for whom they became places to do business, take their leisure or engage in sexual practices, contesting the identity of baths as social as much as healing places (Breathnach, 2004; Mackaman, 1998 cited in Foley, 2014).

Modernity, size and shape and global manifestations

3

The spa industry often promotes its products, treatments and experiences through stories that are rooted in cultures and have historic perspectives providing 'traditions of the brands'. Moving forward into the 21st century, thermal and mineral bathing are experiencing resurgence in popularity, driven largely by consumers who seek traditional and authentic experiences. The definition of authenticity has been much contested and can be described as object or activity related; existential authenticity a concept applied to tourism studies, has witnessed a recent surge in academic attention. Research that has employed the concept of existential authenticity focusses on emotions, sensations, relationships and a sense of self (Rickly-Boyd, 2013), and thus is disposed towards application to spa. Bathing in thermal or mineral waters, through engaging the emotions and senses, present opportunities to explore and experience what it is to be human (Stiener and Reisinger, 2006). Existential authenticity, a potential state of being, comprises personal and intersubjective feelings which can be activated by the process of bathing. Thus, as Wang (1999: 351) suggests, people may feel more authentic and able to self-express than in everyday life because they are 'engaging in non-everyday activities, free from the constraints of daily life'. The concept of authenticity is yet to be studied specifically in relation to spa and as such is an area apt for academic exploration.

Validating the resurgence in bathing, the Global Hot Spring Initiative was formed in 2015; an international wellness think-tank dedicated to exploring the values of geothermal waters for health, recreation, tourism and community. This initiative seeks to connect the global communities involved with geothermal waters and provide a network to foster consumer and political awareness (GWI, 2015). Principally, thermal and mineral spring establishments can be categorised into three main types: recreational, wellness or therapeutic.

- Recreational establishments include: water-based parks, hotels, resorts and swimming pools.
- Wellness establishments include: water-based spas and bathing facilities,
- Therapeutic establishments include health resorts and sanatoria.

Health resort medicine has a long history in Europe and also Asia. It includes modalities such as balneotherapy, hydrotherapy and climatotherapy, often combined with exercise, relaxation and physical therapies, for health promotion, and the prevention and treatment of chronic disease (Steir-Jarmer *et al.*, 2015). Thalassotherapy resorts and spas exist as the latter two types of establishments (GWI, 2014). Thalassotherapy has a long history in Europe, with countries such as France, Italy, Spain and Russia having many centres; it had a resurgence more recently in Asia, in particular in Japan, where urban thalassotherapy centres replace the traditional folkloric bathing (Nomura, 1991).

The current size of the industry can be contested, as its parameters are not clearly defined; one estimation from the Global Wellness Institute (2014) suggests the thermal and mineral spring market is worth of over fifty billion dollars worldwide. GWI (2014) position it under the umbrella of wellness, which also encompasses the spa industry and wellness tourism. The revenue from thermal and mineral springs comes from both their therapeutic and recreational use; there now exist over twenty six thousand thermal and mineral spring establishments worldwide, see Table 3.2 below, which shows their regional distribution and revenue (GWI, 2014).

Region	Number of Establishments	Revenue (US $ billions)	Top Countries
Asia-Pacific	20,298	26.75	China, Japan, Taiwan, South Korea, New Zealand
Europe	5,035	21,65	Germany, Russia, Italy, Austria, Turkey
North America	203	0.49	United States, Canada
Latin America-Caribbean	961	0.87	Brazil, Mexico, Argentina, Costa Rica, Chile
Middle East- North Africa	315	0.23	Tunisia, Israel, Algeria, Iran, Jordan
Sub-Saharan Africa	35	0.05	South Africa, Namibia

Table 3.2: Thermal and mineral springs by region (Adapted from GWI, 2014).

The thermal and mineral spring industry is most mature in Asia-Pacific and Europe, with China being by far the largest thermal and mineral spring economy when measured by revenue (US $14,078.3 billion); furthermore, Japan has the largest number of establishments (17,653), containing over two thirds of the world's total. Together these two countries dominate the industry, in receipt of over half of the global thermal and mineral spring economy's revenue (GWI, 2014). The popular perception in Japan is that *onsen* are specifically used for recreational purposes, however, evidence of their therapeutic effects has been documented in Japan (Serbulea and Payyappallimana, 2012). After China and Japan, other Asia-Pacific countries with significant numbers of thermal and mineral spring establishments are Taiwan, South Korea, New Zealand and to a lesser degree Australia. The Australian thermal and mineral spring industry is one of contrast, with establishments ranging from the majestic to the mundane; at the grand end of the scale are elite resorts such as Hydro Majestic in the Blue Mountains and at the other end of the scale are the many minimalist thermal and mineral spring sites of the Northern Territory (White, 2012). The most comprehensive development of thermal and mineral spring centres in Australia can be seen in the self-proclaimed 'Spa Capital', the central highlands of Victoria (White, 2012).

Most of the countries recorded in the Global Wellness Institute's (2014) top 20 list are in Europe, moreover, Europe has a time-honoured thermal and mineral spring industry, attested by the existence of many spas, health resorts, sanatoria and balneotherapy centres. Countries such as Germany, Austria, Switzerland, Italy, the vast of majority of Eastern Europe and the Baltics have long traditions of *kur*, which involves curative, rehabilitative, and preventive therapy (GWI, 2014, Frost, 2004). Many coastal spa resorts exist along the Baltic and North seas (Albin *et al.*, 2013). In Iceland, the Svartsengi geothermal power plant utilises the high level of geothermal activity in the area to discharge warm saline fluid, and has created an artificial lake known as the Blue Lagoon. Due to the properties of this water and the beauty of the landscape this has now become a thriving spa and tourist attraction (Albin *et al.*, 2013). The European industry is also privileged to receive government support and regulation in many of its countries. This is largely dependent on the recognition of water based modalities within each country, for example the UK, Netherlands, Sweden and Denmark do not recognise any as medical specialisms, conversely, countries such as Germany, Poland, Hungary, France and Austria do recognise them and health insurances provide refunds, at least in part, for health resort treatments (Gutenbrunner *et al.*, 2010). Already buoyant, this market is furthermore seeing resurgence, with examples such as the development of Herviz as a spa resort in Hungary, based around the world's second largest thermal lake, and renewed interest in England where the Thermae Bath Spa re-opened in 2006, resurrecting the age old use of the thermal waters, and the plans underway to re-develop the Crescent Hotel in Buxton, as a five star spa hotel, using the local mineral water.

North America is dominated by day spas, club spas and spa resorts; Canyon Ranch in Tucson Arizona being the largest of the latter. Established in the 1970s Canyon Ranch offers its guests a range of services including: nutrition, exercise, health education, body treatments and aquatics therapies (hydrotherapy) (Frost, 2004). The North American thermal and mineral spring industry is small in comparison to its spa industry, with just over two hundred thermal and mineral spring establishments, with a revenue of just under half a billion US dollars (GWI, 2014).

Latin American and Caribbean thermal and mineral spring establishments are modest in number (961) but this region, rich in natural assets and steeped in tradition, is also experiencing resurgence (GWI, 2014). In Copahue, Argentina, geothermal systems cause the formation of thermal muds with significant content of sulphur and clay mineral; these peloids are applied in the treatment of rheumatic, arthritic and dermatological conditions (Baschini *et al.*, 2010). Most current thermal and mineral spring establishments in this region are recreational; however, extensive thermal resources such as those found in Copahue mean this region is ripe for investment in wellness and therapeutic establishments.

The Middle Eastern and North African thermal and mineral spring industry is small and largely serves local consumers; only 315 establishments exist, with a revenue of under 0.2 billion US dollars (GWI, 2014). However, this is the second fastest growing region for spas, following Sub-Saharan Africa. This growth in spas is largely driven by developing Gulf countries such as Dubai and Saudi Arabia but also by countries such as Morocco and Israel. Many countries in this region, including Tunisia, Algeria and Iran have extensive natural spring resources; however, geopolitical stability would increase the potential of further thermal and mineral spring developments in this region (GWI, 2014).

An even less developed thermal and mineral spring economy is seen in Sub-Saharan Africa; nevertheless, this is the fastest growing region in the world for development of spas (GWI, 2014). An increasing middle class in high-growth economies such as Ghana, Nigeria and South Africa is supporting the fast paced expansion of this market. South Africa is the only country within this region that can currently be considered to have a well-developed thermal and mineral spring market which is largely recreational and based around hot spring resorts (GWI, 2014). However, other developing countries in Sub-Saharan Africa have the natural resources to support the development of thermal and mineral spring establishments, which could be developed to include recreational, wellness and therapeutic resorts (Boekstein and Spencer, 2013). Illustrating the potential for development, Boekstein and Spencer (2013) note that of the 87 documented springs in South Africa, only 30 have been developed into resorts. Western Cape, is one example of a developed region in South Africa, and has eleven thermal springs, which host eight resorts.

Efficacy

Documented evidence attesting the efficacy of balneotherapy, thalassotherapy, hydrotherapy and pelotherapy is widely dispersed. Every region of the globe has given consideration to this task; however, some of the literature has remained untranslated from its language of origin, for example in Japan, and the rest is published in a vast array of academic journals or held by individual establishments, making a challenging task of consolidating the knowledge. Attempts have been made to change this, ESPA, have developed an open access e-library dedicated to evidence-based balneology which aims to disseminate high quality information (ESPA, 2016b). Another example is Wellness Evidence, an online portal designed to unite dispersed medical evidence by providing direct access to four of the most respected evidence-based medicine databases: Natural Standard, The Cochrane Library, PubMed, and the meta-search engine TRIP (Wellness Evidence, 2014).

Despite age old traditions of bathing for therapeutic purposes and modern manifestations around the globe, its role in modern medicine varies and remains unclear (Tenti *et al.*, 2015). In recent decades several research projects have investigated the benefits of bathing and the application of peloids in relation particularly to dermatologic, rheumatologic and arthritic conditions. Some say at present the field is far from evidence-based medicine (Varga, 2010). Many of the studies do display positive outcomes, nevertheless, for every optimistic study equivalent numbers exist suggesting the need for further randomised controlled trails and studies of high methodological quality. Varga (2010) reasons that the preparation of systematic reviews and meta-analyses is hindered by the lack of exact definitions and keywords in this field, a step called for by Gutenbrunner *et al.* (2010). Progress is being made in some areas, one example is the recent systematic review and meta-analysis of clinical trials conducted with Hungarian thermal-mineral waters, conducted by Bender *et al.* (2014). The review identified 122 studies, published in English, 18 of which were clinical trials, and of these nine met the predefined criteria for meta-analysis. The review concluded that Hungarian thermal-mineral water is an effective remedy for lower back pain and knee and hand osteoarthritis (Bender *et al.*, 2014). In many countries detailed analyses of the composition of thermal and mineral waters and peloids have not been conducted and this attests not only to the need to extend studies of the benefits of balneo-therapy, thalassotherapy, hydrotherapy and pelotherapy, but also to the need to develop suitable standards for thermal and mineral waters and peloids in relation to their therapeutic use (Karakaya *et al.*, 2010).

Application of knowledge

1. Consider whether the three main categories of thermal spring listed below, are accurate:

   ■ Relaxation and connection with the environment, as seen in Asian cultures;

   ■ Health based and spiritual treatments, largely seen in European cultures;

   ■ Religious connections, evident in Indian and indigenous cultures.

2. Identify global developments in the use of thermal and mineral spring during the Renaissance period.

3. Compare and contrast thermal and mineral spring establishments in regions around the globe by their number and revenue.

References

Albin, J. N., Huaser, W. and Buskila, D. (2013.) Spa treatment (balneotherapy) for fibromyalgia – a qualitative narrative review and a historical perspective. *Evidenced-Based Complementary and Alternative Medicine*, **2013**, 55-61

Baschini, M. T., Pettinari, G.R., Valles, J. M., Aguzzi, C., Lopez-Galindi, A., Setti, M. and Viseras, C. (2010). Suitability of natural sulphur-rich mud from Copahue (Argentina) for use as semisolid health care products. *Applied Clay Sciences* **49**, 205-212.

Badalov, N.G., and Krikorova, S. (2012). Mud cure in Russia: history, achievements and prospective. *Medical Hydrology and Balneology: Environmental Aspects*, **6**, 171-172

Bender, T., Balint, P.V. and Balint, G.P. (2002). Post Script, A brief history of spa, *Annals of Rheumatism and Disease*, **61**, 947-950

Bender, T., Balint, G., Prohaszka, P., Geher, I. and Tefner, K. (2014). Evidenced-based hydro and balneotherapy in Hungary: a systematic review and meta-analysis. *International Journal of Biometeorology*, **58**, 311-323

Benedetto, A. V. and Millikan, F.L.E. (1996). Mineral waters and spas in the United States. *Clinics in Dermatology*, **14**, 583-600.

Boekstein, M.S. and Spencer, J.P. (2013). International trends in health tourism: Implications for thermal spring tourism in the Western Cape Province of South Africa. *African Journal of Physical, Health Education, Recreation and Dance.* **92**(2), 287-298.

Darian, S.G. (1978). *The Ganges in Myth and History*, Honolulu, University Press of Hawaii

Eck, D. L. (1983). *Banaras: City of Kight.* London: Routledge & Kegan Pau

European Spa Association (ESPA) (2016a). Spa Medicine, Szeged Consensus Statement on Balneology and Health Resort Medicine. Available at http://www.espa-ehv.eu/content/spa-medicine/spa-medicine (accessed 23rd August 2016)

European Spa Association (ESPA) (2016b). E-library. Available at http://www.espalibrary.eu/ (accessed 23rd August 2016)

Feldhaus, A. (1995) *Water and Womanhood: Religious Meanings of Rivers in Maharashtra*, Oxford: Oxford University Press.

FEMTEC (2015). Water and Health - How water protects and improves health overall. FEMTEC World Federation of Hydrotherapy and Climatotherapy, NGO in official relation with WHO (World Health Organisation)

Foley, R. (2014). The Roman-Irish Bath: Medical/health history as therapeutic assemblage. *Social Sciences and Medicine*, **106**, 10-19.

Frost, G. J. (2004). The spa as a model of an optimal healing environment. *The Journal of Alternative and Complementary Medicine*, **10**(1), 85-92.

Global Spa and Wellness Summit (2013). Global Hot Springs. Hot Springs Forum 7 October, New Delhi India

Global Wellness Institute (2014). Global Spa and Wellness Economy Monitor. September.

Global Wellness Institute (2015). Global Hot Spring Initiative. Available at http://www.globalwellnessinstitute.org/hot-springs-initiative/ (accessed 6 March, 2016)

Gutenbrunner, C., Bender, T., Cantista, P. and Karagulle, Z. (2010). A proposal for a worldwide definition of health resort medicine, balneology, medical hydrology and climatology. *International Journal of Biometeorology*, **54**, 495-597

Karakaya, M.C., Karakaya, N., Sarioglan, S. and Koral, M. (2010). Some properties of thermal muds of some spas in Turkey. *Applied Clay Science*, **48**, 531-537.

Nomura, T. (1991). Development project of thalassotherapy in the Japanese Coastal Area. *Marine Pollution Bulletin*, **23**, 339-342

Rickly-Boyd, J. M. (2013). Existential authenticity: place matters. *Tourism Geographies*, **15**(4), 680-686.

Routh, H. B., Bhowmik, K. R., Parish, L. C. and Witkowski, J. A. (1996). Balneology, mineral water and spas in historical perspective. *Clinics in Dermatology*, **14**, 551-54

Serbulea, M. and Payyappallimana, U. (2012). Onsen (hot springs) in Japan – Transforming terrain into healing landscapes. *Health and Place*, **18**, 1366-1373.

Steiner, C. J. and Reisinger, Y. (2006). Understanding existential authenticity. *Annals of Tourism Research,* **33**, 299-318

Stier-Jarmer, M., Kus, S., Frisch, D, Sabariego, C. and Schuh, A. (2015). Health resort medicine in non-musculoskeletal disorders: is there evidence of its effectiveness?. *International Journal Biometeorology*, **59**, 1523-1544

Tenti, S., Cheleschi, S., Galeazzi, M. and Fioravanti, A. (2015). Spa therapy: can be a valid option for treating knee osteoarthritis? *International Journal Biometeorology*, **59**, 1133-1143.

Uherek-Bradecka, B. and Bradeki, T. (2012). Cultural aspects of sauna and SPA architecture in the city – examples of design and execution. *Architectus*, **2**(32), 89-94.

van Tubergen, A. and van der Linden, S. (2002). A brief history of spa therapy. *Annals of Rheumatism and Disease*, **61**, 273-275

Varga, C. (2010). The balneology paradox. *International Journal of Biometeorology*, **55**(2), 105-106.

Wang, N. (1999). Rethinking authenticity in tourism experience. *Annals of Tourism Research*, **26**, 349-370

Wellness Evidence (2014). Evidence-Based Medicine Portal for Wellness Therapies. Available at http://www.wellnessevidence.com/wellnessevidence (accessed 6th March, 2016)

White, R. (2012). From the majestic to the mundane: democracy, sophistication and history among the mineral spas of Australia. *Journal of Tourism History*, **4**(1), 85-108.

3

4 Eco-spas: The Sustainability Agenda in the Spa Industry

Gaurav Chawla

Introduction

As concerns about global warming, climate change and greenhouse gas emissions increase, businesses are actively looking for ways to manage their impact on the environment. Environmental issues are not a new topic in the leisure industries. Stipanuk (1996) notes that the leisure sector has been involved in environmentally friendly practices at least since the late 1920s, though sustainable management has become a key business imperative in the last three decades. Despite this increased attention towards sustainability, the term itself remains broad and ill-defined (Chawla and Ndung'u, 2014). Gardetti and Torres (2016) articulate sustainability as an open concept that continuously leads us to change our objectives and priorities. In this sense, sustainability has been viewed as a journey rather than the destination. Mowforth and Munt (2009) note that sustainability has long been associated with environmental concerns and natural resource management. This statement is reflective of the view that everything we need for our survival and wellbeing depends directly or indirectly on the natural environment. For others, sustainability encompasses the totality of the environment including both the economy and the people within the environment (Elkington, 1997). Sustainability seeks to improve human quality of life by reconciling environmental and ethical concerns with economic growth (United Nations Convention on Climate Change, 2009). In other words, the sustainability concept is underpinned by prudent management of natural resources, economic development and social progress.

The Climate Change Summit in Paris concluded in December 2015 and firmly established sustainability as a prime global concern. However, the indications that industries are building the concerns into their strategic planning is less evident. Porter *et al.* (2008) urge businesses to accept responsibility and suggest that they are in a position to make a substantially greater positive impact on social issues than most other institutions. Porter and Kramer's concept of shared value rests on the assertion that sustainable business practices themselves could be a source of added value and hence competitive advantage (2011). The new yardstick of a businesses' success is not measured by net worth, but by 'net good' (Global Wellness Summit, 2015). Sustainability therefore is increasingly being viewed as an opportunity rather than an obligation that must be fulfilled.

4

Sustainability in the spa industry

Spa services are an integral component of the tourism system and wellness is increasingly being paired with every travel category possible (Global Wellness Summit, 2015). The industry is witnessing strong growth due to greater interest in personal wellbeing. Wellness has long been framed as a lifestyle choice, though this image is changing in light of the cost of healthcare, chronic diseases and ageing (*ibid*). This image makeover is further likely to fuel the growth of the spa industry. The projected growth of the sector is positive news, though it also implies higher demand for non-renewable resources and greater impact on the economy and society. In many ways, the spa industry and sustainability share a unique relationship. Johnson and Redman (2008) suggest that people see spa as serving social purposes and improving quality of life, thereby contributing in its own way to sustainable living. At the same time, the sector depends on natural resources such as clean water, fresh air and uncontaminated soil as the 'spa experience' relies on these. Hence, preservation of the environment is very much in the interest of the industry. Cooper (2009) argues that the physical and social environment directly impact the spa industry. The physical environment can enhance a sense of isolation and peace. The social environment itself can be therapeutic. It can promote wellbeing through learning, de-stressing and social exchange, thereby providing greater sense of fulfilment. Therefore, it can be argued that personal wellness is dependent on the wellness of our planet and everything around us. McMichael (2005) suggests that human experience – that is, happiness, fulfilment, well-being and health – is the actual 'bottom-line of sustainability'. Hence, sustainability in many ways represents a 'back to roots' approach to the spa industry. It may therefore neither be possible, nor desirable to separate spa experience and sustainability.

In its early days, sustainability was adopted by the industry in response to increased pressure by stakeholders such as consumers, employees, governments and communities. Now, the spa sector is strategic in approaching this issue, and sustainability is often embedded in the corporate goals of 21st century businesses. A simple online search reveals detailed sustainability policies of major players such as The Peninsula, Jiva by Taj and Canyon Ranch. Interestingly, independently operated properties such as Rancho Le Puerta (Mexico), Gayana Eco Resort (Malaysia) and The Scarlet (Cornwall, UK) are equally enthusiastic about sustainability. Many other spa businesses have gone a step further and branded themselves as 'eco-spa'. Eco-spa as a business concept is built on the principles of sustainability.

Eco-spas: Living the triple bottom line of sustainability

John Elkington (1997) is widely credited for presenting a holistic view of the sustainability agenda through the triple bottom line (TBL) framework. There are many ways of understanding TBL. It can be seen as an accounting or reporting framework that challenges the popular view that the impacts of an organisation should only be measured on the financial bottom-line (profits). As per TBL, the impact assessment must include social (people) and environmental (planet) bottom lines as well. At a broader level, TBL refers to the entire set of values and processes that organisations must address not only to minimise potential harm, but also to create social, economic and environmental value. TBL advocates a balanced approach (Elkington, 1997; Franknel, 1998), and stresses that true sustainability can only be achieved when profits are made with the purpose of social progress, and without harming the environment. It is easy to conceive of TBL as a sound business philosophy. Figure 4.1 depicts the TBL concept.

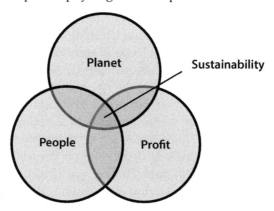

Figure 4.1: The triple bottom line (Elkington, 1997).

There is, as yet, no universally accepted definition of eco-spa. The term eco-spa is often used interchangeably with green spa, sustainable spa or socially responsible spa (Burkholder, 2007), the basic principle being the need for balance between man and nature. According to Green Spa Network, eco-spa refers to a spa where reducing the environmental footprint of the business is a top priority. This commitment to environmentally friendly practices then translates into all the product offerings (Erfurt-Cooper, 2009). Reynolds (2004) defines eco-spa as a retreat where pampering comes with a clean conscience. Johnson and Redman (2008) further clarify and suggest that the business philosophy of eco-spa is based on the belief that the health of the planet is tied to personal health. Eco-spas offer authentic treatments, giving the experience a sense of place. Traditions are revived and age-old practices such as Ayurveda, Hammam baths, meditation and yoga often are a part of the core experience (Spafinder, 2016). Eco-spas invest in community development and the economic welfare of the area. In addition, they invest in educating and developing their employees and locals alike, and actively participate in the community within which they operate (Smith and Puczkó, 2014; Johnson and Redman, 2008). Eco-spas also educate clients on the historical and cultural significance of the treatments they offer. This not only promotes authenticity, but also instils a sense of pride among the locals (Erfurt-Cooper, 2009). Responsible sourcing is another key business concern of eco-spas (Cabie, 2014).

Eco-spas typically consume fewer natural resources, pollute less and produce less waste. Organic ingredients are used, energy is often supplied through renewable sources and waste water systems are built (Brown, 2005). In addition, eco-spas employ ecological building design to minimise any negative impacts on the natural environment and actively contribute towards conservation of natural habitats (Erfurt-Cooper, 2009; Smith and Puczkó, 2014). On the economic (profit) side, eco-spas employ staff from the local area and source supplies from within the local community (Brien, 2009). Such initiatives help to create jobs, promote entrepreneurship and enhance income opportunities. These business strategies improve the economic welfare of the local communities by enhancing income opportunities. Eco-spas offer fair wages and employment benefits to their employees (Johnson and Redman, 2008). Such businesses operate strictly on the principles of responsible investments and franchising (Cabie, 2014). To sum up, eco-spa as a business model is aligned with the TBL. This business philosophy not only benefits the organisation and the destination, but also wider stakeholders such as employees, local communities and customers.

Sustainability in spa design and operations

To be truly sustainable, the principles of TBL need to be embedded in all aspects of the business, including design and operations. Leadership in Energy and Environmental Design (LEED) and the World Green Building Council provide detailed guidelines and exacting standards with respect to designing sustainable facilities. The International WELL Building Institute certifies buildings that conform to healthy-for-human standards. The certification is based on rigorous testing of the indoor environment, including air and water quality, light and comfort.

Research by the Indian Green Building Council (2016) estimates that the cost of including environmental measures into building design can increase the initial expenditure by 8-20%. However, eco-design does result in significant operational cost savings and the payback period is usually between 4 to 5 years. Ufland and Sternfeld (2009) and Sloan *et al.* (2013) provide helpful examples of sustainable ideas with respect to designing of the spa. Some of those are listed below:

- Recycled, reused and re-sorted materials should be used as much as possible. Use of natural materials should be maximised. It is important to integrate cultural and artistic traditions into design. This can provide a sense of authenticity and location to the spa experience. For example, Osmosis Day Spa in Freestone, CA prides itself on using recyclable materials in spa design.

- Use of larger windows and skylights will maximise natural light. This will not only reduce energy consumption, but can also positively impact human health and employees' productivity.

- Alternative energy sources (wind and solar power) should be considered. Such measures are an important part of sustainable initiatives of Spa Snovik (Slovenia), who consider themselves leaders in harnessing renewable energy.

- Water conservation is another prime concern in the spa industry. This can be achieved by reusing grey water, installing low-flow showerheads, dual-flush toilets and sensor-faucets, for example. Rainwater harvesting systems could be an integral part of the spa design. Akasha Holistic Wellbeing Spa in Jerusalem is an outstanding example of effective water conservation practices in a spa business.

- Space should be planned for on-site organic gardens. Such initiatives will allow fresher and healthier produce to be served to the patrons. The Boulders in Arizona and Lake Austin Spa Resort are excellent examples.

- Waste segregation spaces and composting facilities should be considered at the designing stage as well.

However, designing sustainable facilities is only one aspect of the overall plan. Sustainability also needs to be integrated with operational practices. This can be achieved by:

- Buying organic treatment products, biodegradable detergents and cleaning products. Not only are these environmentally friendly, but also are better for human health.

- Procuring supplies locally as this implies lesser transportation and lower carbon emissions. This also represents cleaner surroundings for the spa. For instance, the Bedruthan Hotel and Spa (Cornwall, UK) is fully committed to buying all its supplies from the local area.

- Buying in bulk to avoid excessive packaging.

- Sending waste to recycling instead of landfill. This can help reduce the carbon footprint of the spa.

- Offering vegan and vegetarian food choices. Not only are these sustainable food choices, but they also respond to increased demand by discerning spa goers. Tor Spa Retreat in Kent, for instance, prides itself on offering only vegetarian meal options.

- Training staff and providing education to local communities on sustainability related issues. Chiva-Som International Health Resort is a good example of a spa business where such initiatives are a core part of the operations.

- Paying fair wages and appropriate taxes.

- Investing in developing social infrastructure that will benefit the business and communities alike.

- Screening suppliers based on their commitment to sustainability. This can help to develop a responsible supply chain. St. Michael Hotel & Spa (Cornwall), for example is fully committed to working with local, sustainable suppliers.

Business benefits of sustainability

Sustainable management is likely to benefit the environment and the society, but there are direct benefits to any business that invests in sustainability. According to Choi and Parsa (2006), more and more customers are willing to reward companies that express strong social and environmental responsibility. Others suggest that sustainable management can enhance the brand's image and reputation among stakeholders (Jackson, 1995 cited in Williams *et al.*, 2007). Such 'reputational capital' is of paramount concern to spa operators, especially as their core product, i.e. wellness, is highly intangible. Studies by Berns *et al.* (2009) and Watt and Bayada (2008) establish other business benefits of engaging in sustainability, such as:

- The business can potentially attract more customers and retain existing ones due to an enhanced reputation. There is clear evidence that spa customers are demanding of businesses and expect them to engage in sustainable business practices, and are willing to reward organisations that are seen as responsible by patronising them.

- Stronger brand image can result in greater pricing power. Research suggests that customers are willing to pay a higher price for sustainable products and services (Darnall and Milstein, 2015)

- Higher profits can be achieved through greater efficiencies and less waste (Green Spa Network, 2016). Sustainable business practices imply that the spa will use less energy, water and other supplies. This can result in significant cost savings.

- Sustainability can help enhance relationships with local communities, who are more supportive of businesses that are seen as responsible. It can also help improve business-to-business (B2B) relations.

- Sustainability can also be valuable with respect to human resource management. Sustainable business practices result in greater employee motivation, retention and productivity. In addition, they can enhance the business' ability to attract quality employees (Chawla, 2015).

- Sustainability can help attract ethical investments and improve relations with government regulators.

- Sustainability mitigates environmental, regulatory, physical, competitive and financial risks.

- Spa businesses can take advantage of many incentives such as tax grants and tax reliefs offered by governments.

First steps towards sustainability: where to start?

It is encouraging to note that many international organisations and network groups are actively supporting the spa industry to move forward and adopt the sustainability agenda. The Green Spa Network (www.greenspanetwork.org) is a not-for-profit organisation that develops educational materials for interested operators and shares best practice with them. The National Association of Eco-friendly Salons and Spas (www.naefss.org) publishes a sustainability guidebook to encourage spa owners who might wish to apply sustainable thinking to their business. *Organic Spa* magazine (www.organicspamagazine.com) actively promotes retreats that offer a sustainable spa experience. The International Medical Spa Association (www.dayspassociation.com) and the International Spa Association (www.experienceispa.com) have developed their own codes of business ethics, which serve as excellent guiding principles for businesses interested in sustainability. Measuring sustainable performance is another prime concern for spa managers. The Global Reporting Initiative, or GRI (www.globalreporting.org) publishes detailed disclosure guidelines. In addition, EarthCheck (www.earthcheck.org) and GreenGain (developed by the Green Spa Network) are widely used assessment tools as well. To sum up, whether it is a start-up or a well-established spa business, there is abundant professional guidance and support available with regard to sustainable business practices.

Eco-labels and greenwashing

In addition to the above mentioned organisations that are helping the spa sector to engage in sustainable business practices, the industry can also take advantage of various eco-labels developed specifically for spas. An eco-label is a form of legally protected label that is applied to a product or service, warranting that it complies with certain pre-determined environmental and social criteria (Naumann, 2001). The objective of eco-labelling is to promote consumer confidence in the product, thereby encouraging businesses to adopt sustainable business practices. An eco-label or certification scheme can demonstrate that the spa business is voluntarily and proactively taking measures to incorporate sustainability in the business's vision. There is a multitude of eco-labels specifically for the spa industry. The National Association for Eco-friendly Salons and Spas (www.naefss.org) offers a Certification scheme that evaluates spas in the areas of build out, operations and maintenance. Green Globe (www.greenglobe.com) offers social and environmental benchmarks for tourism and leisure businesses (including spa) and a Certification scheme. EcoCert's label called 'Being' is built on strict criteria around three main concerns – environment, society and health (www.ecocert.com). In a similar vein, TüV Rheinland International Spa Standards provides a seal of approval based on more than 300 specified criteria (www.tuv.com).

It would be fair to say that spa customers are a lot more concerned about sustainability, and eco-labels can further contribute to their knowledge and confidence. However, there is also growing evidence that many clients are more sceptical of the businesses' sustainable initiatives as greenwashing continues in leisure services (Chen and Chang, 2013). Greenwashing refers to the act of misleading consumers regarding the environmental practices of a company or the environmental benefits of a product or service (Parguel *et al.*, 2011). In other words, greenwashing is the malpractice of branding a product as sustainable when that is not the case. Research suggests that clients only value sustainability if it is perceived as genuine and sincere (Kovaljova and Chawla, 2013). Therefore, it is important that spa managers integrate sustainable thinking into their day-to-day operations and transparently communicate such initiatives to the stakeholders (Rahman *et al.*, 2015). The following three case studies demonstrate how sustainability can be embedded into all aspects of the spa experience.

Case studies: Sustainable champions of the spa industry

This section presents sustainable initiatives of three prominent brands in the hotel, spa and wellness sector. It is easy to see that the sustainability programmes discussed below are built on the TBL concept.

Six Senses Hotels & Resorts (2016) craft their entire guest experience on the principles of sustainability. Each property has a unique sustainability programme, addressing environmental and social issues in the area. For example, Six Senses Laamu (Maldives) is fully committed to reduce its environmental footprint. This is achieved by reducing energy consumption, packaging waste and use of plastic bags. The resort offers filtered rather than bottled water. Only eco-certified paper is used for printing (where necessary) and used paper is recycled. In addition, all food waste is composted on site while other waste is sent to recycling centres. The resort educates their guests on responsible snorkelling and diving behaviours. They employ people from the local community and source their supplies from within the area. The resort is committed to comply with Maldivian and international legislations on environmental health, occupational health and safety and employment legislation.

Image 4.1: Source: Six Senses Laamu Website (2016).

In contrast, **Banyan Tree Hotels and Resorts** (2016) adopt a more corporate driven approach to sustainability. This is reflected in their annually published sustainability report (the most recent one was from 2014). The sustainability report focuses on many key stakeholders, such as guests, employees, local communities, the environment, suppliers and investors. Banyan Tree Resorts allow their guests the opportunity to actively participate in sustainable initiatives. In 2007, a company-wide programme called Greening Communities was launched. The objective of this initiative was to engage the communities, employees and guests to reduce their collective footprints. The Seedling Café project was designed to promote vocational skills to at-risk young adults. Banyan Tree also provides scholarships for education to the needy and promotes healthy lifestyles by offering free cooking lessons. Each resort contributes at least 1% of its profits to social and environmental causes.

Image 4.2: Banyan Tree, Ringha (Source: Official Website).

Anantara Hotels, Resorts and Spas (2016) pride themselves on their sustainable initiatives. Their sustainability programme, called '365 Days of Good Deeds' focuses on promoting the local heritage, giving back to the local communities and protecting the environment. Their notable projects include mangrove planting, coral adoption and outreach programmes for orphanages and schools in various parts of the world. The resorts organise beach patrols at night to protect the turtles laying eggs. The hatchery is funded by the donations and protects the eggs from forces of nature and human exploitation. The company offers free therapy sessions for autistic children and built the first elephant hospital in Krabi, Thailand. 'Dollars for Deeds' programme is designed to engage guests in the spirit of giving back and the resort matches every donation made by the guests dollar-for-dollar. Anantara supports entrepreneurial ventures, such as silkworm business for employees' wives, as this allows them financial independence and promotes better quality of life.

4

Image 4.3: Anantara Qasr Al Sarab, Liwa Desert, UAE (source: company website).

It is evident from these three examples that sustainability promotes a better quality of life, while allowing humankind to live in harmony with nature. It is also evident that the focus of each organisation varies, depending on the values of the business. However, these three cases demonstrate that sustainability is seen as serious business in the spa sector. This is a favourable outcome and is reflective of the future of the industry.

Conclusions

To conclude, our discussions so far have produced compelling evidence that sustainability is a complex and multi-faceted agenda. However, it is the need of the hour and can ensure long term viability of the spa industry. Sustainability concerns all stakeholders, and businesses must willingly give back to the societies they dwell among. It is clear that sustainability is a prime concern in the spa and wellness industry, as the sector itself is reliant on environmental and socio-cultural resources. Sustainable initiatives demand absolute commitment and support from the top management. It is important that sustainability is not viewed as an add-on, but is integrated with all aspects of the business strategy. There is no doubt that the spa and wellness industry is already embracing sustainability and concepts such as eco-spas are likely to flourish. This will not only promote wellness, but also preventative health. Only sustainable business practices can ensure that the industry can continue to grow. There is no doubt that the future of the spa industry is 'green'.

Discussion topics

Eco-spa has shifted from being an industry-driven to consumer-driven trend (Spafinder, 2008). This probably explains why many resorts aggressively market themselves as eco-spas. Titanic Eco-Spa in Huddersfield, UK (www.titanicspa.com), Diantree Eco-lodge and Spa in North Queensland, Australia (www.daintree-ecolodge.com.au) and Natura Park Beach Resort and Spa in The Dominican Republic (www.blauhotels.com) are well-known destination spa resorts that pride themselves on their sustainable business practices.

Examine the sustainability programmes of these self-styled eco-spas and answer the following:

■ Outline their sustainable practices and analyse them based on TBL.

■ To what extent do their sustainable programmes reflect a balanced approach between people, profit and planet as advocated by TBL?

■ What is the key focus of these spa resorts from a sustainability perspective? What might be the underlying reasons?

■ How do their sustainability policies compare against one another?

References

Anantara Hotels, Resorts and Spas. (2016) Social responsibility. Available at: http://www.anantara.com/our-projects/ [Accessed 20 January 2016].

Banyan Tree Hotels and Resorts. (2016) A journey of sustainability. Available at: http://media.corporate-ir.net/media_files/IROL/20/200797/Banyan_SR2014_SGX.PDF [Accessed 20 January 2016].

Berns, M., Townend, A., Khayat, Z., Balagopal, B., Reeves, M., Hopkins, M. and Kruschwitz, N. (2009) The business of sustainability: imperatives, advantages and actions, The Boston Consulting Group. Available at: https://www.bcg.com/documents/file29480.pdf [Accessed 16 January 2016].

Brien, C. (2009) The challenge of eco demands on spas, *Financial Times,* 18 April. Available at: http://www.ft.com/cms/s/0/88675f00-2add-11de-8415-00144feabdc0.html [Accessed 22 February 2016].

Brown, A. (2005) Spa trends of 2005, About Travel. Available at: http://spas.about.com/od/spareviews/a/topspatrends.htm [Accessed 21 February 2016].

Burkholder, P. (2007) *Start Your Own Day Spa and More.* Irvine CA: Entrepreneur Press.

Cabie, I. (2014) Sustainable tourism: ten key issues investors should consider, *The Guardian,* 3 April. Available at: http://www.theguardian.com/sustainable-business/sustainable-tourism-10-key-issues-investors [Accessed 22 February 2016].

Chawla, G. and Ndung'u, M.W. (2014) The ethics of an all-inclusive plan: an investigation of social sustainability in the case of all-inclusive resorts, Jamaica. *Research in Hospitality Management,* **4** (1/2), 21-28.

Chawla, G. (2015) Ethical employment in the catering industry, in P Sloan, W. Legrand and C. Hindley. *The Routledge Handbook of Sustainable Food and Gastronomy.* Routledge: London, 145-156.

Chen, Y. and Chang, C. (2013) Greenwash and green trust: the mediation effects of green consumer confusion and green perceived risk, *Journal of Business Ethics,* **114**, 489-500.

Choi, G. and Parsa, H.G. (2006) Green practices II: Measuring restaurant managers' psychological attributes and their willingness to charge for the green practices, *Journal of Foodservice Business Research,* **9**(4), 41-63.

Cooper, M. (2009)Health and wellness spa tourism environment, in: P. Erfurt-Cooper and M. Cooper. *Health and Wellness Tourism: Spas and Hot Springs,* Bristol: Channel View Publications, 156-180.

Darnall, N. and Milstein, M. (2015) Can eco-standards and certification create competitive advantage for a luxury resort? in H.G. Parsa and V. Narapareddy, *Sustainability, Social Responsibility and Innovations in Tourism and Hospitality*, Apple Academic Press: Oakville, 1-46.

Elkington, J. (1997) *Cannibals With Forks: The Triple Bottom Line of 21st Century Business,* Oxford: Capstone.

Erfurt-Cooper, P. (2009) The health and wellness concept: a global overview, in P. Erfurt-Cooper and M. Cooper. *Health and Wellness Tourism: Spas and Hot Springs.* Bristol: Channel View Publications,25-48.

Franknel, C. (1998) *In Earth's Company.* Gabriola Island: New Society Publishers.

Gardetti, M.A. and Torres, A.L. (2016) *Sustainability in Hospitality.* Sheffield: Greenleaf Publishing.

Global Wellness Summit. (2015) Building a well world, Available at: http://www. globalwellnesssummit.com/images/stories/gsws2015/pdf/summit-wrap-up-2015-mexico-final.pdf [Accessed 17 January 2016].

Green Spa Network. (2016) Why choose a green spa? Available at: http://greenspanetwork. org/why-choose-green-spa/ [Accessed 4 July 2016].

Indian Green Building Council. (2016) Green building rating: overrated. Available at: www.cseindia.org/userfiles/04GreenBuilding.pdf [Accessed 22 January 2016].

Johnson, E.M. and Redman, B.M. (2008) *Spa: a Comprehensive Introduction.* Lansing, Michigan: The American Hotel and Lodging Educational Institute.

Kovaljova, P. and Chawla, G. (2013) Can sustainability really add customer value? The case of Hotel Ermitage, Evian-Les-Bains, France, *Proceedings of the International Conference on Hospitality and Leisure Applied Research, Lausanne,* July 4-5, 9-18.

McMichael, T. (2005) Sustainability, health and well-being, in J. Goldie and B. Furnass. *In Search of Sustainability.* Collingwood, Victoria: CSIRO Publishing, 17-31.

Mowforth, M. and Munt, I. (2009) *Tourism and Sustainability: Development, Globalisation and New Tourism in the Third World.* 3rd ed. Abingdon: Routledge.

Naumann, E. (2001) Eco-labelling: Overview and implications for developing countries, Development Policy Research Unit. Available at: http://www.dpru.uct.ac.za/sites/ default/files/image_tool/images/36/DPRU%20PB%2001-P19.pdf [Accessed 5 July 2016].

Parguel, B., Benoit-Moreau, F. and Larceneux, F. (2011) How sustainability ratings might deter greenwashing: a closer look at ethical corporate communication, *Journal of Business Ethics,* **102**(1), 15-28.

Porter, M. E. and Kramer, M.R. (2011) Creating shared value, *Harvard Business Review,* January-February, 1-17.

Porter, M., Sala-I-Martin, X. and Schwab, K. (2008) *The Global Competitiveness Report 2007-2008.* Basingstoke, UK: Palgrave Macmillan.

Rahman, I., Park, J. and Chi, C.G. (2015) Consequences of greenwashing: consumers' reactions to hotels' green initiatives, *International Journal of Contemporary Hospitality Management,* **27**(6), 1054-1081.

Reynolds, G. (2004) At eco-spas, it's nature and nurture, *The New York Times.* 23rd April. Available at: http://www.nytimes.com/2004/04/23/travel/journeys-at-eco-spas-it-s-nature-and-nurture.html [Accessed 10 July 2016].

Six Senses Hotels & Resorts. (2016) Sustainability. Available at: http://www.sixsenses.com/resorts/laamu/sustainability [Accessed 20 January 2016].

Sloan, P., Legrand, W. and Chen, J.S. (2013) *Sustainability in the Hospitality Industry.* 2nd ed. Abingdon: Routledge.

Smith, M. and Puczkó, L. (2014) *Health, Tourism and Hospitality.* 2nd ed. Abingdon: Routledge.

Spafinder. (2008) Spafinder 6th annual full trends report, Spafinder. Available at: http://www.spafinder.com/blog/press-release/spafinder-issues-6th-annual-full-trends-report-top-10-spa-trends-to-watch-in-2009/#4 [Accessed 21 February 2016].

Spafinder. (2016) Spa and wellness glossary, Spafinder. Available at: http://www.spafinder.com/blog/content/spaguides/spa-glossary/#E [Accessed 22 February 2016].

Stipanuk, D. (1996) The U.S. lodging industry and the environment, *Cornell Hotel and Restaurant Administration Quarterly,* **37**(5), 39-45.

Ufland, A. and Sternfeld, L. (2009) Eco design, *Spa Management,* **19**(3), 86-94.

United Nations Framework Convention on Climate Change. (2009) The Copenhagen Accord, Available at: https://unfccc.int/meetings/copenhagen_dec_2009/items/5262.php [Accessed 25 February 2016].

Watt, M. and Bayada, B. (2008) Environmental and social benchmarking, in M. Cohen and G. Bodeker, 2nd ed. *Understanding the Global Spa Industry.* Abingdon: Routeldge, 303-316.

Williams, P., Gill, A. and Ponsford, I. (2007) Corporate social responsibility at tourism destinations: toward a social license to operate. *Tourism Review International,* **11**, 133-144.

5 The Wellness Industry: From Therapy to Hedonism

Pascal Mandelartz and Isobel Stockdale

"Time and Silence are the most luxurious things today." Tom Ford

Introduction

Bathing in thermal waters, massages, beauty treatments, alternative medicine – the spectrum of products and services offered by the wellness industry is large, as outlined in this book. Boundaries between self-indulgence and therapeutic necessity are blurred. The intention of this chapter is to further the debate on the conceptualisation of classifications of wellness products and services offered by the industry. The aim is to provide insights into the broad variety of products and services offered by the wellness sector, catering for market specifics from products, including medical elements to products that include elements of hedonism. To enable the visualisation of such a scale, wellness products have been placed within a spectrum to allow a differentiation of products that cater for medical wellbeing in comparison to offerings that cater for the decadence of pampering and luxury. The chapter discusses the broader lines of providing remedies and cures in comparison to services which have no scientifically proven or at least questionable impacts on the physical health of guests, in an industry that faces increasing competition, forcing further product segmentation and development.

Why do people choose wellness services?

The reasons for choosing wellness services are as multifaceted as their consumers: from people trying to revitalise, maintain their beauty, escape from their daily lives, treat themselves to something extraordinary, to the ones who want to work on their well-being holistically, but also those who have aches and pains up to serious illnesses. In a postmodern society the categories can be kaleidoscopic, meaning that they can merge and change for each person also during time, and are partially influenced by their sociocultural environment. Imagine winning the lottery, would you treat yourself to more extravagant forms of wellness?

Unfortunately not everybody can win the lottery but many people still want the special treatments offered by the industry, so we might take what our time and budgets allow us. This implies that there must be added levels of luxury in the spectrum of wellness products and services. Furthermore one might suggest that if the economic situation of an individual allows it, there may be increased levels of hedonism as well as enhanced forms of treatments when being treated in health related issues. So what does the term hedonism actually imply? As there are varying definitions of hedonism we would like to go with Veenhoven's (2003:437) definition: "for a way of life in which pleasure plays an important role. Hedonists are people who are positive about pleasure and who pluck the fruits of pleasure when possible."

Also interesting is the concept of hedonism by Crisp (2006: 620-621)

'It is not psychological hedonism, the view that human action or perhaps rational and deliberate human action is motivated by a concern for the greatest expected balance of pleasure over pain. Nor is it a view about morality, such as hedonistic utilitarianism, according to which the right thing to do is maximize impartially the balance of pleasure over pain. Nor is it a view about the good, since the kind of hedonism I have in mind is consistent with the view that there are non-hedonist values, such as aesthetic values. Nor is it a view about what makes for a good life, or a good human life. Nor, even, is it a view about happiness, which may well be understood most plausibly in a non-hedonistic way. Rather, I wish to discuss hedonism as a theory of well-being, that is, of what is ultimately good for any individual.'

Thereby, socio-cultural understanding plays an important role in how the individual defines what is ultimately good for them.

Despite several scholars having argued that spa visitation caters to 'hedonistic sybarites' (Dann and Nordstrand, 2009: 127) or suggesting that spa visitors are focused on the "superficial quest for merely feeling 'well' rather than on 'true' well-being" (Steiner and Reisinger, 2006: 12) or describing spiritual retreat visitors as pursuing more meaningful and worthy experiences, portraying them as the 'true' wellness tourists (Smith, 2003; Steiner and Reisinger, 2006), Voigt *et al.* (2010) in their study on hedonic and eudaimonic experiences of wellness tourists suggest that from a positive well-being point of view, it is "too simplistic to view hedonic tourism experiences as shallow, or to equate spa visitors with unhealthful, overindulgent individuals who seek meaningless pleasures". Hedonic well-being or positive affect should not be regarded as unsubstantial, meaningless, or even destructive and that "the lines between hedonic pleasure and more 'meaningful pursuits' should not be drawn too rigidly" (King *et al.*, 2006: 191). Instead they note that positive psychologists regard hedonic and eudaimonic well-being as equally important in achieving a state of optimal positive psychological well-being.

Society increasingly recognises the importance of experiential leisure and the significance of the pause, furthering the understanding of leisure as a state of mind, perceived freedom vs. relative freedom, intrinsic motivation and self-determination in leisure. Within contemporary society there are numerous reasons for seeking soothing, calming environments and escapism from the daily routine, with terms like work-life balance, burnout syndrome and depression becoming increasingly important in the work environment. Depression and anxiety are the most prevalent global mental disorders, with an estimated 350 million people of all ages being affected (WHO, 2016) The World Health Organisation (WHO) estimates that by 2020 depression alone will be the most prevalent single cause of disability in both the developed and the developing world, affecting more woman than men (Lopez *et al.*, 2006; WHO, 2016).

As a remedy, the role of well-being/wellness in improving mental health is of increasing interest, not only to the spa and wellness industry, but also to psychologists and medical sciences. More than 30 years ago, Butler and Wall (1985) suggested that potential relationships exist between tourism and mental as well as physical health, stating the need for more explicit attention.

Aside from improving mental health, wellness can be regarded as a holistic approach to improving well-being. Within a public health framework, the activities that can improve health include the promotion of health, the prevention of illness and disability, and the treatment and rehabilitation of those affected. These are different from one another, even though the actions and outcomes overlap. They are all required, are complementary, and no one is a substitute for the other (Herrman *et al.*, 2005: 6). As categories overlap and merge together, it is becoming increasingly difficult to differentiate the variety of wellness services and offerings available from the industry, possibly due to the fact that the World Health Organisation since 1946 has followed a more holistic approach to define health as physical, psychological and social well-being, signalling the move away from purely treating illnesses towards increasing the well-being of each individual.

Competition in the market is also increasing, and similarly to other service industries new niches are created and established thereby diversifying the wellness market. Within the spa industry, the definitions of the terms wellness and health are inconsistent and they vary significantly as well as being used interchangeably, even though they often describe different concepts.

From therapy to hedonism

Dunn (1959: 4) as a pioneer in the field defined wellness as "an integrated method of functioning which is oriented toward maximizing the potential of which the individual is capable. It requires that the individual maintain a continuum of balance and purposeful direction within the environment where he is functioning." He also stated that "wellness is a direction in progress toward an ever-higher potential of functioning" (1959: 6). Dunn also described wellness as health being, "much more than the absence of disease remains a cornerstone concept of wellness today" (1959: 7). Dunn saw wellness as hierarchical: there were lower levels of wellness and higher ones, and the aim was to move everyone up from where they started to high-level wellness (Dunn, 1961) (see Figure 5.1).

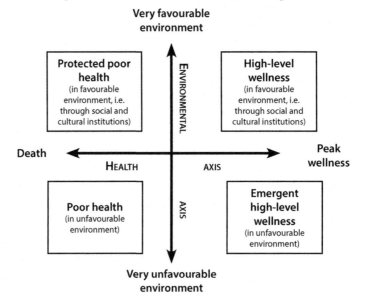

Figure 5.1: Dunn (1961) The health grid

Connected to this narrative, nowadays there is a multitude of offerings, treatments and products designed by the spa and wellness industry to cater for each market segment. The concept of holistic wellness is defined as an integrated method of functioning that is oriented towards maximising the potential of which the individual is capable within the environment where he or she is functioning. Furthermore, it is essential for destinations, resorts and spas in contemporary society to support their unique selling points and positioning within the market by offering differentiated, individualised products within the global wellness market. Local products, tangibles and ambience provide individuality and also the exclusivity that may provide a higher level of difficulty to be copied by the competitors. Hotels and wellness providers, and sometimes the tourist destination, play a role in the creation of these offerings. So when in Ottawa, Canada, to maximise this potential, guests of the Holtz Spa can indulge in 'white chocolate truffle wraps' or 'maple luscious' maple syrup peelings and body wraps (holtzspa. com,) underlining the trend for individualised local/regional experiences.

Wellness is seen as an active process through which individuals can become aware of and make choices that will lead to a more successful existence in social, occupational, spiritual, physical, intellectual and emotional dimensions (Hettler, 1976). By these definitions wellness is occupying most aspects of our life and there is seemingly no end to the process of diversifying the products and services offered to create unique selling points that distinguish a company from the rest of the market.

It has to be said that spa and wellness, in the historic sense, are elitist as an industry, catering for the middle and upper classes. This is especially the case for services dedicated to self-indulgence and hedonism rather than providing cure and relief from certain illnesses, although services in that area do exist. Some of the strange treatments enable the customer to experience something that no one else has. Although even when it comes to medical treatments, the boundary lines are blurred as levels of luxury (that may include aspects of pampering and holistic wellness) are added wherever possible.

Schuster *et al.* (2004) note that individuals may use certain methods of complementary and alternative medicine as an alternative to conventional medical care or supplement their treatment on medical complaints. For others complementary and alternative medicine are part of a health lifestyle that places emphasis on preventive health care. They also find use in lifestyles that promote wellness through elements of disease prevention practices, a healthy diet, stress reduction and regular exercise.

The interpretations of the terms within the spectrum of wellness are many-sided. The GSS report (2011) on Wellness and Medical tourism asked: where do spas fit? There are again multiple answers to the question dependent on the institution, culture, society and scholar that is asked. The report also encompasses socio-cultural understandings leading to regional concepts and initiatives. The association of German health resorts (Deutscher Heilbäderverband e.V.) for example has created a model (see Figure 5.2) for wellness quality that embeds four pillars, namely, medicine and therapy, nature and culture, exercise and relaxation, communication and experience.

Figure 5.2: Wellness in a health resort (Deutscher Heilbäderverband e.V, 2002)

It is interesting to note that social aspects such as culture and communication as well as clinical aspects such as medicine and therapy have been included to achieve the goal of holistic wellness for the guest. It further indicates a link between the wellness and the medical element.

Distinctions between the clinical and the social have been made by Philo (2000) and Greenhough (2006). Little (2012) uses the term 'pampering' to describe the link between health and wellbeing and the appropriate body, admitting that the term is often used as 'a 'catch-all' term for describing a range of practices in which the individual is indulged, and through which their bodies are 'treated' using a variety of (often small scale) luxuries. Such luxuries take the form of products (oils, lotions, towels) and environments (use of music, comfortable seating, attractive décor). Pampering sometimes incorporates a sense of the exotic and is generally seen as something that the client does not receive at home or in their daily lives. Straddling the boundaries between the medical and the cosmetic body in well-being practices, it draws attention to "the fluidity of such boundaries in contemporary gendered subjectivities" (p.5). Price and revenue as a factor have been considered by Kimes and Singh (2008) who discuss the effectiveness of facility and capacity management.

Yeoman (2011), in his research of changing behaviours of luxury consumption, remarks that as a society becomes wealthier its definition of luxury changes. Luxury, indulgence and hedonism become more accessible to a wider market spectrum, creating difficulty for luxury products to defend their exclusivity. "Smaller, affordable luxuries and quality products are strengthening their appeal as consumers continue to satisfy their need for regular treats and indulgences in their lives. At the same time, luxury products have set out to protect their exclusivity through premium pricing and authenticity" (p.50) whilst also trying to capture their market share by offering accessibility to consumers via the high street and the World Wide Web which could lessen the exclusivity of the brand.

Providing new extraordinary experiences to those that can afford them is a difficult endeavour. Azara, in Chapter 6, brings Maslow into the debate, and the hierarchy of needs can certainly assist in explaining the move away from the safety and security element to self-actualisation and experiencing purpose. It accumulates in spas, hotels and resorts upping their game to levels of 'Extreme Wellness' where the offering now includes ridiculous health perks (Details, 2014).

To clarify this, the wellness industry diversifies on all levels but where further investment is made possible there is a seemingly never ending strain of new ideas and services that might add to the customer's wellbeing, be it vinotherapy or vitamin C infused showers. The industry is trying to educate the guest and suggest lifestyle changes to prevent the yo-yo effect; the continuation of the wellness lifestyle experience post destination being incorporated into everyday life (GSWS, 2013). The difficulty being that, as Conradson (2005) states, wellness has a self-care factor and when the medical link and therefore advice is lacking we make lay decisions based on our cultural and social identity.

Husain and Pheng (2010) lament the fact that in contemporary society the consumer is overwhelmed by the information and marketing material provided by the industry. They conducted a study on enhancing the wellness recommendation services available on a wellness community portal to find the best technique(s) for matching users' wellness concerns with appropriate wellness therapy, and making reliable wellness recommendations based on individual preferences and wellness conditions. This underlines the fact that there is further demand for conceptualising the spectrum of products and services offered by the industry.

The following sections will be concerned with conceptualisations of wellness products and services, adding to the debate by suggesting a model that builds on previous attempts of shedding light onto the multiple facets of an industry that is becoming increasingly diverse, and which incorporates not only the self-care and medical element but also portrays the levels of luxury added to services provided.

Added levels of luxury – conceptualising the wellness industry

Heterogeneity, segmentation and product diversification characterise the vast number of products and services offered under the umbrella term 'wellness'. Schweder (2010), for instance, compares the previous millennium fitness centre model to the new millennium holistic wellness sanctuary with therapeutic values. Instead of a gym, pool, sauna and aerobics, one now hopes to find high-energy fitness, holistic exercises and specialty programmes, water and wet area experiences, spa treatment services, nutrition expertise, spa merchandise, lifestyle event series, and unique trend-setting designs, making it a substantial business driver for businesses such as hotels and spa centres.

Categorisation and conceptualisation of the industry are hence of increasing importance in guiding industry decisions and furthering the understanding of motivational factors and customer decision-making processes.

The Global Spa Summit (2011) in their model differentiate between wellness and medical tourism when categorising different offerings. (See Figure 2.3, p. 18.)

The intersection, combination and distinction does however seem to be far more varied than suggested. What about hotels offering thalassotherapy, what about cosmetic surgery clinics that are attached to hotel complexes or Ayurvedic clinics within eco resorts? These all do happen.

There is a North Sea clinic that offers tourists the package *Sylt gesund*, currently for €1369, including seven nights "in a lakeside cottage with up-market ambience". Included are relaxing massages, hydrojet treatments mud baths, Kneipp therapy, nordic walking and water aerobics. Treatments by medical staff are not required. Even medical check-ups are optional. Several offers by the clinic have been disapproved by the county council, including ones which partially use the hospital facilities but which are not part of the primary care or rehabilitation regime. The hospital now wants to further its product mix by adding rehab and prevention services for private payees, that are medically identifiable and can be differentiated from touristic products (SHZ, n.d)).

The case underlines the blurred boundaries between wellness and medical products that also include added levels of cost and luxury. To visualise the added levels of luxury in wellness products a model has been created. (See Figure 5.3)

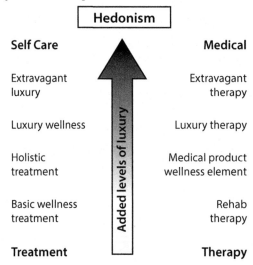

Figure 5.3: From therapy to hedonism: Added levels of Luxury.

The model differentiates between the self-care element which does not include the cure of illness as a motivational factor to visit. The medical spectrum includes the cure of illness as a push factor to visit. It has the wish for a treatment or the need to undertake therapy as a starting point, but treatment can be complemented with added levels of luxury.

The components for self-care include:

- **Basic wellness treatment**: As a form of escapism from the stresses of day-to-day life, relaxation. It includes products and services such as the day spa, wellness weekends, massages etc.

- **Holistic treatments**: These include aspects that benefit the wellness dimensions, i.e. reflexology, aromatherapy, social, spiritual, nutrition, tranquillity, stimulation of the senses.

- **Luxury wellness**: Include aspects of indulgence, more tangibles, value-added components, brands, wider range of facilities, appearance

- **Extravagant luxury**: Top-of-the-range products, special treatments, extraordinary facilities that distinguish and differentiate themselves from the rest of the market. High service levels, extraordinary treatments sometimes with questionable health benefits. Consultation on various aspects of wellness. Certified excellence.

The components for medical wellness include:

- **Rehab therapy**: The need for rehabilitation, physiotherapy, medical regimes that require prolonged stays away from home. Here the services can be basic and focussed on the medical recovery but luxury can be added through better facilities, interior design or tangibles offered to the guest.

- **Medical product that includes wellness elements**: There is a medical underpinning as a motivational factor, however many aspects of luxury are included that make the experience more comfortable and enjoyable as well as having benefits for holistic well-being.

- **Luxury therapy:** There is a medical aspect but the services and products are of a very high standard, special treatments, extraordinary facilities that are not seen as a necessity for curing an illness. Consultation from specialists. Holistic treatments, tranquillity.

- **Extravagant therapy**: Top-of-the-range products, new treatments, special treatments, tangibles, value-added, prevention, holistic consultation, expected professionalism, experts.

The model suggests that there is a move away from the necessity to take a treatment and the basic standards of self-indulgence, to higher levels up to "non-essential items or services that contribute to luxurious living and indulgence or convenience beyond the indispensable minimum" (Webster, 2002). Kapferer (1997:253) states that: "Luxury items provide extra pleasure and flatter all senses at once". It is interesting to note that this is the case for taking self-care treatments as well as for medical therapy. Luxury elements can be added on all levels, and services are sometimes even provided within the same facilities. Within the model, the added level of luxury hence increases through the stages. The added wellbeing benefit for the customer requires further debate. It seems like a comparison between cars. How beneficial is it for a driver to drive a luxury car when any car could fulfil the main purpose of bringing a person from A to B? Well, the luxury car might offer better ambience, heated seats, a better sound system and higher quality products that adds value to the overall experience.

Conclusion

Wellness can be a hedonistic indulgence as well as a therapeutic endeavour to get relief from physical and psychological discomforts, and to some it is both. Those who can afford it are likely to add levels of luxury to their preferred choice of products and services. As these become more diversified and heterogenous we shall not exclude the holistic idea behind wellness that is of importance to each individual within a society. Looking at the variety of interpretations of terms within the wellness spectrum amongst cultures and standings, perhaps we need to embed wellness further in our culture and society, for example to include wellness at work. There is now an expectation that an individual's wellbeing is being valued and developed. The GWS (2016) state that wellness at work will explode in the next five to ten years, and that the current programmes will be replaced by a new culture of wellness. There will become an expectation that organisations have to be responsible for wellness and how the work environment and ethos affects it. The changing of mind set, work to live rather than living to work, more balance/harmony. Employers doing right by their employees and the community. A move away from an industrial ethos into a postmodern delineated way of life that acknowledges individuality. This will eventually lead to even further permutation of the wellness industry from therapy to hedonism as products, facilities and services diversify, offering a new spectrum of niches but also collaborations.

Discussion questions

- Is hedonism part of the wellness customer decision-making process?

- Differentiate the terms: health treatment, medical treatment, wellness treatment and spa treatment.

- Would the consumption of wellness services change if a person were more wealthy?

- Why is there an ongoing process of wellness product and service diversification?

- Do cultures interpret wellness differently?

References

Butler, R. and Wall, G. (1985) Introduction: Themes in research on the evolution of tourism, *Annals of Tourism Research*, **12**(3), 287-296.

Conradson, D. (2005) Landscape, care and the relational self: therapeutic encounters in rural England, *Health & Place*, **11**(4), 337-348.

Crisp, R. (2006) Hedonism reconsidered, *Philosophy and Phenomenological Research*, **73**(3), 619-645.

Dann, G. and Berg Nordstrand, K. (2009) Promoting wellbeing via multisensory tourism, *Wellness and Tourism: Mind, body, spirit, place*, 125-137.

Details (2014) http://www.details.com/fashion-style/grooming/201402/luxury-hotels-amenities-fitness-and-wellness, accessed on 5/9/2015

Deutscher Heilbäderverband e.V (2002) http://www.deutscher-heilbaederverband.de

Dunn, H. L. (1959) High-level wellness for man and society, *American Journal of Public Health and the Nation's Health*, **49**(6), 786-792.

Dunn, H. L. (1961) *High-level wellness: A collection of twenty-nine short talks on different aspects of the theme "High-level wellness for man and society."* Slack.

Global Spa Summit (GSS) (2011) *Wellness Tourism and Medical Tourism: Where Do Spas Fit?* from: http://www.spaindustry.ca/files/file/Business%20Tools/spas_wellness_medical_tourism_report_final.pdf

Greenhough, B. (2006) Tales of an island-laboratory: defining the field in geography and science studies, *Transactions of the Institute of British Geographers* (31), 224-238.

Global Spa and Wellness Summit (GSWS) (2013). Global Hot Springs. Hot Springs Forum 7 October, New Delhi India

Herrman, H., Saxena, S. and Moodie, R. (2005) *Promoting mental health: concepts, emerging evidence, practice: a report of the World Health Organization, Department of Mental Health and Substance Abuse in collaboration with the Victorian Health Promotion Foundation and the University of Melbourne.* World Health Organization.

Hettler, B. (1976) The six dimensions of wellness, National Wellness Institute (www.nwi. org), and http://www.hettler.com/sixdimen.htm.

Husain, W. and Pheng, L. T. (2010) The development of personalized wellness therapy recommender system using hybrid case-based reasoning, In *Computer Technology and Development (ICCTD), 2010 2nd International Conference* (pp. 85-89). IEEE.

Kimes, S. E. and Singh, S. (2008) Spa revenue management, *Cornell Hospitality Quarterly.*

King, L. A., Hicks, J. A., Krull, J. L. and Del Gaiso, A. K. (2006), Positive affect and the experience of meaning in life, *Journal of Personality and Social Psychology*, **90**(1), 179–196.

Little, J. (2013) Pampering, well-being and women's bodies in the therapeutic spaces of the spa, *Social & Cultural Geography*, **14**(1), 41-58.

Lopez, A. D., Mathers, C. D., Ezzati, M., Jamison, D. T. and Murray, C. J. (2006) Global and regional burden of disease and risk factors, 2001: systematic analysis of population health data, *The Lancet*, **367** (9524), 1747-1757.

Philo, C. (2000) The birth of the clinic: an unknown work of medical geography, *AREA* **30**, 11-19.

Schuster, T. L., Dobson, M., Jauregui, M. and Blanks, R. H. (2004) Wellness lifestyles I: A theoretical framework linking wellness, health lifestyles, and complementary and alternative medicine, *The Journal of Alternative & Complementary Medicine*, **10**(2), 349-356.

Schweder, I. (2010) The emergence of a new global luxury business model: a case study of the spa at the Mandarin Oriental, in M. Cohen and G. Bodeker (eds) *Understanding the Global Spa Industry: Spa Management*, Oxford: Butterworth-Heinemann,171-180.

SHZ (n.d) http://www.shz.de/lokales/sylter-rundschau/schluss-mit-wellness-urlaub-in-der-nordseeklinik-auf-sylt-id10007526.html, accessed on 5/9/15

Smith, M. (2003) Holistic holidays: Tourism and the reconciliation of body, mind and spirit, *Tourism Recreation Research*, **28** (1), 103–108.

Steiner, C. J. and Reisinger, Y. (2006) Ringing the fourfold: A philosophical framework for thinking about wellness tourism, *Tourism Recreation Research*, **31**(1), 5-14.

Veenhoven, R. (2003) Hedonism and happiness, *Journal of Happiness Studies*, **4**(4), 437-457.

Voigt, C., Howat, G. and Brown, G. (2010) Hedonic and eudaimonic experiences among wellness tourists: an exploratory enquiry, *Annals of Leisure Research*, **13**(3), 541-562.

Webster, (2002) Third International Dictionary, Merriam Webster

WHO, (2016) Depression, WHO Media Centre, http://www.who.int/mediacentre/factsheets/fs369/en/

Yeoman, I. (2011) The changing behaviours of luxury consumption, *Journal of Revenue & Pricing Management*, **10**(1), 47-50.

5

6 Principles and Practices of Spa Consumer Behaviour

Iride Azara

Introduction

The spa industry is complex and multifaceted, encompassing a variety of markets, each with specific consumer behavioural characteristics (SRI, 2008; Beattie, 2011). Spa consumer behaviour research is still in its infancy, and to date there remains a need to develop a deeper understanding of consumer behavioural characteristics. This chapter provides students with an understanding of the principles of consumer behaviour as applicable to spa consumers. The chapter begins with a discussion on the current and emerging regional patterns of demand for spa, discussing some of the key stimulants. It then moves on to highlight the challenges in identifying types of demands for spa. The chapter then presents and discusses the main concepts of consumer behaviour in spa, including key models derived from related disciplines of marketing, business, tourism and hospitality, which can be used to understand the complexities of spa guests' behaviour. The chapter concludes with a discussion on how the understanding of consumer behaviour in spa is vital for marketers and business operators alike.

Regional patterns of demand in spa and key stimulants for growth

In this section we look at current regional patterns of demand in spa. In so doing we aim to begin unpacking some of the reasons behind the demand differentiation and fragmentation of the spa products and practices encountered today. The latest report produced by the Global Wellness Institute (GWI, 2014) highlights how Europe, Asia Pacific and North America account for 86% of the world's spa markets. Europe, with its history of therapeutic bathing and wellness traditions dating back Roman and Greek civilisations, is considered to be the largest and most mature regional spa market in the world. It primarily services a demand for preventive, therapeutic, curative and rehabilitative services, many of which are built around or complement thermal and mineral springs resorts (SRI, 2007; GWI, 2014). The industry accounts for an estimated 25,000 spa facilities, generating a €20 billion turnover. The region directly employs 500,000 people and supports an additional 1.2 million jobs in related fields (Beattie, 2011). The Asia- Pacific market is currently the second largest market after Europe in terms of spa revenue, with an estimated €18.8 billion turnover. Yet the region now surpasses Europe in terms of the number of operating spa businesses, with a further potential for growth as more and more traditional wellness practitioners cross over into the spa market (SRI, 2007; GWI, 2014). Spa demand is predominantly made of international tourists staying in hotels, resorts and destination spas, pursuing wellness, health preservation and promotion, and increasingly interested in culturally-based healing and wellness therapies, such as Ayurveda, Thai and Chinese massages and Aboriginal treatments.

Growing international demand is also directed towards medical tourism facilities, combining health treatments with recuperation, healing and convalescence-specific spa treatments. Domestic demand for day/club/salon spas continues to grow in middle and upper income countries, such as Japan, Korea, Hong Kong, Singapore, Australia, and New Zealand (SRI, 2007). However, it is worth noting how similar trends are being registered in relatively newly industrialised countries, such as China and India (GWI, 2014).

Incorporating two well-established markers such as the USA and Canada, the North American spa industry, with 20,660 spas and $13.5 billion in revenues, currently ranks third in terms of revenues and in the number of spas. Although traditional demand concentrates around day/club/salon spas and hotel/resort spas, new industry segments and new business models continue to emerge in both countries. The GWI (2014) report mentions an increase in demand for spa services offered on the premises of a customer's home or office, as well as demand for cruise ship spas.

Finally, fast growth is registered in regional markets such as the sub-Saharan Africa and South America spa markets; a growth that arguably exposes well the societal changes underway in those regions. Broadly speaking, notions of differentiation and internationalisation of demand in spa can be ascribed to macro-economic, technological and socio-cultural changes which, gathering pace towards the latter part of the last century, continue to impinge upon the global spa industry today (see Table 6.1).

At a simple level, globalisation, understood here as a contemporary growth in goods and services, information communication, people and cultures' mobility across frontiers, can be seen as problematising the current industry trends and spa consumption activities we observe today. For example, the proliferation across the globe of products such as Garra rufa fish spas, Hamman experiences or even hot stone massages, reflect an increased tendency towards cultural homogenisation and standardisation of the spa offer. Yet, simultaneously, globalisation can be seen as a major enabling force behind these changes, for example fuelling global demand for once cultural-based, locally-specific traditions and practices such as Indian Ayurveda (Azara and Stockdale, 2012). As spa as a concept and experience becomes an integral part of consumers' everyday life and consumers become more discerning, greater demands are placed on businesses and destinations to offer new and unique local practices capable of stimulating consumers' senses and desires. As Suzie Ellis, founder of SpaFinder, said "There is no more powerful consumer trend across the developed world than the hunger for all things authentic and indigenous, impacting what we now most want to eat […], to where we most want to travel" (Spafinder Wellness UK, 2015).

Increases in disposable income
Growth of global middle class (especially in emerging economies such as China, India, Russia, Brazil, etc.)
Advances in technology and improved scientific research dealing with health and appearances and quality of life
Ease and availability of travel
Increased in leisure time
Increased democratisation of health access
Ageing population and rises of lifestyle diseases
Economic recessions in traditional markets and expansions into new ones
Threats of global pandemics
Growth in specialised intermediaries/ suppliers
Differentiation of offers/ products, services
Improved presentation of the product/ increased importance of semiotic
Increase in consumer culture and de-differentiation of cultural spheres leading to the incorporation of spa as everyday practice

Table 6.1: Macro factors fuelling differentiation of demand for spa

Typologies of spa demand and challenges in market segmentation

Much research has been produced over the years attempting to advance knowledge and understanding of contemporary forms of spa demand (Mueller and Kaufmann, 2001; Mintel, 2004; Smith and Laszlo, 2009 and 2014; GWI, 2014). Despite these works, spa consumer behaviour research is still in its infancy and to date there still remains a need to produce a more thorough and rigorous understanding of consumers' behaviour and characteristics (Beattie, 2011). Demand has traditionally been thought of as divided into two broad types: demand for medically oriented spa services or experiences such as galvanic treatments, mud packs and inhalation therapies, typically offered in many European thermal spas; and demand for spa products or services designed to foster a holistic sense of wellbeing, such as Swedish and Thai massages, and colour and crystal therapy. Yet, it is clear that consumer demand today is tremendously varied, in a way reflecting the relentless globalisation and hybridisation of the industry and of the spa offer altogether. Accordingly, it is difficult to group consumers into one of these mutually exclusive categories. Building upon the conceptual models presented by Bywater (1990), Hall (1992), SRI (2010), Johnston *et al*. (2011) and GWI (2014), it is perhaps best to conceptualise spa consumer demand as moving along a 'health demand continuum', where at one end of the spectrum we position demand for medically-oriented spas and treatments, and at the other we locate demand for experiences and treatments oriented towards the preservation and holistic maintenance of health. Moving from the periphery to the centre of the continuum, we place demand for all the myriad of activities, treatments and experiences which may offer a degree of combination between the medical and wellness paradigms.

Health demand

Medically oriented spa demand

Consumers primarily motivated to engage in spa activities/ treatments/ facilities aimed at treating ailments and other medical conditions.

Wellness oriented spa demand

Consumers primarily motivated to engage in spa activities/ treatments/ facilities as part of their healthy lifestyle and desire to maintain their health.

Figure 6. 1: The health demand continuum

Imagining spa demand in such a way enables us to account for those consumers who, for example, may stay at a medispa and engage with both medical beauty procedures such as body sculpting, facials and personal coaching sessions. In other words, it allows for the recognition that whilst some spa consumers (which we may call *core*) may engage with specific treatments or experiences designed to foster a sense of wellbeing (whilst other will be in need of recuperation); many spa consumers may pick and mix a multitude of available experiences and activities. Similar discussions have been forwarded by Beattie (2011) who, in renewing a call for more accurate research in relation to specific spa consumer behaviour, reminds us how the greatest challenge and opportunity for the industry worldwide lies in its ability to identify and effectively attract consumers who show weak to moderate level of engagement with the products. Correct segmentation, she argues, will aid managers and marketers to provide a marketing mix capable of addressing the needs of these consumers. Despite this recognition, segmentation exercises remain limited and consumers are currently simply grouped in line with their level of involvement with the product (see Table 6.2). Accordingly, core spa consumers could be defined as those showing active involvement with either medical or wellness oriented spa products and experiences; whereas middle level and peripheral consumers as those tending to have a more ad-hoc involvement with spa products and experiences (SRI, 2010; Beattie, 2011).

Health and Wellness Consumer Segments		
Sickness reactors, not active spa-goers	Wellness focused, moderate-to-active spa-goers	
Periphery	Mid-level	Core
■ 'Entry level' health and wellness consumers ■ Aspire to be more involved in health and wellness, but their behaviors do not yet follow their aspirations ■ Are mostly 'reactive' rather than 'proactive' when it comes to matters of health and wellness	■ Moderately involved in a health and wellness lifestyle ■ Tend to follow some of ■ the trends set by the Core ■ Purchase large amounts of both conventional and health and wellness- specific products ■ Still somewhat concerned with price and convenience, but also driven by knowledge and experience	■ Most involved in a health and wellness lifestyle ■ Serve as trendsetters for other consumers ■ Health and wellness is a major life focus for them ■ Driven by sustainability, authenticity, and local sources

Source: GMDC and The Hartman Group, Consumer Shopping Habits for Wellness and Environmentally Conscious Lifestyles Study: Insights for Health, Beauty and Wellness, September 12, 2009, http://www.pacific.edu/Documents/ school-pharmacy/acrobat/Consumer%20Shopping%20Habits%20for%20Wellness%20-%20Presentation.pdf.

Table 6.2: Spa consumer segments. Adapted from SRI, 2010, and Coyle Hospitality Group, 2011.

It is clear that further research needs to be carried out to understand each of these segments' behaviour and spending patterns, especially so that each group can be targeted effectively.

Principles of consumer behaviour

Consumer behaviour is commonly defined as "the study of individuals, groups, or organizations and the processes they use to select, secure, use, and dispose of products, services, experiences, or ideas to satisfy needs and the impacts that these processes have on the consumer and society" (Solomon *et al.*, 2016: 5). As a discipline and a key marketing function of an organisation, consumer behaviour attempts to understand the role a variety of factors play in influencing consumers to behave in a particular way towards products and practices, such as spa.

Broadly speaking consumer behaviour can be thought of as a process requiring a consumer to go through a sequence of problem-solving activities which eventually lead him/her to make specific decisions towards a product. Blackwell *et al.* (2001) suggest a consumer (here a spa consumer) will go through seven decision making stages including the act of consumption, evaluation and disposing of the product. These are:

1 **Need recognition**: the development of a want or need.

2 **Information search:** involving an internal search (remembering prior experiences and knowledge) or an external search (exposure to marketing/ advertising activities) or both.

3 **Evaluation of alternatives**: with an aim to ultimately identify the best solution for the individual.

4 **Purchase**: involving going through the act of selecting and paying for it.

5 **Consumption**: engaging in the fulfilment of the need/ want.

6 **Post consumption evaluation**: reflecting on the product's ability to fulfil the initial need and considering repeat buying.

7 **Divestment**: disposing of the product or any of its residues after consumption.

Yet, spa consumer behaviour is complex, as are all the processes leading an individual to consume, and thus to conceptualise spa consumption in such a linear fashion is to potentially ignore the role that a myriad of factors may play on a consumer's decision to buy. Indeed a spa consumer may decide to skip some of the stages altogether and buy the product or experience they were looking for in the first place. Thus, whilst the model presented by Engel *et al.* is a useful starting point in the discussion, it is best to turn our attention to the factors, both internal and external to the individual, that may play a part in influencing his decision making process. Swarbrooke and Horner (2006) call these factors *motivators* and *determinants*.

Motivation is defined as a set of internal drives that force an individual towards the fulfilment of a need. Thus it is the reduction of a need-induced state of tension that will 'drive' the individual to engage in a particular behaviour. Motivational research is generally considered a useful tool for marketers attempting to understand the complex patterns of spa consumer behaviour observed today. One of the best known frameworks for the study of motivation is the one developed by Maslow (1954,) also known as the hierarchy of needs framework (see Figure 6.2).

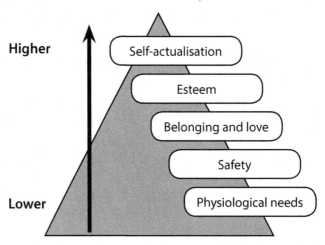

Figure 6.2: Maslow's hierarchy of needs. Adapted from Maslow, 1954.

Maslow's model postulates that an individual will go through life engaging in a sequence of need-fulfilling activities, starting from the realisation of basic physiological and safety needs (also known as *biogenic* needs) and gradually moving on to the fulfilment of more complex needs such as the need for belonging, esteem and self-actualisation (also known as *psychogenic* needs). In other words, as needs become satisfied, new and more complex needs will emerge for the consumer to fulfil. Although in itself not devoid of criticism (especially because of the difficulty in empirically testing), Maslow's model can be used to begin discriminating among some of the basic motivators that may influence consumers to engage with spa, as indeed some consumers may be looking for a massage to relieve stress (thus responding to physiological needs), or may be, for example, attending a meditation course aimed at spiritual enlightenment (thus seeking to satisfy psychogenic needs). Obviously, it is clear that processes of consumption are not that simple and linear, as indeed a consumer may be looking for and engaging with a particular sets of spa products or experiences in the attempt to gain physiological, emotional and spiritual benefits simultaneously. Therefore, whilst Maslow's model can be used as a starting point in the identification of spa consumer needs, greater recognition needs to be given to the fact that that every consumer is different in his/her ways of consuming spa and that this diversity is reflective of the complexity of the industry and the range of spa products and practices available worldwide. In this context, it is important to remember that additional factors (determinants) internal to the individual, such as the consumer's personality, lifestyle, past experience, memory, perception, self-image, lifecycle stage and other personal circumstances, will affect motivations and the decision to act upon them (see Table 6.3). Furthermore, there will always be a multitude of motivators influencing a spa consumer choice. For example, spa consumers on "a mum and daughter day spa package" may be looking for de-stressing, physical relaxation and fulfilling socialisation needs simultaneously. This not only points at the existence of primary and secondary motivators which may be specific to the individual; but also to some forms of internal negotiations that will inevitably take place at the level of the individual. Whilst some of the key motivators are outlined in Table 6.3 below, it is worth noting that to date there exist no definitive list of motivators for engaging in spa activities and practices (SRI, 2008 and 2010).

Physical	Relaxation, exercise, fitness and health
Cultural	Sightseeing, experiencing new cultures and traditions
Status	Exclusivity, fashionability, obtaining a good deal
Emotional	Nostalgia, romance, pampering, exploration, escapism, fantasy, spiritual fulfilment, personal rewards
Personal	Visiting friends and relatives, make new friends, need to satisfy others
Personal development	Increase knowledge, learning new skills

Table 6.3: A basic typology of spa motivators. (Adapted from McIntosh and Goeldner, 1986; Swarbrooke and Horner, 2006; and Smith and Laszlo, 2009).

Personal circumstances	Health Disposable income Available time Work commitments Family commitments Car ownership
Experience of	Types of spa Different destinations The products offered by different organisations Spa with particular individuals or groups Attempting to find discounted prices Individual spa consumer
Knowledge of	Destinations The availability of different spa products Price differences between competitor organisations
Attitudes and perceptions	Perceptions of destinations and spa organizations Political views Preferences for particular countries and cultures Fear of certain modes of travel and diseases How far in advance they like to plan and book a trip Ideas on what constitutes value for money Their attitudes to standards of behaviour as a spa guest

Table 6.3: Internal determinants. (Adapted from Swarbrooke and Horner, 2006)

Clearly, it is important to remember that determinants will affect consumers differently depending on spa consumers' attitudes, personalities, beliefs and prior experiences, and will inevitably vary over time. However, it is also important to remember that ultimately spa consumer behaviour will also be affected by a number of external factors outside the control of the individual, such as economic recessions, political turmoil, social unrest and terrorism, which may ultimately play a role in hindering or completely blocking the consumer's decision to buy a particular spa product or experience.

Spa consumer behaviour models

As spa as both a cultural and global industry practice continue to grow, the need to develop a deeper understanding of the subject remains paramount, yet as stated throughout the chapter, attempts to systematically understand and model processes of consumer behaviour in spa are to date limited. This is clearly a result of the relatively young age of the discipline. In this section of the chapter we want to briefly present some of the consumer behaviour models developed the context of other disciplines such as psychology and marketing, tourism and hospitality. In presenting these theoretical models, we are well aware that they should simply be treated as such, that is, generalised, grand attempts at describing consumer behaviour. However, we feel they could be used in the context of this chapter to convey the present challenges in understanding the influences that multiple factors have on spa consumers' behaviour.

Since the development of the discipline of marketing (see also Chapter 10) by the mid 20th century, many theoretical models had been produced. One of the most often quoted model is that of buyer behaviour developed by Howard and Sheth (1969), see Figure 6.3. The model highlights the importance of recognising the effects various internal processes have over the individual's decision to buy a product or a service. Specifically, the model suggests that in making a decision to buy, the consumer (here the spa consumer) will be exposed to a series of factors. These are:

1 **Input variables**: all of the stimuli that a consumer is exposed to, for example, from marketing and branding activities of spa organisations, family and reference groups, and the physical characteristics of the product, such as price and other attributes.

2 **Hypothetical/ intervening variables**, which serve as both filtering and processing the stimuli and influencing future decisions to either buy or look for further information. The authors separate these variables into two categories:

  ■ Perceptual constructs, which include the consumer' sensitivity to information, perceptual bias and the active seeking for information.

  ■ Learning constructs, such as generic and specific motives, evoked sets, decision mediators, and predispositions of the consumers; as well as inhibitors (e.g. time and money) and satisfaction from post-purchase activities.

3 **Output variables**, representing the noticeable consumer responses to the internal negotiation of the above forces, resulting in the consumer's five stages

to buy. These are attention, comprehension, attitudes, intention to buy and actual purchase behaviour.

4   **Exogenous (external) variables** or those forces specific to the consumer to include the importance of buying the product for the consumer; where he is positioned in terms of culture, social class, his or her personality traits, etc.

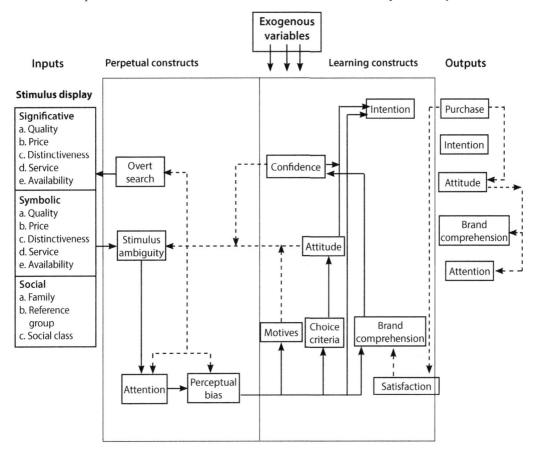

Figure 6.3: The theory of buyer behaviour. Source: Howard and Sheth, 1969.

Originally developed in 1968 by Blackwell, Engel and Kollat, the Consumer Decision model is often used to illustrate the complex interplay of internal and external forces on the consumer's decision to buy. Whilst raising similar criticisms in relation to the grand generalisations it inevitably suggests about consumers, the model is generally praised for having gone through modifications with the passing of time, responding to advances in understanding of consumer practices and buyer behaviour (acknowledging for example the role of divestment influencing contemporary consumer practices). The model is organised around the seven decision making stages of buyer behaviour: need recognition, search, pre-purchase evaluation, purchase, consumption and divestment. Assuming consumption as a problem-solving exercise, the model highlights a series of factors that will influence the consumers' decision at the level of needs recognition. These are external stimuli (such as the advertising of a product, which will be processed by the consumer against memories of previous experiences); environmental factors such as the culture where is the consumer situated; his or her social class; and a series of individual factors such as his or her motivation, knowledge, attitude, personality and lifestyle.

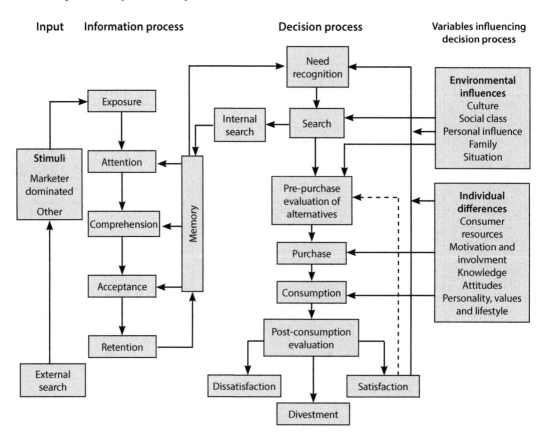

Figure 6.4: The consumer decision model. (Source: Blackwell, Miniard, and Engel, 2001)

Researching spa consumers: a call to action for better marketing research

It is clear from the discussion presented thus far, that research in spa consumer behaviour is still in its infancy. This said, the study of consumer behaviour in the context of spa is key to the foundation of any marketing activities used to advertise, and sell spa products, services and experiences. The understanding of how spa consumers make choices, buy and use products and services, their behavioural patterns and the factors that influence their purchase gives spa businesses the ability to influence, satisfy and anticipate shifts in demand. The development of a more robust and rigorous subject knowledge is therefore not simply a wish, but rather an imperative call to action as the industry continues to fragment and new, sophisticated forms of demand come to play.

Read this short case study and identify the motivators and determinant factors behind Sheila Williams's decision to travel to and use a Centre Parcs spa.

Case study

Hi my name is Sheila. I am a 49 year old mother of two wonderful teenage daughters. Mary will be 13 in a couple of months and Anna has just turned 17. This year we have gone back for the fourth time to Centre Parcs as they run lots of activities for my active family. Yes, I know it is a bit crazy! To be back for the fourth time in nine years may seem odd, especially as it is a luxury. But, I can honestly say in my opinion it's worth every penny! My kids and I really enjoy the experience as you get a chance to do things together and get some time alone if you wish.

This year I am taking Anna for her first spa experience whilst Mary is on her introduction to orienteering course. Anna is really looking forward to this as she has heard me talking about it and caught on my enthusiasm! As this is her first time, I may guide her in choosing what experience to have. I know she is a bit a shy and self-conscious as she suffers from eczema, so I think a manicure and a facial will be more appropriate until she knows the ropes. I have had a word with the spa receptionist when I made the booking and made sure they know it is a special treat for my daughter. It does help that the staff here are so friendly and attentive. I am looking forward to my treatments also!

Spas are wonderful, relaxing spaces where you can escape from your everyday life and it is so nice to have one on your doorstep and with such a wide range of treatments! My preference used to be for body massage with a facial, but now since holistic therapies have become more common, I go for crystal therapies followed by hot and cold stone massage. I feel it has more of a relaxing effect on my mind, which is really what I need with my busy job. The spa facilities have recently been upgraded too so it is a big bonus! I love using the steam room and the pool before my treatments, just a pity they can get so busy and noisy. But the staff is so helpful, and they make you feel so comfortable so I guess that's just something you have to put up with. Overall I'd absolutely recommend going there as you can really have a great time.

6

References

Azara, I. and Stockdale, I. (2012). Spa tourism. In P. Robinson, *Tourism, the Key Concepts* (pp. 198-201). Abingdon: Routledge.

Beattie, C. (2011). *Spa Tourism, International.* Mintel Oxygen.

Blackwell, R., Miniard, P. and Engel, J. (2001). *Consumer Behaviour* (9th ed.). London: Harcourt college publishers.

Bywater, M. (1990). Spas and health resorts in the European community. *EIU Travel and Tourism Analyst,* **6**, 56-67.

Coyle Hospitality Group. (2011). *Priorities of Today's Spa Consumers.* Coyle Hospitality Group.

GWI. (September, 2014). *Global Spa and Wellness Economy Monitor.* New York: Global wellness institute.

Hall, C. (1992). Adventure, sport and health tourism. In B. Weiler, and C. Hall, *Special Interest Tourism* (pp. 141-58). London: Belhaven Press.

Howard, J., and Sheth, J. (1969). *The Theory of Buyer Behaviour.* New York: Wiley and Sons.

Johnston, K., Puczko, L., Smith, M. and Ellis, S. (May 2011). *Wellness Tourism and Medical Tourism: Where Do Spas Fit?* Global Spa Summit.

Maslow, A. (1954). *Motivation and Personality.* New York: Harper and Row.

McIntosh, R. and Goeldner, C. (1986). *Tourism, Principles, Practices and Philosophies* (5th Edition ed.). New York: John Wiley and Sons.

Mueller, H. and Kaufmann, E. L. (2001). Wellness tourism: market analysis of a special health tourism segment and implications for the hotel industry. *Journal of Vacation Marketing,* **7**(1), 5-17.

Mintel. (2004). *Health and Wellness Tourism, Global.* Mintel Oxygen.

Smith , M., and Laszlo, P. (2009). *Health and Wellness Tourism.* Oxford: Butterworth and Heinemann.

Smith, M. and Laszlo, P. (2014). *Health, Tourism and Hospitality: Spas, wellness and medical travel.* Abingdon: Routledge.

Spafinder Wellness UK. (2015). *2015 Trends Report, Wellness Traditions from the Islamic World.* Retrieved June 2016, from Spafinder: http://www.spafinder.co.uk/blog/trends/2015-report/wellness-traditions-from-the-islamic-world/

SRI International. (2007). *Global Spa Economy Report.*

SRI International. (2010). *Spas and the Global Wellness Market: Synergies and Opportunities.* Global Spa Summit.

Swarbrooke, J. and Horner, S. (2006). *Consumer Behaviour in Tourism* (2nd Edition ed.). Oxford: Butterworth Heinemann.

7 Guest Service and the Guest Journey

Angela Anthonisz, Tim Heap and Lorraine Baker

Introduction

In an experience economy, people want to consume services that provide memories rather than simply functions, so in the spa industry, as in all service sector organisations, it is vitally important to fully understand the needs and aspirations of your customers. The customisation of the experience is therefore essential to avoid problems in even the most basic customer services. The key to success is in recognising the needs of guests before, during and after their visit, and is therefore process driven. The industry does have the benefit of each spa having its own guest profile, which makes the fine tuning of the individual's spa experience much easier, as it is often based upon an existing profile of the consumer's needs and wants.

The industry is within a competitive fast moving environment and so the constant monitoring of those changes is imperative for the sustainability of a company. The change of emphasis from a model of spa, to wellness and spa is a classic move by the industry to reposition itself in a growth area of the service sector. It is then imperative to assess and predict the changing needs of the guests in order to maintain a spa that exceeds the goals and expectations of those guests. Consumption emotion, which is seen as an emotional reaction that an individual has in response to product consumption or service experience (Richins, 1997), must be linked to the quality processes which in themselves create the spa experience (Lin and Mattilda, 2010).

The guest experience

Traditionally the planning and quality of the emotional experiences have been monitored by the spa management team, conducting monthly reviews, both internal and external in terms of services, staff interaction, retail options and operational structure. Analysing both the positive and negative strategies used in the competitive market has traditionally been the rubric upon which to create a spa that more intuitively understands and reacts to the guest's needs and aspirations. The problem is that in the current environment this is seen as being old fashioned and reactive, and not proactive, as everyone is waiting for everyone else to move. This can lead to inertia in existing provision, and act as a barrier for new entrants into the market.

As with many service sector organisations, spa businesses have built up historic structures, policies and procedures ('the way we have always done it') and employees too often simply accept and inherit those practices, or guidelines, on how work is performed, from their predecessors. This acceptance of the status quo means it is difficult to challenge current methodologies, improve users' experiences or create efficiencies (Hammond et al., 2006).The same is often true with regards to the hierarchies that exist within spas, which in turn reinforce organisational behaviour and often produce unique environments in relation to the service encounter. This familiarity has often been welcomed by customers, but in today's marketing environment guest choice and guest loyalty are seen as part of a much more complex process.

This chapter reviews the processes involved in the guest service and guest journey and their association with the guest experience. This is encapsulated in the concept of customer journey mapping (CJM) as related to the consumer decision journey (CDJ). Lingqvist et al. (2015) explain that there is a sequence of events in the consumer decision journey where customers experience touch-points through which they interact with the service organisation, and where they review the purchase process. It is important therefore that those touch-points are identified and listed in the service exchange process for the specific spa, treatment and/or product. By understanding the spa guest touch-points, management can then work with team members to employ tactics that foster service innovation. The aim is obviously to enhance customer service provider interactions and so to improve the guest experience associated with each touch-point.

Each touch-point is then part of their horizontal customer journey map which is linked to the process timeline. Each touch-point, which can be many faceted within the spa guest, should then include a vertical axis that includes the emotional journey of the customer. This may include their thoughts, beliefs, feelings and emotions which are difficult to observe, and therefore to measure in accordance with a process timeline (Lingqvist et al., 2015). That measurement was attempted by Lo et al. (2015), when looking at hotel spa experiences where they found that responsiveness was the most important determinant factor in explaining positive emotions from service quality, followed by reliability, empathy, and tangibles. This emotional emphasis transforms CJM into a very specific management tool namely, an empathy mapping exercise (Tschimmel, 2012).

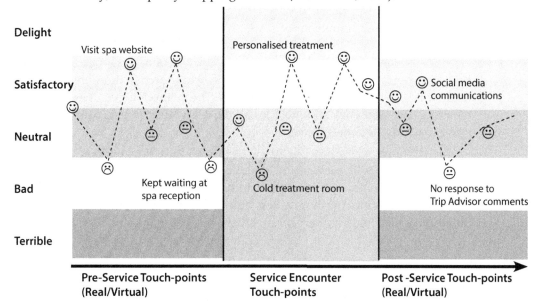

Figure 7.1: Customer service touch-points

Identifying and measuring those empathetic responses may, perhaps, only come with the level of experience of the spa employees. The importance of customer expectation and satisfaction in the spa industry are the key ingredients in maximising customer loyalty and driving business growth, so it is essential that they are identified. The industry has traditionally relied upon adopting industry standards across the sector for service level to define product related guest service standards. These are then often benchmarked against competitors to assess the spa's competitive position.

The number of customer touch-points, and hence potentially reduced control of the experience, requires firms to integrate multiple business functions, including information technology (IT), service operations, logistics, marketing, human resources and even external partners, in creating and delivering positive customer experiences. So it has become increasingly difficult for firms to create, manage, and attempt to control the experience and journey of each customer (Edelman and Singer 2015; Rawson *et al.*, 2013). It is easy to make the point that customer experience measurement is essential for identifying and actioning insights, but it is more difficult for the industry to create meaningful metrics on guest experience from so many touch-points. Brakus *et al.* (2009), for example, identified that customer experience measurement needs to test sensory, affective, intellectual, and behavioural patterns so to examine the relationships between brand experience and brand personality, satisfaction, and loyalty.

The SERVQUAL model has been used extensively over time as a measurement tool in the service sector, and continually adapted since its development by Parasuraman *et al.* (1988), including attempts to validate and improve the scale (Roberts, *et al.* 2014). Other ideas such as 'service blueprinting' where Bitner *et al.* (2008) identified 'moments of truth', 'critical incidents' and the importance of 'atmospherics' and the 'environment' as being essential for the success of the journey. In some ways the latter two have always formed the basis of the spa experience and continue to do so, but it is the breakdown in those that may lead to the critical incidents and moments of truth. The methodology is therefore a customer focused approach and includes all those involved in the customer service provision and is internally focused.

The CJM provides a timeline that is separated into three periods with touch-points associated with each period, and for the spa experience it can be identified as spa pre-service through spa service to spa post-service. Urban Healing (2011), define a Guest Service Journey as "the journey guests experience in our spas, from the moment they make a reservation until they leave the spa after their treatment".

Pre-service

The touch-points include guest experiences and expectations built before the service begins. These can be from initial contact (real or virtual), arriving at the spa, and the customer's relationships with the brand. Lemon and Verhoef (2016) call these 'brand owned touch-points' or 'partner owned touch-points', and state that both influence customer attitudes and preferences. The partner owned touch-points are jointly managed by the individual spa employees and the brand, but following procedures outlined by that brand. The pre-service stage also includes 'social and external touch-points' which include peer influences, social environment (including online examples such as Facebook) and more structured virtual touch-points such as Trip Advisor.

Most spa consumers are primarily motivated to engage in spa activities/ treatments/ facilities as part of their healthy lifestyle, and desire to maintain and preserve their health. The pre-service process therefore involves a pre-cognisant information search involving an internal search (remembering prior experiences and knowledge) and/or an external search (exposure to marketing/ advertising activities). This then leads to evaluation of alternatives with an aim to ultimately identify the best solution for the individual with the purchase as the end point. 'Online' used to simply mean a web site, but now booking online is a basic expectation, whilst enabling guests and consumers to book a service or experience within minutes. The reality is that the industry may not be fully engaged with the change agenda, and is waiting for others to point to the changes necessary.

Reasons for guests returning to a spa are recognition, feeling valued and 'important' through their journey, seeing results, getting value for money and having had a great experience that matches or exceeds their expectations. With more guests commencing their journey online, or via mobile app, the initial touch-points present the danger of the guest becoming lost at the beginning of the journey (Spa Life, 2013). The company must ensure that the guest digital touch-point at the start of that journey is controlled by the company. It is no longer possible to 'build it and they will come', the journey must include the story of the build, the outcomes and the expectations that the story creates within the potential customer. The Hilton group, for example, search for some customers via airline bookings, as they have identified that if a customer books a flight to a destination they have 40 minutes maximum to get them to book a hotel bed. A spa journey is therefore one that touches a guest's senses, allowing the physical connection with spa's facilities and services, but it cannot reach that stage without building the expectations. The simple addition of spa treatments to the package online could then continue to build expectations.

Service

These are a combination of partner owned and customer owned touch-points and include introduction to and/or re-engagement with your brand values. The touch-points will be individual to each spa, but include the pre-treatment, treatment and post-treatment phases which are allied to the environmental and therapist touch-points.

Tobin (2013) explains that it can be difficult to achieve a unique experience in the service encounter and to recreate what Gallo (2008) calls 'customers for life' (Vlad, 2015), but as the individual is by definition unique then the experience must be unique. What is more important is that each touch-point should be excellent and Angelo and Vladimir (2011) believe that each interaction between employees and guests represents a critical moment, or should that be 'critical moments'? They believe these touch-points must be treated as vital elements of guest engagement, by adopting Jan Carlzon's concept of 'moments of truth', which then form part of the vertical axis that includes the emotional journey of the customer decision journey (CDJ).

Carlzon explains that a company has no value without customers; it is customers that bring the company value therefore the real value being the perception of the customer. For example if all the touch-points that the customer has with the various employees in the service encounter, i.e .spa receptionist, spa host, spa therapist, are positive, the CDJ emotional journey is positive. These touch-points are often explained as a mix of objective and existential authenticities (Wang, 1999) and they must satisfy customers' needs in terms of both the product on sale and service provided. Brown (2013) explains existential authenticity as the authentication of the self through experiences and activities within the spa journey. The primary focus of objective authenticity is that of the genuineness of the

7

objects ranging from the structures to the customs, appearances and rituals of the spa (Steiner and Reisinger, 2006). Taegoo *et al.* operationalize this, as they provide the link between emotional labour helping to produce emotional intelligence, but without producing emotional exhaustion.

The methodology connects the virtual and real world to create outstanding and consistent customer journeys through all channels that are continually being 'authenticated' by the customer. It is important to link different touch-points together in order to understand the dynamics of the customer's visit and ultimately their experience. This stresses the importance of planning and monitoring the customer's entire visit, also capturing data and information at each point of contact with a member of staff or self-service point to manage the operation and drive efficiency.

According to Alo and Tsai (2015) previous spa studies have failed to investigate the impact of the specific dimensions of spa service quality on consumers' emotions. They attempted to fill that gap by identifying the dimensions and attributes of spa service quality and investigating their impact on consumers' positive emotions attained from a hotel or resort spa experience. Responsiveness (by staff and customer) was found to be the most important determinant factor in explaining positive emotions, followed by reliability, empathy, and tangibles. The results demonstrate the importance of spa service quality in enhancing the attainment of positive emotions by spa customers. Well-designed service process, standardised service procedures, and training, need to inform and guide the enhancement of spa service quality, generate positive emotions, and ultimately create a better spa experience for customers.

"We lay the stage for each guest's own piece of interactive theatre. It's about creating an environment and atmosphere that is quite special and then acting as facilitators for our guests' own out-of-the-ordinary experience" (Ho Kwon Ping, Chairman Banyan Tree Hotels and Resorts Spa). Customer experience is about creating the right environment, 'back-stage' support and technology and then enabling your staff to facilitate an experience that will be valued by your guests. It is difficult not to simply script your staff, or prescribe exact behaviours in an industry that has traditionally followed a strict set of procedures/techniques by typology of treatment; or from the strict adherence to brand values and identity. The answer has to lie within being aspirational in how your employees deliver that experience in order to differentiate your brand.

It is important to build on the framework of guest expectations from the pre-service stage so that the service stage then converts these into your own values. It is important to assess how your spa team is performing against these expectations and values. This leads to guest values that in themselves drive retention and advocacy. It becomes your own brand promise that delivers excellence and differentiates your spa from competitors. It can be difficult to differentiate with those that deliver the same branded products. But localism or the glocalisation of the product can only be changed through those employees that understand

and buy into those values. It is important to experience your own guest journey through the spa so that you can begin to empathise with their experiences. This in itself is difficult, as it is not easy to look at the journey through the guests' and not the organisation's perspective.

Richard Chase and Sriram Dasu (2001) identified five rules to ensure that customers focus on the positives of the customer journey and not the negatives:

- **Finish strong**: Do something unexpected at the final touch-point, e.g. a small gift at the end of treatment or on checking out. This will help to create positive memories.

- **Build customer commitment through choice**: Ensure guests have full information of charges within the spa in brochures and websites in the pre-service stage so they are transparent. Guests can then make informed choices and will not be surprised by and perhaps embarrassed by having to pay them in the final touch-point.

- **In selling the idea, overcome objections as soon as they arise.** For example, guests find consultation or health forms onerous so, give them the opportunity to complete in the pre-service stage, either on line or by taking away the form from the last treatment in the post-service stage. This enables you to have knowledge of guest expectations, lifestyle and health status.

- **Stick to rituals**: Create 'on-brand rituals' that guests associate with your spa, for example, something that reinforces their sense of time and place within your locality. Perhaps something made locally to highlight your/their support for the local community, again as part of a constructed and existential authenticity.

- **Segment pleasure, combine the pain**: Spread the pleasure by providing those little touches, eg complimentary drinks with cookies being a guilty pleasure. These are often called 'spikes' of pleasure. Combine the 'pain' by bundling other facility charges into the guest rate so that they experience them in one step rather than every time they wish to use them.

These are simply some ideas, but they need to be added to, and turned into principles that relate to your specific spa values and experiences.

Spas primarily sell 'experience' and as this spa service section of the customer's journey has the most touch-points, it has the most opportunities for generating positive and/or negatives emotions. It is this stage of the journey that converts the customers from new one-off customers into repeat customers who will encourage other customers to seek the same positive experience in the future. The power of trip advisor, Facebook and other social media now form an integral part of the post-spa stage, so it is essential that the customer enters the stage with those positive emotions.

Post-service

These are experiential and based upon the consumption of the product and include the engagement through, brand owned, customer owned and social and external touch-points. A simple ending to the journey can be to create signature retail items infused with the aromas of the spa that allow the guest to take the spa emotions and experiences home with them. This can encourage them to introduce the spa to friends and colleagues, and self-gratification can result if those friends book with the spa, as they then become the potential influencers for your spa. The identification of key influencers should form part of the evaluation of the customer's journey. Links to Facebook, Twitter etc. are now seen as essential post service touch-points in identifying Post consumption evaluation. This means that the virtual engagement needs to be constantly updated, provide added value to the customer (perhaps in special offers only available on line) and enable you to identify the key influencers in several social network groups.

It is important at the post-service stage that the monitoring of the individual journeys is mapped against the brand values of the spa. The results of monitoring the customer journey through the use of touch-points helps to conceptualise the customer experience, understand the key drivers of success, provide better metrics that link to improved firm performance and match expectations with experiences.

Conclusion

This chapter has looked at the spa as a series of experiences through the lens of the customer journey and touch-points throughout the journey. It is not an attempt to identify individual touch-points, but to encourage individuals to identify their own spa specific touch-points and journeys from a customer and industry perspective.

The literature indicates that customer experience is holistic and a multidimensional construct focusing on a customer's cognitive, emotional, behavioral, sensorial, and social responses. The emphasis is upon the whole journey from pre-spa to post-spa and the confirmation of existentially and objectively authenticating the experiences through that journey. This leads to customer satisfaction through increased service quality that is concentrated at the touch-points. Looking at pre and post spa reinforces that every aspect of the company's offering and business practices should be reviewed. This is nothing new, but the spa industry needs to concentrate upon experience design that is customer driven and this can only happen by continuous monitoring of the customer journey.

Application of knowledge

Stage one: Undertake a review of a Spa (one you work for or have access to) and attempt to identify the key touch-points with the customer through the three stages of the Customer Service Journey (see Figure 7.1)

Stage two: Review the input into those key touch-points by the organization with regards to customizing the experience.

Stage three: Attempt to analyse the potential customer's emotional responses to those inputs as to how they benefit the customer experience. There are the 'vertical' axis of the journey.

Stage four: Suggest how the company could improve on the customer service journey.

References

Angelo, R.M. and Vladimir, A (2011) *Hospitality Today: An Introduction*, Educational Institute of the American Hotel Motel Association

Bitner, M. J., Ostrom, A. L. and Morgan, F. N., (2008), Service blueprinting: A practical technique for service innovation, *California Management Review*, **50** (3), 66–94.

Brakus, J. J., Schmitt, B. H. and Zarantonello, L. (2009), Brand experience: what is it? How is it measured? Does it affect loyalty? *Journal of Marketing*, **73** (May), 52–68.

Brown, L. (2013). Tourism: A catalyst for existential authenticity. *Annals of Tourism Research*, **40**, 176-190.

Chase, R. B. and Dasu, S. (2001) Want to perfect your company's service? Use behavioral science. *Harvard Business Review*, **79**(6):78-84.

Edelman, D and Singer, M. (2015) Competing on customer journeys. *Harvard Business Review*, Nov.

Gallo, C. (2008) Employee motivation the Ritz-Carlton way, *Business Weekonline*, 24

Hammond, J.S., Keeney, R.L. and Raiffa, H. 2006. The hidden traps in decision making. *Harvard Business Review*, **84**(1):118–126.

Kim, T.T., Kim, W.G. and Kim, H.B., (2009) The effects of perceived justice on recovery satisfaction, trust, word-of-mouth, and revisit intention in upscale hotels. *Tourism Management*, **30** (1), 51-62

Lemon, K.N, & Verhoef, P. C. (2016). Understanding customer experience throughout the customer journey. *Journal of Marketing*: *AMA/MSI Special Issue* **80**, 69–96

Lo, A. S., Wu, C. & Tsai, H., (2015). The impact of service quality on positive consumption emotions in resort and hotel spa experiences, *Journal of Hospitality Marketing & Management*, **24**(2), 155-179.

Lingqvist, O., Plotkin, J. & Stanley, J. (2015) Do you really understand how your business customers buy? *McKinsey Quarterly*, **1**, 74–85

Parasuraman, A., Zeithaml, V.A. and Berry, L. (1988), SERVQUAL: A multiple-item scale for measuring consumer perceptions of service quality, *Journal of Retailing*, **64** (1), 12–40.

Rawson, A., Duncan, E. and Jones, C. (2013), The truth about customer experience, *Harvard Business Review*, **91**(September), 90–98.

Richins, M. L. (1997). Measuring emotions in the consumption experience. *Journal of Consumer Research*, **24**(2), 127–146.

Roberts, J. H., Kayand´e, U. and Stremersch, S. (2014), From academic research to marketing practice: exploring the marketing science value chain, *International Journal of Research in Marketing*, **31** (2), 127–40.

Spa Life, 2013) ... MISSING ... p 77

Steiner, C. J. and Reisinger, Y. (2006). Understanding existential authenticity. *Annals of Tourism Research,* **33,** 299-318.

Tobin, T. (2013) Service Leadership, *Sales & Service Leadership*, 13(11), 10-11

Tschimmel, K. (2012) Design thinking as an effective toolkit for innovation. Proceedings from the XXIII ISPIM Conference: Action for innovation: Innovating from experience, ISPIM, Manchester, UK.

Vlad, M. (2015) Exceeding guest expectations, in J. Feng (ed) *Educational Strategies for the Next Generation Leaders in Hotel Management*, IGI Global

Wang, N. (1999). Rethinking authenticity in tourism experience. Annals of tourism research, 26, 349-370.

8 Spa Operations Management

Faith Samkange, Amon Simba and Lorraine Baker

Introduction

Slack *et al.* (2004) define operations management as a process used in organisations to produce goods and service. This process based notion of operations management, confirmed by Karlson (2009), is then made more explicit by Roth and Manor (2003) who argue that operations management transforms inputs into goods and services based on customer needs and interests with obvious associations with spa products (see Chapter 9). Porter (1991) and Slack *et al.* (2013) then present a view that operations management is the activity of managing the resources that create and deliver services and products creating a specific guest experience. The rationale is that to achieve the ultimate customer satisfaction, the spa organisations need to operate as unified systems combining various operational processes and procedures to deliver a complete customer experience. This chapter, therefore, examines spa operations management from a systems perspective.

A systems perspective of spa operations management

The role and function of operations management involves the coordination of a broad range of spa processes and procedures in an effort to meet the needs and interest of the consumer. For example spa pools, aromatherapy rooms, sauna and steam rooms allied to treatment offers such as sports massage, Thai massage, Watsu, and all dependent on the type of spa, whether it is a health club facility, a day spa, a destination spa or even a wellness centre or wellness incorporated in with the spa environment. Spa facilities and treatments will also be dependent on geographical area and consumer type for that specific spa. A systems perspective provides spa operations with the methodology to convert inputs such as materials, labour, proprietary information into outputs such goods, services and value-added products. This then constitutes the design and development element to achieve the ultimate guest experience. This perspective requires a detailed examination of the theory from a framework initially developed by Ludwig Von Bertalanffy (1968) and later developed by other scholars including Lovelock and Wirtz (2003) and then refined by Senge (2014)

Systems Analysis Thinking Theory

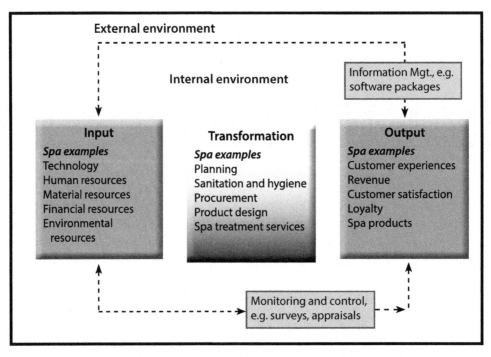

Figure 8.1: The systems analysis thinking perspective and its application to spa operations.

A systems thinking perspective perceives an organisation as a complete system consisting of inputs, transformation, outputs, monitoring and controlling, as well as information management processes. These elements exist in an internal environment which is the organisation itself. However, the organisation exists in a larger and external system often described as the external environment (Porter, 1991; Senge, 2014). The organisation can therefore be viewed as a subsystem of the external environment, but as each spa is essentially different, e.g. location, type, age, size etc. then each subsystem must be different. This means that each spa must produce its own subsystem to survive in the service economy.

■ The input element of the spa operations

The input element consists of resources to develop products and deliver the customer services. Slack *et al.* (2013) and Mullins and Dossor (2013) break down resources into two major categories, namely the transformed and transforming resources (see Figure 8.2). Transformed resources include material and product, management information systems including customer databases, financial, and environmental resources. Transforming resources refer to those human and technological resources capable of manipulating other resources in the process of developing the necessary customer experiences. These include the spa staff and management including related digital technological applications of spa therapies performing specific operational tasks.

In order to establish transferred resources to outputs requires adequate efficient and professional staff training, sufficient and efficient resources both human and technological for example the staff delivering and maintaining services and operations in order to produce consumer satisfaction which equally could build customer loyalty.

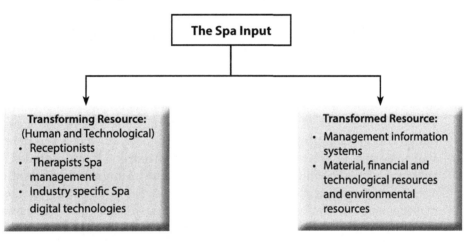

Figure 8.2: Categorisation of spa inputs

Human resources includes managers and employees who work within various areas of a spa delivering specified experiences and treatments. These include front of house operational staff, such as receptionists and spa hosts, as well as different levels of therapists such as senior therapist to treatment therapist, who deliver various treatments whilst some specialise in specific treatments. Services dependent on the type of facility can range from, and include, different types of body and facial treatments, hand and feet treatments, holistic and wellness treatments and programmes to incorporate health and wellness such as nutritional and detoxification programmes. Back of house staff include cleaners, contracted personnel maintaining the facilities and accountants, human resources and marketing staff, who may not always be visible to the guest.

Technological resources continue to play an increased role and are often used to help facilitate operational efficiency and effectiveness because of the convenience and the various possibilities they offer towards the automation and standardisation of operational processes and procedures (Slack and Lewis, 2015, Boardman *et al.,* 2006; Bocij *et al.,* 2008; Bryjolfsson and McAfree, 2014). The technology is not just the hardware, from laptops to smart gadgets, but more importantly the various application systems used to perform specialised functions such as reservations, point of sale, inventory and stock control, purchasing, customer relationship management, marketing and other service functions. Technology systems are used increasingly in the design of a spa to provide sensory stimulation, ambiance and mood. For example, technology provides visual stimulus, through lighting systems, and auditory stimulation, through sound systems. Spa facilities and equipment are highly technical and can include anything from monsoon showers to hannan beds and flotation tanks. The systems based approach does, therefore, have to work with a complex range of inputs, outputs and scenarios.

■ The transformation element of the spa operations

The transformation process is how the organisation takes the above inputs/ resources and delivers the necessary products and services (Figure 8.3). According to Slack and Lewis (2015), this is justifiably the major part of the operations management process. It is the performance element. Arguably the key process function of the spa, this unit is made up of the procurement, inventory control, such as stock control, maintaining of equipment, sanitation and hygiene, pool testing, maintenance of spa facilities and equipment service delivery, product design and development, including development of treatments and training the staff to be able to effect those treatments cost effectively. It also includes reservations, such as booking guests into facilities and treatments or different packages or programmes; facilities design and maintenance, customer relationship management, e.g loyalty schemes, membership, staff training on guest and spa etiquette, human resource management, employing the right staff for the correct roles, staff induction and training; accounting and revenue management, such as daily and monthly takings and targets, budgeting for equipment and products and laundry etc. If there are failings in these areas, then the customer experience suffers. Transformation is dependent upon staff training in customer relationship management and spa treatments, as customer loyalty and repeat purchases are the cornerstone of long-term succes.

Figure 8.3: The spa operations as transformation process

The output element of the spa operations

The spa outputs are essentially the customisation and creation of the customer experience be they tangible (effective treatments) or intangible (experiences). Examples of outputs include the completed therapies and treatments such as massages, pedicures, manicures, facial treatments, healthy meals. The output element also reflects the levels of revenue and profit margins and therefore the success or otherwise of the business operations.

The systems approach to operations management therefore recognises the relationship between the complex elements of the spa operations systems and how they impact the results and in particular service quality, related customer satisfaction and loyalty.

The control and information management elements

Relationship between the elements of spa operations are sustained by the control element (Hannagan, 2008); Mullins and Dossor, 2013). The control element establishes mechanisms to ensure that products and services conform to the standards required, not only by the spa but also by professional bodies and product brands, as demanded by the customer and stipulated by the organisation. For example the function of the control element determines the extent to which the treatments booked meet expectations, and the quality of the therapies performed by the therapist. Control systems in this area include, thorough staff training; staff huddles prior to each shift for staff to ascertain their targets, the set up for the day, for example their treatment times and discussion of any products that may be out of stock or as a number 1 seller, etc.; and team work to ensure a smooth running of the spa journey. A control system for each treatment is recommended by the product companies and forms part of staff training. Control systems are also necessary for gathering data on customer service perceptions and satisfaction (Gronroos, 2007). This is confirmed by others (Slack and Lewis, 2015, Kotler and Armstrong, 2010 and Torrington *et al.*, 2005). Control processes indicate the critical aspects of resources utilisation and relate this to financial accountability. The measurement of revenue outputs and profit margins are further explained in customer feedback surveys, bookkeeping and accounting tools such as cash flows, balance sheets, profit and loss accounts, and employee performance management tools, such as job descriptions and performance appraisals, all of which show the complexity of the control element.

The external environment is made up of stakeholders outside the spa organisation, but they are hard to identify and track from the economic, political, social, cultural and technological contexts that make up that external environment. Operational boundaries should therefore be porous, adaptable and flexible enough to allow its workforce to engage with the outside world to keep abreast with the ever-changing external market developments (De Wit and Meyers, 2014; Johnson *et al.*, 2008; Mintzberg, 1993). Failure to understand and apply the laws on

8

safety and hygiene for instance would have legal consequences for the organisation. Conversely evidencing compliance can be used as positives within sales and marketing. The extent to which operational boundaries are porous can determine the extent to which the organisation remains functional and sustainable.

The systems analysis thinking perspective is a body of knowledge which recognises that organisations as whole entities can only be operationally efficient and effective if they are able develop functional units (Senge, 2014) that co-exist with others within the external environment. Operations managers therefore need to coordinate organisational units, as they play their role in delivering the required products and services.

The link between operational strategy and spa operations management

Operations management translates corporate vision and strategy into specific customer experiences, so spa operational activities must include understanding the organisation's strategic objectives which help to develop products and services that constitute the customer experience. Strategic objectives, related key performance objectives and indicators provide the basis upon which spa operations are planned executed, controlled, monitored and evaluated. Specific processes and procedures are developed from key operational objectives and indicators which leads to establishing performance and productivity boundaries. An effective operations management plan is guided by the strategy and data from the management information system (market research etc.) This is a customer-oriented approach (Kotler and Armstrong, 2010; Jobber, 2002) which specifies the market segment targeted and then deliberately seeks intelligence to understand what drives this segment of the market (Jobber, 2002). The impact of such market research initiatives on operations management plan shapes operational processes and procedures and how they are managed (Hill, 2005). The benefits of market research however need to be current and linked to digital and social media to ensure currency for the spa services. The process of operations management and related activities is reflected in Figure 8.4.

Operational activities

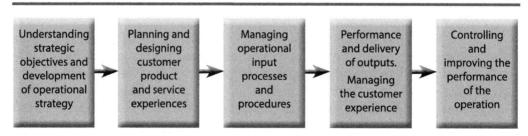

Figure 8.4: Summary of spa operational activities

Understanding strategic objectives

The case study below helps illustrate and analyse this critical stage in operations management

Application of knowledge

At corporate level a conglomerate of luxury hotels called Leisure Springs Inclusive wants to expand their hospitality experience with an emphasis on state of the art spa, health and wellness. Consistent with this vision the corporate strategic unit decides to open 10 spa resorts per year over a period of five years targeting Europe (including the UK), Africa, America and India.

What could be the role of operations management in the research, planning, product development, marketing and staffing?

Operational management in Leisure Springs needs to determine the specific spa facilities required in terms of structure, size, shape and capacity. The operations unit determines the resources required, such as technologies and telecommunications, plant and equipment (Slack *et al.*, 2005). The unit also considers the nature of the spa services and products to be delivered. This inspires the specific facilities design details including the floor plans, interior and exterior landscaping. It is the role of spa facilities design to decide on the location, development and presentation of specific spa areas. Spa areas may include the reception or front of house, the retail boutique, health and wellness restaurants lockers and dressing rooms, pre-treatment hydrotherapy areas, waiting areas, salon areas, treatment spaces including dry and wet areas, exercise studios, fitness rooms, administrative offices and the staff lounge. Storage, laundry, housekeeping facilities and utility spaces are part of the process. Operations management determines the human resources demands and facilitate recruitment, selection, hiring, training, induction and engagement of staff into the new spa resort operations (Mullins and Dossor, 2013) and the section of products and treatment packages.

The involvement of operations management at this stage provides an assurance that the customer needs and interests remain at the centre of developments. Coordination with management units such as human resources, marketing, information technology, technical support and accounting is the key to successful operations (Baines and Lightfoot, 2013).

Operational objectives together with a resources mix including expertise decide how many specific spa units should be offered and in which specific areas, shape form and size. The type of spa services vary significantly ranging from medical, day club, mineral spring, resort and hotel, cruise ship to destination and residential spa service. Specific units could include spa therapy and massage centres, nail lounges, hairdressing facilities, fitness centres, nutrition centres

8

including nutrition restaurants, baths and springs, swimming pools, saunas and even desired sports facilities. Spa products include a wide range of specialist treatments and of skincare products.

Spa operations function on the basis of key operational objectives as reflected in Figure 8.5.

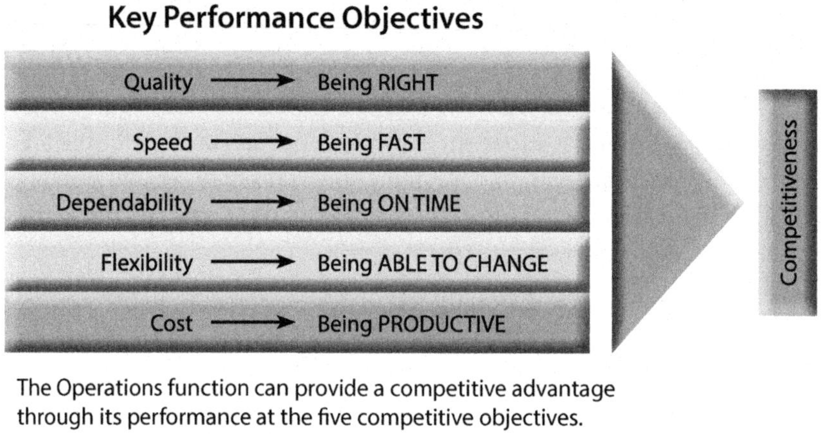

Key Performance Objectives

The Operations function can provide a competitive advantage through its performance at the five competitive objectives.

Figure 8.5: Key performance objectives. Source: Slack *et al.* (2013)

This service delivery constitutes the key function of operations management. Key performance objectives are critical to operations management as lack of guidance can equal high development costs. Key performance objectives hinge around quality, timeliness, dependability, flexibility and price. In setting out an action plan for spa operations, managers need to determine the quality of the services and products to be delivered. Specific performance standards need to be developed to help control and improve the operations. These are translated into standard operational procedures which include the time taken to produce and deliver the experiences and to schedule the prompt delivery of products and services. In doing so the organisation creates an image of dependability and reliability. The next phase is to maintain consistency in that service delivery. Product companies will detail the required service delivery standards for specific treatments to ensure that the treatment is carried out in a set way by all spa therapists. From the above spa operations are broken down into specific tasks and employees assigned to these tasks as individuals or teams. This leads to specific job descriptions and standard operations procedures and finally work schedules designed to facilitate the delivery. The objectives themselves need careful planning.

■ Planning

The impact of performance objectives on the planning processes is crucial, as is the link to training and development. Operational planning allocates appropriate resources, including time, money expertise and technology to ensure tasks are performed (Porter, 1991), and requires developing specific performance targets.

Spa therapists have a required number of key performance targets that set out how many treatments they are required to perform in a certain time, and how much time is spent consulting with the client before a treatment and providing post treatment advice and product recommendation. Therapists are also set retail targets and customer feedback targets. Incentives and performance related bonuses are usually linked to these targets. Standard operating procedures are needed for all areas of treatment, including support services, operational budgets, employee schedules and related time schedules (Hill, 2006). Planning also involves developing specific and functional ideas around purchasing, procurement, inventory control, sanitation and hygiene, health safety and security, production and service delivery processes (Porter, 1991; Slack *et al.,* 2005).

The role of the operations manager in this case is to coordinate all the business units towards the achievement of specified operational objectives. The hammam, for instance, must be in a position to determine the potential number of customers likely to utilise the service in a given time period. Booking and reservations systems must be planned in advance, and account for any surge in customer numbers. Additionally, an appropriate time scale for product development and service delivery should be drawn up.

Product and service design and development

8

Product and service design of operational processes involves determining the physical form, shape and composition of products, services and procedures. This requires an understanding of the target markets and consumer. Understanding specific consumer behaviour and determining the profile of the spa guest is a prerequisite of the design and development process. (Slack *et al.,* 2005, Aghdaie and Alimardani, 2015).

Spa guests present diversified needs and interests based on cultural, economic, social, educational and geographical backgrounds, and so reflect a dynamic customer profile (Mullins and Dossor, 2013). The factors of health and wellness in customer interests is driving growth in the sector, but also increasing these dynamics. The advent of knowledge-based economies with increased levels of education, impacts of social media, increase that unpredictability for product (Mullins and Dossor, 2013). This informed customer is, however, increasingly prepared to pay a premium price for unique and value added products and services but equally will seek last minute offers and deals. This discerning consumer is also more assertive in terms of service quality delivery representing increased levels of dynamism, selectivity and complexity in managing those consumers. Organisations need attention to detail, being transparent and informative in their product design and development.

Another emerging trend is personal indulgence accompanied by the pursuit of unique experiences. This implies operational processes must be continuously evolving in order to create innovative experiences for the customer. The converse is that the customer is more conscious of the impact of spa operations on the environment. The customer is probably more willing to explore culturally assimilated products in the pursuit of unusual experiences. Spa operations are therefore challenged to meet the evolving needs of these customers. This requires sophisticated levels of creativity in implementing relevant operational management systems.

Drivers of the growing wellness industry not only directly impact the spa industry and its consumers but are also opening new opportunities for spas to play a leading role towards a more proactive way of people taking care of themselves, for example older and unhealthy people, failing medical systems (SRI International, 2010). It can be argued that this is changing the nature of the product and service delivery. It is not surprising that this design, development and delivery process has become an innovative operations management function. Designing guest experiences consistent with the current profile of the consumer is a process demanding an articulation of the link between operational input processes and related outputs (Slack and Lewis, 2015).

■ Managing input processes

Operational input processes relate to the procurement of resources necessary to provide the above organic product growth. Examples of resources necessary in a treatment room for instance include: treatment couch, stool, cabinet or trolley, hot cabbie, skincare products, oils, consumables, laundry, mits and towel. A list of resources is determined and a budget plan drawn up as part of the planning process to facilitate procurement, monetary and financial control (Porter, 1991). The procurement process ensures prices are negotiated and delivery is expedited just in time (JIT). Success is dependent upon maintaining up-to-date networks within the supply-chain (Slack and Lewis, 2015) and managing inventory linked to procurement systems. The purchasing function works closely with the accounting unit to ensure prompt and accurate payment of supplies. Inventory control functions determine storage requirements and space norms so tracking usage is essential (Kumar and Suresh, 2009). An analysis of inventory function underscores the significance of transforming and transformed resources and impact on the transformation process (Slack *et al.*, 2013). Augmented spa inventory management would therefore require a robust system to ensure a continuous service provision.

■ Delivering outputs and managing performance

Operations managers are expected to execute stipulated plans to perform specified tasks as they endeavour to deliver customer product experiences. This is a highly technical part of operations demanding specific expertise as various treatments require specific technical skills, knowledge and competencies. Training, development and updating knowledge and skills consistent with current trends and new product development is essential. Operational effectiveness and efficiency determines the extent to which resources utilisation is cost effective (Johnson *et al.,* 2008). In this regard, operations management aims to maximise outputs while limiting operational costs without compromising the quality of the service.

Operation management therefore needs to engage employees productively (Hannagan, 2008) and research often links employee motivation and engagement to productivity (Porter, 1991; Slack and Lewis, 2015) the accomplishment of tasks within given time frameworks do require articulate and motivated staff.

Operational procedures are the summation of the management process and provide guidelines regarding product and service delivery. For a guest to receive a massage within a treatment room the ambience needs to be correct, the therapist requires the correct training and professionalism and skills updated, awareness of a guests lifestyle in order to ascertain and give a correct treatment for the guest to receive benefits from the treatment are all important aspects. Building a rapport with the guest to be able to build a picture of how to treat and recommend products and advise with aftercare. The manner and sequence of staff actions form the customer experience and ensure upselling and customisation. Packaging and presentation of customer experiences is reflected in standard operational procedures (see Figure 8.6). These appear somewhat simplistic in terms of step stage models, but it is the 'why' and what 'outcomes' that result from the procedures that are important.

8

	Spa reception operational procedure
1	Check all bookings and prepare to receive guest as they arrive. *Confirms that the therapists have capacity, identifies any shortfall and new versus existing guests. The receptionist is likely to have taken the booking so this is the second part of the customer journey and therefore relationship marketing.*
2	Greet guests by name with a smile on arrival, if you are otherwise engaged, for example taking a telephone call, make eye contact with the guest to acknowledge their presence. *You are ensuring that the expectation of service quality is being realised.*
3	Confirm the treatment the guest has booked. *This initial conversation provides the opportunity for link and up selling, through discreet questioning for example the aim of the guest's visit and to gather information that can be used to personalise the service. Information vital for marketing*
4	Seat guests comfortably and ask them to complete a personal details form if required. *Essential for relationship marketing, digital data and the sense of belonging on the part of the guest.*
6	Offer the guest a drink as determined by the availability list or their chosen treatment. *The receptionist then becomes part of the treatment process and the sense of holistic product.*
8	Inform the relevant therapist that their guest has arrived. *Pass on any information gathered through the initial conversation, is the client anxious, receptive, excited etc.,*
9	Relax the guest by providing appropriate reading materials and make conversation professionally. *Again the reading material should perhaps include details of new treatments available.*
10	Introduce the guest to the therapist and allow the guest to be shown to their treatment room or the changing room. *This ensures the guest is never left to be influenced by anything else but the journey that the product ensures through the operations management process.*

Figure 8.6: Sample operational procedure: Reception

Control and performance improvement

The example in Figure 8.6 is all about the seamless nature that should be customer satisfaction that comes from operations management (Gronroos, 2007; Lovelock and Wirtz, 2007; Zeithaml *et al.*, 2010).

Figure 8.7 links the 'why' to the 'how' in terms of exploring revenue management in terms of the journey introduced in Figure 8.6.

Spa service standards
Staff are professionally presented, meeting the agreed grooming standards. *The key word is 'professionally' and is linked to the expectations generated in part 2 from pampering through guest journey to selling the total spa.*
Staff are attentive, helpful and professional in their dealings with guests. *Comes from the training and development, knowledge of revenue streams and marketing ethos outlined in part 3.*
Appointments are efficiently booked, *if requested services are not available, alternatives should be offered. Link and up selling suggestions are made to guests.*
Staff are observant of all guests within the spa and provide help and assistance throughout the spa journey. *The knowledge of the total product offer is again essential.*
Staff are knowledgeable and describe all treatments and procedures to guests before they are delivered and offer individual privacy. Treatments commence and finish on time. *The customisation of the product, with the guest feeling safe, individual, but also satisfied with the cost of that treatment.*
Therapists are informed and interact with guest during treatments, where appropriate giving useful information. *The training and development ensure product knowledge and process.*
Treatment rooms should be fully prepared, meeting the required specification prior to guests entering them. Spa is clean, tidy, hygienic and safe at all times. *This should be seamless, but conversely confirmed by the actions of the staff during the treatment.*
Spa should have extra information in the form of up-to date brochures, pamphlets leaflets and posters. *This is essential to ensure the upselling.*

Figure 8.7: Sample spa services standards

As we have seen, operations management is involved with forecasting customer demand and creating optimum conditions under which spa products and services are translated into monetary outputs. Essentially this is the pricing from the marketing into the service delivery. Monitoring, measurement and assessment of the productive capacity of the spa constitute the control process, but can only be assessed through an identified process. Service delivery analysis is based on observations, guest surveys or personal interaction with staff.

Assessment and evaluation reports, including employee performance appraisals, are easy to standardise if linked to the processes indicated in Figures 8.6 and 8.7. These are then linked to performance indicators and targets. Good practices are shared among teams in order for staff to improve performance (Zeithaml *et al*, 2007). This assessment identifies when certain spa operations may be under-performing in terms of revenue management, and identifies the areas where this may be happening.

Principles and practices in managing spa operations

Operations management therefore designs and delivers service experiences as demanded by the customer. The success and/or failure can be attributed to the five basic principles of spa operations management.

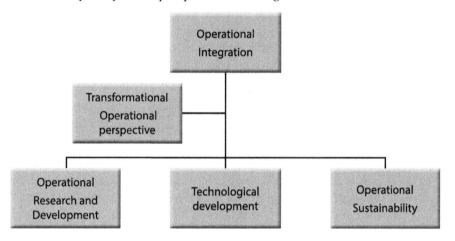

Figure 8.8: Basic principles of spa operations management

■ Integration

Integration is a basic principle that ensures all aspects of the spa are well designed, effectively connected and operate alongside other business elements and units in a integrated way. Integration means harnessing the expertise and knowledge, including the creative capacity of employees within the organisation, towards value creation. The current spa consumer seeks experiences beyond the usual expectations towards unique services of value.

■ Transformational leadership

Operations managers need to share knowledge and, especially in spas, the prescriptive models of management with inherent barriers need to change. There is a certain old fashioned hierarchy that still pervades in some parts of the spa industry, but this does not match with today's customers demanding higher levels of flexibility and creativity. The details in Figures 8.7 and 8.8 show how the sharing of knowledge is essential within the processes and procedures in spas. Operations managers therefore need to drive transformation so as to keep pace with the ever changing needs of the consumer.

■ ### Research and development

Operations management needs to inculcate a culture of research and development. Continuous research and development is necessary to keep customer experiences fresh while remaining competitive.

■ ### Technological strategic development

Among other principles and practices, operations management in spa needs to be underpinned by technology. It is no longer just an operational tool to enhance operational efficiency and effectiveness, it is now a strategic development tool. It is clear organisations will need to create their own capacity to develop technologies that suit their own needs and interests, rather than simply import generic applications. This could imply that organisations need to develop their own sustainable technological solutions to own operational problems.

■ ### Sustainability

Sustainability is a broad principle that resonates with efficient, user- and environment-friendly resource utilisation including the development of appropriate, yet relevant, management systems. Sustainability should not only refer to utilisation of resources but also embrace the mechanisms that are deployed to address managerial and operational issues. Managerial systems should be driven by relevance and ability to offer lasting solutions and developments that add value to the organisation. Sustainability includes fostering lasting relationships and partnerships with stakeholders including the communities in which spas are located. Communities should provide a reliable human resources base for the spa operations.

The challenges of managing spa operations

Spa operations present quite a number of challenges. The development of customer driven by technologies requires a workforce that keeps pace with those developments. The difficulty is to identify which technologies can help drive the business forward, given their proliferation, and what access they give to the consumer. The customer has evolved over the years, so how can the spa industry, and in particular operations management, keep pace with such developments? Designing an appropriate customer experience is becoming more and more challenging. The answers to these questions should be found within the organisations. It is clear the spa industry will need to continuously reinvent itself to remain viable in the face of intensive competition. Operations management will need to come up with creative ways of providing innovative customer experiences while maintaining appropriate levels of profitability. This is no mean task.

Conclusion

Operations management constitute the heart and soul of the spa business. Not only does operations management define the nature and scope of business but it also designs and delivers customer experiences based on their needs and interests. Perceiving operation management from a systems perspective (Senge, 2014) reflects the integrated and interdependent nature of product and service design and delivery. Unpacking operational strategy into specific goals, standards and related processes and procedures remains a fundamental function of operations management. Spa operations are therefore viewed as transformational, based on the understanding that they convert organisational inputs into desirable outputs consistent with specified operational processes and procedures derived from performance objectives and related indicators. Performance objectives and indicators reflect standards through which product design, development and service delivery are measured, assessed and evaluated thus forming an integral part of the control processes. Control processes not only reflect the success or failure of the spa business but also indicate areas of performance improvement. Operations management as a complex function is underpinned by the principles of integration, technological awareness, innovation, sustainability, research and development. Progressive spas find creative ways of applying these principles to develop networked, coordinated, cohesive and functional systems. This is the way in which the spa organisation as a whole entity can effectively articulate its internal environment in response to the pressures imposed upon them by the external environment.

References

Aghdaie, M.H. and Alimardani, M. (2015). Target market section based market segmentation evaluation: A multiple attribute decision making approach. *International Journal of Operational Research,* **24**, (3) 3691-3700.

Baines, T. and Lightfoot, H. (2013). *Made to Serve: How manufacturers can compare through servitization and product service system,* Chichester: John Wiley and Sons.

Bertalanffy, L. (1968). *General Systems Theory: Foundations Development Applications.* New York: George Braziller

Boardman, A.E., Greenberg, D.H., Vining, A.R. and Weimer, D.L. (2006). *Cost Benefit Analysis: Concepts and Practices.* Pearson.

Bocij, P., Greasley, A. and Hickie, S. (2008) *Business Information Systems: Technology development and management for the e-business.* Prentice Hall, Harlow.

Bryjolfsson, E. and McAfree, A. (2014). *The Second Machine Age: Work, Progress and prosperity in a time of brilliant technologies,* New York: W.W. Norton and Company.

De Wit, B. and Meyers, R. (2014). *Strategy, Process, Content and Context.* London: Cengage Learning.

Gronroos, C. (2007). *Service Management and Marketing: Customer Management in Service Competition*, Chichester: John Wiley and Sons.

Hannagan, T. (2008). Managing in the public sector, in *Management Concepts and Practices* (5th ed) FT Prentice Hall, Harlow, p 104-135.

Hill, M.J. (2005). *Public Policy Process*. Pearson, Longman.

Jobber, J.F.D (2002). *Foundations of Marketing*. Mc Graw Hill, New York.

Johnson, G., Scholes, K. and Whittington, R. (2008). *Exploring Corporate Strategy Text and Cases*. FT Prentice Hall, Harlow.

Karlson, C. (2009) *Researching Operations Management*. Routledge, New York.

Kotler, P. and Armstrong, G. (2010). *Principles of Marketing* (13th Global Edition), Pearson Education inc., Boston.

Kumar, S.A. and Suresh, N. (2009). *Production and Operations Management*. New Age International.

Lovelock, C. and Wirtz, J. (2003) *Services and Marketing: People, Technology and Strategy* (5th ed), Pearson.

Lovelock, C. and Wirtz, J. (2007) *Managing People for Service Advantage*. FT Prentice Hall.

Mintzberg,H. (1993). *Structure in Fives: Designing effective organisations*. FT Prentice Hall

Mullins, L.J. and Dossor, P. (2013). H*ospitality Management and Organisational Behaviour*. Pearson, Harlow.

Porter E.M. (1991). Towards a dynamic theory of strategy. *Strategic Management Journal* **12**, (52), 95-117.

Roth, A.V. and Manor, L. J. (2003) Insights into service operations: A research agenda. *California Journal of Production and Operations Management* **12**, (2) 145-164

Senge, P. (2014) Systems thinking for a better world. Paper presented at Systems Analysis Laboratory 'Being Better in a World of Systems', Aalto University, available at https://micor9.wordpress.com/2014/12/18/peter-senge-systems-thinking-for-a-better-world/

Slack N, Lewis, M. and Bates, H. (2004). The two worlds of operations management research and practice: can they meet, should they meet? *International Journal of Operations and Production Management*, **24**, (4), 372-387.

Slack, N. and Lewis, M. (2015). *Operations Strategy*. Pearson.

Slack, N. Lewis, M. Brandon Jones, A. and Howard, M. (2010). Competing through operations and supply. The role of classic and extended resource-based advantage. *International Journal of Operations and Production management*, **30**(10), 1032-1058.

Slack, N., Brandon-Jones, A and Johnston R. (2013) *Operations Management*. Pearsons.

SRI International. (2010). *Spas and the Global Wellness Market: Synergies and Opportunities*. Global Spa Summit.

Torrington, D. Hall, L. Taylor, S. (2005) *Human Resource Management*. (6th ed), FT Prentice Hall.

Zeithaml, V. Bitner M.J. and Gremler, D.D. (2010). Services marketing strategy, in R.A. Peterson and R.A. Kerin (eds.) *Encyclopaedia of Marketing: Marketing Strategy, Vol 1*. Chichester: John Wiley and Sons.

9 Selling the Total Spa Product

Louise Buxton

Introduction

Retail sales can contribute significantly to a spa's revenue, however, many spas do not realise their full retail potential. This chapter presents strategies to maximise retail sales, including: brand selection, brand ambassadors, incentives, training, retail design and visual merchandising to provide a tool kit for success. Consideration is also given to the importance of integrating retail throughout the entire customer journey. A case study is presented at the end of the chapter to encourage the application of knowledge.

Selling experiences is seen as the principal function of a spa (Wuttle and Cohen, 2008), nevertheless, retail and other sales such as up-selling and link selling can all make significant contributions to a spa's revenue. In exploring approaches to selling, the benefits of, and barriers to, selling are presented as well as strategies to maximise sales. The chapter is therefore essentially a more practically based one, but needs to be read in conjunction with the chapters on consumer behaviour, guest service and journey and marketing spas.

Approaches to selling

As spas are synonymous with both pampering and healing (Deswal, 2014), they present a dichotomy when considering the appropriate approach to sales. With many spa consumers citing relaxation and rest as motivators for their spa visits (Monteson and Singer, 2004, cited in Lo and Wu, 2014), a key factor for spas to take into consideration, when deciding which approach to adopt, is the importance of balancing selling with the need to relax and escape (Tabacchi, 2010). Contrasting consumer motivations such as pampering and indulgence could be viewed as more conducive to a sales environment. Moreover, understanding the behaviours of individual consumers is the ultimate goal of suppliers of products and service (Lo and Wu, 2014), thus, adopting sales approaches allied to those behaviours is a key challenge for spas.

Depending on the individual spa's approach, selling can be placed high on the agenda or seen in a supporting role. Differing approaches towards sales are evident in the culture and ethos of a spa and are generally born out of the spa's vision and philosophy. Moreover, various types of spa may take differing approaches to sales. Considergthe ISPA (2013) typologies of spa: club, cruise, day, destination, medical, mineral spring and hotel spas; each may place a different emphasis on sales. Spas that place sales high on their agenda set exacting targets for individuals, teams or both and attainment of those targets are closely monitored, in contrast, some spas with a more relaxed approach choose not to set any sales targets.

Benefits of selling

The benefits of successful sales can be viewed on three levels, benefits for the organisation, benefits for spa professionals and benefits for the spa guest.

■ Benefits for the organisation

One of the most obvious benefits for a spa is increased revenue. It is widely accepted within the spa industry that retail sales should contribute at least 20% towards a spa's overall revenue. Figures of around 20 to 25% are often cited as achievable, but in reality for many spas are aspirational, as a large proportion achieve retails sales of well below these figures. A principal benefit of achieving good retail sales is that they provide a greater contribution towards the spa's overall profitability than many spa treatments, as margins are higher. Fundamentally, retail success plays a significant role in a spa's financial sustainability, therefore, adding retail areas or increasing the focus on retail, are fairly simple but effective ways of increasing revenue for spas (Johnson and Redman, 2005).

A proactive approach to sales also benefits the organisation in respect of increasing its reputation for professionalism and customer care, by offering the guest additional services such as the purchase of retail products (Wuttle and Cohen, 2008); and through recommendations of additional or more luxurious treatments or experiences, via up-selling and link selling, the guest experience is personalised. Furthermore, retail extends the guest journey and the benefits of treatments beyond the physical environment of the spa.

■ Benefits for spa professionals

Spa professionals can benefit from selling in a number of ways. Depending on the practices operated within their organisation, these may include increased salary and/or other rewards and recognition schemes; furthermore, enhanced employability is a supplementary benefit.

Commission is the most commonly used incentive within spas (ISPA, 2013). Commission is a financial incentive, whereby staff earn a percentage of the price of the products they sell. Commission rates can vary but are largely of between 10% and 20% (ISPA, 2013), thus providing the potential to significantly increase a spa professional's salary. Other rewards for retail success include free or discounted products, gifts, holidays and training; furthermore, recognition schemes and awards such as 'retailer of the month' reward excellence in retail sales.

Spa professionals who are confident sales people and can demonstrate a successful record in sales are also highly sought after within the industry. Retail is an area often highlighted when skills gaps within the spa and associated industries are discussed. The Global Spa and Wellness Summit (2012) highlighted sales and retail as being top training priorities for spa directors and managers. Furthermore, the UK-based Hair and Beauty Industry Authority (HABIA) reported in its most recent survey of skills within the spa industry that 70% of spas reported the ability to increase retail sales as a skills gap (HABIA, 2006). As this is an area which some spa professionals find challenging, anyone who excels in sales significantly increases their employability.

■ Benefits for spa guests

Spa guests also benefit in a number of ways from visiting a spa with a successful approach to sales, as they are provided with an additional service (Wuttle and Cohen, 2008). Those who visit spas with specific skin or body care aims will find the provision of product recommendations essential in addressing their concerns. The retail products they take away with them provide solutions to their concerns, moreover, extending and enhancing the benefits of any treatment they have received. The provision of this service by knowledgable specialists gives a more personal and powerful introduction to products, which greatly exceeds that of alternatives such as the department store counter (Polla, 2014). Furthermore, the guest can experience a more personalised service via the recommendation of alternative treatments and experiences, based on their original choices through up-selling and link selling practices.

Barriers

Spas face a number of barriers to sales which can be both practical and psychological. *Professional Spa and Wellness* (2013) note retail particularly is a challenging area to navigate, however, being aware of those challenges and having strategies to address them can go a long way to helping spa retail thrive.

■ Practical barriers

The main practical barrier to retailing is space; in many spas the physical limitation of the size of the building dictates the space available for retail. As with any retail environment, balancing selling and non-selling space is key (Cox and Brittain, 2004). Careful examination of the space available, clever design of visual merchandising and creative thinking about the placement of retail are important strategies to help overcome this barrier.

The most common place for a spa retail area is within a reception; however, many spas do not have the luxury of a large reception space. Hence, retail displays are often placed in areas where space is tight and even behind reception desks, which in themselves pose physical barriers.

Time is another barrier to sales success. Setting aside time to facilitate regular training, time to set and monitor targets and time for staff to engage in the rich conversations with guest required to increase sales is time taken away from other activities. Acknowledging the importance of dedicating time to carry out activities such as training is essential in achieving sales success, however, from a manager's perspective documenting return on the investment in training is historically viewed as a challenge (Lassk *et al.*, 2012); see Chapter 13.

■ Psychological barriers

Much is written about spa therapists' reluctance to engage with sales and in particular retail, with resistance coming from individuals who view themselves as caring practitioners rather than sales people (Wuttle and Cohen, 2008). A variety of factors are frequently identified as barriers including: lack of confidence, limited training, lack of product knowledge and the desire not to be seen as being 'pushy'. Many of these perceived barriers are psychological; Scott (no date) cited in *Professional Spa and Wellness* (2013) suggests the first step in overcoming them should be to draw on the reasons therapists come into the spa industry in the first place; many are keen to work closely with people and want to help people. If therapists see retail as making recommendations and providing solutions to guests' concerns, they move away from viewing retailing as a negative aspect of their role towards a positive one. Training is one of the key aspects in overcoming these perceived barriers and is discussed later in this chapter.

Integration within the spa journey

Spas have the benefit of a built-in retail cliental, and the spa environment is extremely conducive to selling. In traditional retail environments staff have seconds to connect with the customer, in contrast, spa professionals have contact with their guests for an extended period of time, which is virtually unprecedented (Wuttke and Cohen, 2008), thus allowing for strong relationships to be built. It is these opportunities for relationship building via conversations throughout the spa journey, which help to build rapport and develop trust, essential components of sales success (Weitz *et al.*, 2009).

The terms 'up-selling', 'link selling' and 'retailing' are used frequently when discussing sales; therefore, it is useful to provide a definition of each.

- **Up-selling** is the act of encouraging a guest to purchase a more expensive treatment or experience, for example a guest who has booked a Swedish massage may be encouraged to upgrade to an aromatherapy or hot stone massage, alternatively, a guest who is purchasing a product from a basic skincare brand may be encouraged to purchase the same product from a luxury brand.

- **Link selling** is when a guest is offered an additional treatment, experience or product that is linked to their original choice, for example a guest who has booked pedicure may be persuaded to also have a manicure and alternatively, a guest who purchases a facial cleanser may also be persuaded to buy the matching toner.

- **Retailing** refers to process of encouraging guests to buy products to take away with them, for example a guest who has had a facial treatment is encouraged to purchase the products used to continue to benefits of the treatment at home.

There are many touch-points throughout the spa journey (see Figure 9.1) where the awareness of sales can be raised, recommendations made and reinforced. Each spa in distinguishing its approach to retail must decide which of these touch-points are appropriate. Some may choose all of them, for others as noted by Tabbachi (2010) the wisest course may be to take a gentle approach and have a more discreet style.

9

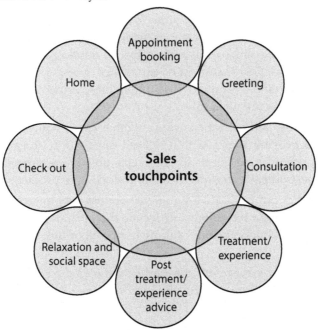

Figure 9.1: Sales touch-points within the spa guest journey

Even before a guest arrives, the exposure to the retail brands carried by the spa can begin via marketing material and through the appointment booking process; in particular if online booking is available, images of retail products can be positioned on the booking page. Appointment booking also gives rise to the opportunity for up-selling and link selling; having a script for the receptionist to follow ensures a consistent message.

Upon arrival, well placed displays within the reception area draw a guest's attention to the retail products available to them. The initial greeting presents a further opportunity for up-selling and link selling. At this point, spas may also open dialogue with guests to ascertain the aim of their visit before they are given a consultation, brief questionnaires or discrete questioning by spa reception staff can elicit information that is subsequently passed on to the therapist to inform further conversations with the guest, in turn providing a personal touch to the spa experience.

Consultation is the next touch-point, and this is where therapists' product knowledge and professional expertise are significant factors in sales success. As Wuttke and Cohen (2008) note, spas are perfectly set to maximise the retail exposure as they have an almost unprecedented opportunity to engage in rich conversations with their guests and establish long, intimate and highly profit-able relationships. Identifying any concerns the guest may have and establishing the purpose of their visit allows for recommendations to be made and products prescriptions to be provided.

During the spa treatment or experience, retail products can have a subtle pres-ence in the environment; Harmsworth, interiewed in *Spa Business* (2014) promotes the concept of 'in-room' spa amenities to support the promotion of spa products. Furthermore, therapists discretely drawing a guest's attention to the features of products they are using (scent, texture, feel on the skin) reinforces the product in the guest's mind. Post treatment or experience, guests should be provided with aftercare advice and a product prescription; these conversation provide a perfect opportunity to secure retail sales.

Social spaces and relaxation areas are other touch-points; tester stands within these areas provide guests with a relaxed opportunity to experience products. Providing products for guests to use in changing areas offers a further opportu-nity for guests to have an experiential introduction to products.

Guest check out provides a significant opportunity to secure the sale; this can be a role for the spa receptionist or for the therapist depending on the structure of the spa. In addition, the opportunity to up-sell or link sell should not be over-looked here.

When a guest leaves with the products they have purchased, this provides them with the excellent opportunity to extend their spa journey, relive their spa experience and continue the treatment benefits at home (Wuttke and Cohen, 2008). The scent of products has been shown to increase the recall of associated information (Krishna *et al.,* 2010 cited in Krishna, 2012) and therefore can remind guests of their spa treatment and experience, encouraging repeat bookings and retail sales.

Maximising sales

■ Brand selection

One of the most important decisions for a spa to make is which product brands to carry. As with deciding which approach to take to selling, the choice of which product brands to offer should be determined by and aligned to the spa's ethos and philosophy. The vast array of spa product companies makes the choice all the more challenging, from high end luxury to handmade, futuristic to organic – the choice is virtually limitless. Moreover, correct brand selection is fundamental as it provides a means to engage guests with your spa, guests who do not merely what to purchase products and services, they also want to buy the products' and services' stories and engage emotionally with them (Gobe, 2001, and Keller, 2003 cited in Morrison and Crane, 2007).

Selecting a brand which exhibits a shared philosophy with the spa can consolidate the spa's position within the guest's mind. Spas that attract results driven guests will be drawn to brands that can attest to such results, therefore, established brands able to invest in research and development and evidence this, will meet the needs of these spas. Spas with an ethos that focusses on sustainability, green issues or being eco-friendly will find organic brands or locally sourced products more closely aligned to their philosophies. Another avenue to explore is the 'own brand', although this should be approached with caution as the appeal of the unknown product can be limited. Carrying two or more complementary product brands can also be beneficial as it allows spas to cater to a range of market segments, appealing to different age groups and genders, plus aligning to different guest values and spend.

■ Brand ambassadors

Once the choice of product brand(s) is made, establishing buy-in from all spa professionals is essential. The channels available for guests to purchase spa products have never been more diverse. Mintel (2015) identifies high street chemists, department stores and supermarkets as the leading providers of skincare and toiletries, moreover, one in five people buy products via the internet or from discount stores. Therefore, spas must ensure their approach to sales is distinctive and provides added value by exploiting the extensive knowledge that spa professionals possess. In doing so, those with responsibility for sales within a spa, whether they be therapists, reception staff or others, should be ambassadors for the brands carried by the spa. As ambassadors all spa professionals should know the story of the products they use and sell so they can engage the guest in compelling, authentic and relevant ways (GSS, 2010).

Spas are very relationship oriented, thus the spa environment fosters the development of rapport and trust between therapist and guest, two fundamental components of a customer-oriented selling approach (Chakrabarty *et al.*, 2013). In turn, this provides spas with the opportunity to encourage brand loyalty from their guests; however, this loyalty can only be established if spa professionals have passion for the products and conviction for the brand. Spa guests' purchasing decisions and brand loyalties have become more aligned with their personal values; they have interests in sustainability and ethics, and therefore telling a product story that corresponds with these values, in addition to matching products to guests' concerns, are convincing approaches to sales (Wuttle and Cohen, 2008). Furthermore, an adaptive selling approach is required to successfully adjust the sales message to respond to different guests and situations (Goad and Jaramillo, 2014).

People buy knowledge as much as they buy a product (GSS, 2010); nevertheless, guests' ability to learn about products no longer depends solely on the sales person, with the availability of information on the internet, spas must ensure they can provide guests with valuable insights into products that differentiates the selling experience. As brand ambassadors, spa professionals should know the key features of any product, for example its unique ingredients or geographical origins and the product's benefits.

■ Training

Training is frequently highlighted as a significant factor for effective selling (Polla, 2014). However, as training costs are significant, due to the time training takes and high staff turnover in spas (Polla, 2014) it is often a neglected area. In many cases sales training is provided as part of a staff induction or the launch of a new product and never repeated.

The extent to which an organisation designs and implements training can be referred to as the learning climate (Wang, 2013); the learning climate exhibited within a spa is fundamental to successful sales training. Staff should be encouraged to develop their sales knowledge through activities, such as formal learning, imitation and self-directed learning (Wang, 2013) with a focus on both hard and soft skills. Many spas and product companies provide sales training that focusses on product knowledge (hard skills), assuming this will be sufficient for people to sell. But as with any retail sector, staff not only need to know *what* they are selling, they also need know *how* to sell it. To be successful, soft skills, such as selling skills should be developed to the point where they are equal to or greater than product knowledge (Gitomer, 2012).

There is a consensus that selling-related knowledge, aptitudes and adaptive selling skills are significant determinants of a salesperson's success (Chakrabarty *et al.*, 2013). Ultimately spa professionals are salespeople, as up-selling, link selling and retailing are essential aspects of their roles. The interpersonal nature of the interaction between the customer and employee may be key to customer satisfaction in the retail environment (Puccinelli *et al.*, 2009, cited in Otnes *et al.*, 2012), but customer knowledge is also a factor (Wang, 2013). For over three decades scholars have asserted that ideal sales encounters are adaptive and interpersonally dynamic (Roman and Iacobucci, 2009). A broad range of literature exists focusing on personal, relationship and adaptive selling and many empirical studies have been conducted, though none focus specifically on the spa environment.

Spa customers are distinguishable individuals, rather than anonymous masses with homogenous desires, and therefore, knowledge of customers is the most productive capital (Wang, 2013). Customer oriented salespeople are focussed on learning about their customers and offering solutions to their needs and concerns (Goad and Jaramillo, 2014); furthermore, this solution focussed approach fits perfectly with the spa environment. Spa professionals have opportunities to gather information about their guests and to respond with a sales message tailored to their needs – this is an adaptive selling approach. (Roman and Iacobucci, 2009, Chakrabarty *et al.*, 2013, Wang, 2013, Goad and Jaramillo, 2014).

The concept of customer orientation was introduced three decades ago and contrasts with the traditional high pressure approach to sales – the selling orientation (Goad and Jaramillo, 2014). The approach of customer orientation relates to the salesperson's concern for others, having the customer's best interests in mind and the use of solution selling approaches, and therefore aligns closely with many spa therapists' motivation to enter the industry. Training which encourages spa professions to adopt a customer oriented approach can alleviate the feeling of being 'pushy' often cited as a barrier to selling. Furthermore, the acquisition of adaptive selling skills coupled with product knowledge builds the confidence of spa professionals, who are then better placed to utilise these skills and increase their sales productivity.

Experiential learning approaches, such role play, are useful techniques to help develop confidence, as they allow the trainee to practice and receive feedback from the trainer (Murthy *et al.*, 2008). Self-directed resources to reinforce the training message, provided in the form of online applications utilising social media, such as YouTube, and a library of sales tasks or role plays can then be created (Lassk *et al.*, 2012).

Coaching is a traditional approach to prolong support for sales training. It is essential that those with responsibility for training are prepared to listen and make recommendations via coaching conversations. This integration of reinforcement tools with coaching are markers of successful sales training (Richardson, 2014) and allow the training message to be extended, thereby fostering a positive learning climate.

■ Incentives and recognition

Incentive schemes are used to motivate staff and boost sales and can be aligned to professional and personal development activities alongside remuneration (Wuttle and Cohen, 2008). Commission is the most common used within spas; therapists often earn between 10 and 20% for retail sales and slightly less for up-selling and link selling. Other rewards include free or discounted products, gifts, holidays and training, and awards such as 'retailer of the month', and are applied to teams as well as to individuals

■ Retail design and visual merchandising

There are several components to good retail design, including: layout, merchandising, and display. The space dedicated to retail should be well planned as it has a powerful impact on retail success. Good design also creates atmosphere, establishes the brand and guides people through their shopping experience. Shopping has become an experience in its own right; therefore, the design of retail space is paramount. Kent (2007) notes that great significance should be placed on the opportunity for interaction, socialising and communication in the retail environment, and this is nowhere more important than in a spa retail environment. As spaces for consumption and play, retail environments also provide openings for interaction and communication between guests and spa professionals, giving rise to the opportunity to further develop profitable relationships. Sensory stimuli can improve the experience in retail environments, as people perceive the world through their senses, the more sensory the experience the more engaging it will be (Soars, 2009).

Successful retail layout encourages guests to move through the space in a way that feels comfortable and encourages browsing. The placement of the retail area should not impede the general flow within the spa, creating a bottle neck in the reception area or an obstacle to transition from one area to another. It is important to consider the effects of atmospherics in *retail design*, the term coined by Kotler (1974 cited in Ballantine *et al.*, 2010) and which is concerned with the purposeful design of retail environments to produce specific emotional effects in shoppers, hence, increasing their probability of purchasing. Colour has been shown to influence shoppers' moods; varying lighting in the retail environment can influence how long people linger (Soars, 2009); dim lighting can create a mood where guests want to interact and play (Ballantine *et al.*, 2010). Music can also influence the dwelling time of shoppers, however, the key is achieving the right fit of music style to the retail environment, Milliman (1982, cited in Soars, 2009) found that slow music increased supermarket sales by 38%.

Visual merchandising requires an understanding of customers, product ranges and how to segment them to present retail products to their best advantage. Products should be segmented in various ways including by: brand, gender, type (facial and body care) or age (anti-aging and teenage). Several merchandising techniques can also be employed such as creating themes or stories, using colour, symmetry and balance, repetition and grouping. When deciding how much space to dedicate to each product category, the size given over should be relative to expected sales, for example if you expect to take 50% of sales from facial skincare, then you should dedicate 50% of the retail space to that.

The way merchandise is displayed can communicate a lot about the product and brand; overcrowded shelves containing large quantities of each product can have a devaluing effect as opposed to creating a perception of quality and exclusivity through displays using singular products.

Consideration should also be given to non-visual aspects of display, several studies demonstrate that allowing customers to smell (Davies *et al.*, 2003; Mitchell *et al.*, 1995; Spangenberg *et al.*, 1996; Ward *et al.*, 2003 cited in Abhishek *et al.*, 2014) and touch (Argo *et al.*, 2006; Morales and Fitzsimons, 2007; Muller, 2013; Peck and Childers, 2003a, cited in Abhishek *et al.*, 2014) products orients them towards making a purchase. However, if guests are able to smell and touch spa products the retail displays should be regularly checked; keeping retail areas looking attractive is imperative, cluttered displays and messy tester stands are not conducive to sales and are identified has having negative effects on retail consumers (Ballantine *et al.*, 2010).

Case study

This case study examines how a new skincare company approached retail when establishing their brand. The overview of the company is presented, then descriptions of the decisions the company made, challenges faced and the next steps they are taking.

Questions are presented at the end of the case study.

About Ishga

■ The Ishga brand was developed on the Isle of Lewis in Scotland by a team of people with a passion for creating the highest quality skincare, and launched to the market in August 2013.

■ Ishga's products harness the natural anti-oxidant, healing and anti-ageing properties provided by the purest Scottish seaweed.

■ The Hebrides, where the Isle of Lewis is located, has some of the cleanest waters in the world.

■ Ishga sustainably hand harvest seaweed to produce a 100% organic ingredient for their skincare range.

Target market

Ishga did not set out to target a specific market with their brand, but aimed at the luxury end of the skincare market, by price. The range was designed to appeal to most skin types. Since the launch of the brand in 2013, the thirty years plus age group have emerged as the main consumers. Ishga also highlight the great results their products have achieved for acne skin, so the brand is now also appealing to a younger demographic.

Consideration given to retail

When developing the Ishga brand, retail was a fundamental part of the plan for Ishga for two reasons: first, to build brand awareness, and second to provide partners with the opportunity to drive more revenue, hence more revenue for Ishga. One key decision for Ishga was to keep their range simple, whilst also being effective. The collection was kept small, therefore, even though the products have a fairly expensive price point, consumers would be more inclined to buy the whole retail range.

Success

Ishga believe one reason they have had great success in the spa skincare market is due to their choice of the simple but effective strategy. This strategy contributes to the ability of the Ishga brand to sit alongside and complement other skincare brands within spas.

Retail packaging

Image is a vital aspect in creating a brand; Ishga were very keen to establish a luxury look and feel for their product packaging but at the same time, they wanted to convey the heritage of the brand. As a new skincare company the challenge when launching the brand was finding appropriate partners, due to minimum order quantities imposed by packaging producers.

Selecting and supporting Ishga partners

Ishga identified some key features to look for when deciding which prospective partner to work with:

- High standards;
- Passion for the Ishga brand;
- Ensuring they can provide a degree of exclusivity and uniqueness for the partner.

Part of the Ishga retail strategy was to provide their partners with merchandise to support retail sales, this includes product prescriptions, brochures and a bespoke Harris Tweed to make gift bags for their products.

Ishga did not want to be too prescriptive, so they do not specify how their retail products must be displayed, hence, providing a degree of flexibility and allowing partners to be creative. However, a recent move to support retail sales is the launch of tester stand light boxes; these have been well received.

Ishga provides support to partners in the collation and distribution of their average retail to treatment conversion rates. This allows partners to keep track of their retail sales and monitor their progress. Ishga note that the variation in the average retail to treatment conversion rates for their partners is large, ranging from 4 to 50%.

Ishga do insist on the Ishga logo being on websites, social media and emails. Brand guidelines are the next initiative.

Growth strategy

Ishga have used a market development strategy to grow the brand; with brand awareness in selected UK street retailers, whilst establishing themselves almost exclusively in spas. The strategy included branching out to new markets beyond the UK by retailing online both domestically and internationally. Ishga's two key market penetrations include the People's Republic of China and the United States of America. Further markets include Australia, Scandinavia, Middle East and Russia. This retail strategy has emerged as a key growth area and strength, and they predict that increased brand awareness will lead to exponential growth. One other new market being considered by Ishga is 'white labelling'; this would see them developing products that are branded for a specific spa or company to sit alongside and complement other Ishga products.

Current and future developments

Ishga are developing retailing training, and currently provide flash cards containing key features and benefits of products to support staff with retail sales, but further support is necessary.

A number of product developments are planned:

■ Extending their current range with a rejuvenating eye balm, shampoo, conditioner, shower gel and candles;

■ Introducing a medically focused range to address skin conditions such as eczema and psoriasis;

■ Developing supplements.

Ishga plans to stay at the forefront of the skincare industry by emphasising the wellness features of the brand to include: sustainability, spirituality linked to where the seaweed is harvested and simple but effective nature. More information will be shared with consumers regarding the science and benefits behind their ingredients.

Application of knowledge

Identify what stories brand ambassadors for Ishga could tell.

■ Consider how Ishga could develop their retail training and outline ways they should deliver sales training.

■ Consider which sales touch points Ishga currently support and ways they could develop their support.

References

Abhishek, S., Sinha, P. K. and Vohra, N. (2014) Role of haptic touch in shopping: some methodological contributions. *Decision,* 40(3), 153-163.

Ballantine, P. W., Jack, R. and Parsons, A. G. (2010) Atmospheric cues and their effect on the hedonic retail experience, *International Journal of Retail and Distribution Management,* 38(8), 641-653.

Chakrabarty, S., Widing, R. E. and Brown, G. (2013) Selling behaviours and sales performance: the marketing and mediating effects of interpersonal mentalizing, *Journal of Personal Selling and Sales Management,* 34(2), 112-122.

Cox, R. and Brittian, P. (2004) *Retailing an Introduction* Harlow: Pearson Education Limited.

Deswal, V. (2014) Spa services: healing or pampering (a study on significance of spa service to individuals), *International Journal of Innovative Research and Development* 3(4).

Global Spa Summit (2010) Bridge to a Huge Opportunity: Spa Retail. Conference Breakout Session, Istanbul, Turkey, 19 May.

Global Spa and Wellness Summit (2012) *Spa Management Workforce and Education: Addressing Market Gaps,* SRI International.

Gitomer, J. (2012) The hard side of training and the soft side of learning. *The Enterprise* June 25-July 1.

Goad, E. A. and Jaramillo, F. (2014) The good, the bad and the effective: a meta-analytic examination of selling orientation and customer orientation on sales performance, *Journal of Personal Selling and Sales Management,* 34(4), 285-301.

HABIA (2006) Skills Survey for the Spa Industry, http://www.habia.org/PDF/industry/ Skills_Survey_for_the_Spa_Industry_Report_March_20061.pdf (accessed 16/07/2015)

Johnson, E. M. and Redman, B. M. (2005) *Spa: A Comprehensive Introduction,* Michigan: The American Hotel and Lodging Institute.

ISPA (2013) *Retail Management for Salons and Spas,* New York: Cengage Learning.

Kent, T. (2007) Creative space: Design and the retail environment, *International Journal of Retail and Distribution Management,* 35(9), 734-745.

Krishna, A. (2012) An integrative review of sensory marketing: Engaging the senses to affect perception, judgement and behaviour, *Journal of Consumer Psychology,* 22(2), 332-351.

Lassk, F.G., Ingram, T. N., Kruas, F. and Di Mascio, R. (2012) The future of sales training: challenges and related research questions, *Journal of Selling and Sales Management* XXXII(1), 141-154.

Lo, A. S. and Wu, C. (2014) Effect of consumption emotion on hotel and resort spa experience, *Journal of Travel Marketing,* 31(8), 958-984.

Mintel (2015) Beauty Retailers at a Glance, Mintel Group Limited

Morrison, S. and Crane, F. G. (2007) Building the service brand by creating and managing an emotional brand experience, *Brand Management,* 14(5), 410-421

Murthy, N. N., Challagalla, G. N., Vincent, L. H. and Shervani, T. A. (2008) The impact of simulation training on agent performance: a field based study, *Management Science,* 54(2), 384-399.

Otnes, C. C., Ilhan, B. E. and Kulkarni, A. (2012) The language of marketplace rituals: implictions for customer experience management, *Journal of Retailing*, **88**(3), 367-383.

Polla, A. (2014) The spa market as a distribution channel, *Global Cosmetics Industry Magazine*, Allured Publishing Corporation.

Professional Spa and Wellness (2013) Income Additions, Feb. professionalspawellness.com

Richardson, L. (2014) The new sales pitch, *American Society for Training and Development*, March, pp 46-51.

Roman, S. and Iocabucci, D. (2009) Antecedents and consequences of adaptive selling confidence and behaviours: a dyadic analysis of salespeople and their customer', *Journal of the Academy of Marketing Science,* **38**, 363-382.

Soars, B. (2009) Driving sales through shoppers' sense of sound, sight, smell and touch, *International Journal of Retail and Distribution Management*, **37**(3), 286-298.

Spa Business (2014) ESPA, interview with Sue Harmsworth, Issue 4, available at: http://www.spabusiness.com/detail.cfm?pagetype=featuresonline&featureid=29431&mag=Spa%20Business

Tabbachi, M. (2010) Spa management: Current research and events in the spa industry, *Cornell Hospitality Quarterly*, February, p114.

Wang, M. L. (2013) Adaptive to customers: The roles of learning climate and customer knowledge, *Human Systems Management*, **32**, 171-180.

Weitz, B. A. Castleberry, S.B. and J. F. Tanner Jnr. (2009) *Selling: Building Partnerships,* 7th edn, New York: McGraw-Hill Irwin.

Wuttle, M. and Cohen, M. (2008) Spa retail, in Cohen, M. and Bodeker, G. (2008) *Understanding the Global Spa Industry: Spa Management*, Oxford: Elsevier Ltd.

9

Acknowledgements

With thanks to Leon Trayling, Director of Hebridean Spa Ltd

10 Marketing for the Spa Industry

Eleni Michopoulou

Introduction

This chapter examines marketing practises and concepts as applied within the spa industry. It uses the traditional 4Ps framework – with a twist. In particular, it looks into the
nature of the product, as it evolved from goods to services to experiences. Then it rede-
fines place and its importance for consumer decision making with regards to spa related
consumption. It moves on to discuss how promotion is performed today, and its core
links to relationship management. Lastly, pricing is reviewed within the context of value
creation and consumption, and its dynamic formulation in the experience co-creation
process.

Product

Discussing the spa product can be tricky, as it is multifaceted and complex. To
better understand it, we can apply the very prolific model of servicescape, which
is often used to explain similar service sector industries (e.g. hospitality) (Durna *et
al.*, 2015; Hooper *et al.*, 2013). While the model is not free of criticism – customers
and employees are not part of the service landscape even though the physical
setting is formed by the people who are in this setting and act and interact with it
(Bitner, 1992; Daunt and Harris, 2012) – it can still be a useful tool to unpack the
complexities of the spa servicescape.

It demonstrates, for instance, that spas as service settings are bound to their
physical dimensions (ambient conditions, signs, artifacts, etc.) as well as the intangible dimensions (service design, quality, friendliness, etc.) (Kwon *et al.*, 2015). It

is important therefore, to address both in terms of defining the 'product'. There is a distinct difference between the goods logic and the service logic with regards to product offerings. The goods logic assumes that the company produces goods and the customers generate value from their use. Similarly, as goods are value supporting resources, services are value supporting processes. Both are important within a servicescape, and even more so, within the spa context.

For example, considering the physical space, all tangible aspects of the spa contribute towards developing customers' view of the spa. Ambient conditions such as temperature, colours, lighting, are important in creating the 'image' of the spa. This can be one way of differentiating spas, for instance 'modern and sleek' versus 'calm and traditional' and anything in-between. There are more items that further contribute towards developing the spa image, such as signs, symbols and artefacts. For instance, these can be quite specific to the particular spa, and can include anything from staff uniforms, name badge design and business card logos to the type of china used for serving teas and coffees and the sheets' thread count. Therefore the tangibles are an integral part of the product, as the image, appeal and USP of a spa are highly dependent on those elements for differentiation and a competitive edge.

There is however, one of the tangibles that warrants separate attention, as it is so central to the spa product notion that is often used as a synonym. That is, the products used for different types of treatments. There are myriads of lotions, creams and oils used around the world for performing treatments that range from massages and facials to hay baths, beer baths and bull semen as hair care (Telegraph, 2016). These products are often valued more than any other tangible, for many reasons.

10

First, these products are a promise of something usually elusive and possibly unattainable. For example, "use this oil for radiant skin" (Figure 10.1) or "use this cream to fight the signs of ageing" (Figure 10. 2), and they promise to do things like make our skin feel "soft, springy, with a healthy looking glow" (Figure 10. 3) and even help us "rediscover emotional equilibrium, calm nerves and give a sense of optimism" (Figure 10. 4). Hence, the actual lotions, creams and oils constitute a critical factor for spa consumption, particularly when consumer decision making is influenced by the promise of the products, so much so as to drive motivation for spa consumptions in the first place.

Further, when these products are branded, they influence directly customer expectations. The brand name and brand identity of these products is used as a standard for predicting the quality of the spa. Some of these products are international powerhouses, with extended visibility and recognition across the globe and across markets. The brand name element is regarded as being of significant importance to consumers within the literature (Barker *et al.*, 2015; de Chernatony and McDonald, 2006; Gázquez-Abad and Martínez-López, 2016; Keller, 2013). According to Fitzsimons *et al.* (2008) the type of brand and consumers' perceptions of the brand can influence their behaviour. The use of a particular product brand by a spa signifies the level of quality a customer may expect from the spa. Therefore, within the spa context, it is often the use of the branded products that sets customer expectations for the wider spa servicescape, including the quality of the other tangibles.

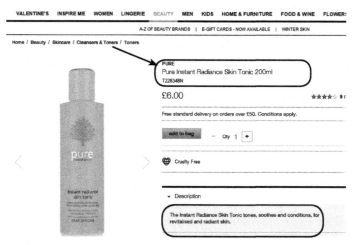

Figure 10. 1: Example of product promises (radiant skin)

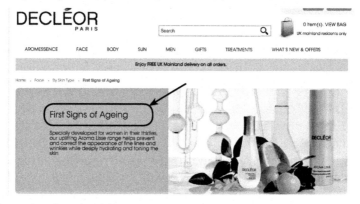

Figure 10. 2: Example of product promises (anti-ageing)

Figure 10. 3: Example of product promises (healthy glow)

Figure 10. 4: Example of product promises (emotional equilibrium and optimism)

This phenomenon is intensified by the fact that there is limited congruence towards a spa rating system. According to the Global Wellness Institute (GWS, 2015), there are major discrepancies between standards and practices in spas across the globe. This argument is further evidenced by the existence of numerous international standards associations (GWS, 2015). For example, in the UK, spa standards can be examined and interpreted according to the AA (2015), Spa Finder Wellness 365° Reader's Choice Award (Spafinder Wellness 365, 2013), or The Good Spa Guide and the 'Bubble ratings' accreditation (The Good Spa Guide, 2016). Therefore, as assessing spa standards can be problematic and bewildering, customers form their expectations based on the anticipated qualities of the product range (as conveyed by its brand) used by the spas. Thus, for example, a customer could consider a spa servicescape, for which little is known, acceptable and maybe desirable, when the product brand they are using is ESPA (i.e. a well-recognised, fairly up-market brand). The inherent assumption would be that the spa servicescape would reflect the brand values of the product range. Hence, the choice of products to be used within a spa is of utmost importance, as the quality and brand image of the products can be the main determinants of customer expectation; not just more than the rest of the tangibles but even of the spa brand itself.

The value of the product brand does not only refer to the tangible lotions, creams and oils. It extends to the treatments and therefore to a big part of the service element of the spa servicescape. The skill and technique required to perform a treatment is equally significant for the customer experience, and perhaps even more than the products applied. Many big and recognisable brands develop signature treatments that require the person delivering them to be trained to their standards. In doing so, they can ensure that the quality of the experience for the customer is not wildly variant between spas. Considering the fragmented approach to standards accreditation (GWS, 2015), and the inherent difficulties in recognising them and setting expectations, the brand value of the product becomes an even more critical factor for consumer choices. When the standards are so different, and each accrediting body uses different criteria (GWS, 2015), consumers often turn to spas that use branded product ranges, because that suggests consistency in both the actual product (creams and lotions) as well as the service (treatment) quality.

Thus there is an argument for the use of branded product ranges within spas to ensure some sort of standardisation of product and service quality. While this section provided an overview of the nature of the spa product, it is important to examine consumers' attitudes towards that product. There have been several motivations listed in the literature as to why customers go to spas (Gustavo, 2010; Mak et al., 2009; Tsai et al., 2012). These motivations can vary considerably between markets, ages, genders and cultures. However, there is one trend that is evident across the globe, and is not only relevant to the spa industry, but across many service industries; and that is experiences.

From the early days of Pine and Gilmore (1998), we know that the type of economy has changed over the years and can be categorized into four stages. The first was agriculture, followed by manufactured goods, then services, and finally experiences. Customers today want to consume experiences. These experiences are underpinned by the tangible and intangible elements of the servicescape, but the focus has moved from the goods and even services available, to the lived experiences. Hence, when discussing the spa product, it has to be done under the contemporary viewpoint of experiences.

Customer experience is "the cumulative impact – both emotional and practical – of all the encounters and interactions a customer has with a company" (Soudagar et al., 2012: 3). As such the outcome of all direct and indirect interactions can be very subjective and personal (Gentile et al., 2007). That these experiences are the result of this interaction, underlines the customer's role, participation and involvement in creating the experience. People buy goods and services as a means to fulfil deeper emotional, sensory and hedonic aspirations (Maklan and Klaus, 2011). With this lens, what matters to customers is "how they experience the extended process of acquiring, integrating and deploying that which is necessary for them to achieve their aspirations and generate value-in-use" (Maklan and Klaus, 2011: 3).

This section examined the spa product as it can be understood within a servicescape framework. Key elements of the spa servicescape include its tangible and intangible aspects. What became apparent is that for both, the value of the branded product range used is critical for consumer decision making. With the apparent lack of spa standards assurances, spas can capitalise of the brand image of their chosen products to offer customers products and services according to expectations formed by the product brand. So, the whole servicescape with all its tangible and intangible elements is the baseline for developing what customers are after – experiences. However, these experiences do not happen in a vacuum; some will occur within a given spa servicescape, but there are wider place considerations to contemplate.

Place

The traditional understanding of place within the 4Ps, refers to the place where the goods are made, stored, transported, and made available and sold to the customer. With services, place becomes a bit more complex because services are characterised by intangibility, inseparability, heterogeneity and perishability (Kotler and Armstrong, 2011). Spas are places were both products and services are made available to the customers, and this section will look at the importance of place within the spa servicescapes.

In the last section an argument was made for the use of branded product ranges within spas to ensure some sort of standardisation of product and service quality, and then moved on to suggest that the focus of the spa product transcends the tangibles and intangibles and should be firmly placed on the experience. One of the potential inherent conflicts of designing spa experiences is the search of authenticity as a key determinant for unique and memorable experiences on one hand, and the need for standardisation and quality assurance on the other. These concepts seem contradictory, but could be complementary in a spa context.

To better understand the argument, the concept of authenticity and its relationship with experiences and place needs to be discussed. Extant literature has examined authenticity under numerous definitions (Shepherd, 2015; Sims, 2009; Taylor, 2001; Verhoef *et al.*, 2009), and in several contexts, including heritage (Chhabra *et al.*, 2003; Zhu, 2012), film (Buchmann *et al.*, 2010), foods (Robinson and Clifford, 2012) and destinations (Knudsen and Waade, 2010; Steiner and Reisinger, 2006; Wirth and Freestone, 2010). However, the concept has not been adequately examined within the context of spas.

Authenticity within the spa servicescape can relate to both tangibles and intangibles. With regards to the tangibles it can link to all elements of place, from the symbols and artefacts (dress code, colours, décor) to the products used (lotions, creams and oils). It also links to the intangibles and services provided, including treatments. For instance, perceived authenticity can be found in olive based skincare products (Figure 10.5) or authentic Arabian hammam rituals (Figure 10.6). For the customer seeking authentic experiences, both tangibles and intangibles need to convey a sense of uniqueness and differentiation. However, authenticity of experiences extends beyond the tangibles and the intangibles of the spa; Authenticity brings consumers to destination attractions (Lindberg *et al.*, 2014; Lu *et al.*, 2015). So spas often borrow messages of authenticity from the environment as well as stories and tales inherent at the destinations, which are then interwoven with the spa servicescape. For instance, the unique properties of the physical environment of Dead Sea allows Jordan to present it as "the largest natural spa in the world" (Kitchen, 2015), and the traditional Mexican Temazcal ritual (VisitMexico, 2016) is capitalising on Mayan traditions. Hence, spas, particularly destination spas, need to incorporate the elements of authenticity as relevant to the particular *place* they operate in.

Figure 10.5: Example of authentic products. Source:http://aphroditeskincare.com

Figure 10.6: Example of authentic rituals. Source: http://arabianhammam.com/

It is important therefore for spas to understand the particularities of the *place* they are located at, so that the proposed offerings are congruent with the destination elements that constitute authentic traditions. For example, it may be acceptable to have a Thai massage anywhere in the world, but for those seeking authentic experiences, the products and treatments need to be linked to their traditional and local contexts. This means that this type of consumer will not be enticed, for instance, by the provision of Ayurveda therapies in Norway, or a Lomilomi (Hawaian) massage in Morocco. For this market, the experience is inadvertently linked to the destination. Within this market there is a sub-segment, for which the authenticity of the experience is so paramount, that even the destination becomes irrelevant. In essence, the destination is not the key determinant in consumer decision making process when choosing a spa experience; it is the authenticity of the experience in itself, regardless of the *place* it occurs. Hence, for a proper mud volcano bath, consumers can choose destinations all around the world, from Malaysia to Colombia.

At this point, the complementarity of the uniqueness of experience and the branded standardisation need to be addressed. The typologies of spas as well as the typologies of spa-goers have been well established by the Global Wellness Institute (GWI, 2015) and also in other chapters in this book. It is clear therefore that there are considerably different types of spa servicescapes and multiple roots to markets. While target markets and catchment areas can vary significantly, a dichotomy between authentic versus standardised is not compulsory. In fact, it could be seen as a spectrum where there are advantages at both ends, and the balance between them is a matter of trade-offs. Hence, spas can decide the extent of authenticity and differentiation they want to bring into the experiences they offer; or alternatively, decide upon the level of standardisation they want to integrate into their offerings. Thus, upon positioning the spa provision within its competitive context, a balance between authenticity and standardisation can be established.

The discussion on the place so far was focused on the experiences as they occur during the spa consumption, at the location. Spa consumption at the location is very important as spa provision is bound by the characteristics of services. Customer experiences, however, are not only formed while at the location, but throughout all interactions before, during and after the spa consumption. Ofir and Itamar (2007) argue that customer expectations have a significant effect on post purchase evaluations, which suggests that customer brand perceptions (of the retailer), might significantly influence the customer's experience. Therefore, it is important to consider a wider perspective of *place*. As the experience of the customer is formed by the encounters and interactions a customer has with a company (Soudagar *et al.*, 2012), the encounters before and after the consumption are also significant. It is important to acknowledge that in today's multi-channel environment, customers' experiences in one channel (e.g., a store) may be affected by experiences in other channels (e.g., the internet) (Konus *et al.*, 2008; Law *et al.*, 2014; Neslin *et al.*, 2006; van Birgelen *et al.*, 2006). Hence, when considering the place, the distribution channels and network (including intermediaries) need to be taken into account, especially as intermediaries do not only mediate the sale or transaction, but also customers' experience.

Promotion and price

The traditional understanding of promotion dictates that advertising, personal selling, sales promotion, public relations, and direct marketing are seen as integral parts of it (Gay *et al.*, 2007). The contemporary view of promotion is directly linked to relationship marketing, encompassing the notion of relational exchanges (Hoppner *et al.*, 2015; Stephen *et al.*, 2014). These exchanges are more than just transactional; they convey commitment, shared values, trust, and reciprocity (Beck *et al.*, 2015; Harmeling *et al.*, 2015; Samiee *et al.*, 2015). These relationships are the baseline for co-creating experiences, using the multiple points of contact between the customer and the organisation as a platform to interactively and jointly create value (Minkiewicz *et al.*, 2014; Vargo and Lusch, 2004). By realising that customers are active participants into creating and designing the experiences they want to consume (Grönroos, 2008; Grönroos and Ravald, 2011), it becomes evident that promotion needs to be informed – if not in a sense co-created – by the relationship between the consumer and the firm. Hence, to better promote value to the customers, customers need to participate, contribute and engage.

These co-creative relationships are particularly evident within services, including hotels (Chathoth *et al.*, 2013), tourist services (Binkhorst and Den Dekker, 2009), medical services (Bove *et al.*, 2009) and personal services, such as hairdressers and hair removal services (Silva *et al.*, 2013); and it is safe to assume that these can also encompass spa services. However, the nature of these relationships can differ between hedonic and utilitarian services. Utilitarian relationships focus on delivering core, generic and standardised products (Jones and Mccleary, 2007; Pels, 1999), while hedonic relationships are more customised and complex, as the interaction itself is part of the value delivered (Bowden *et al.*, 2015; Larsson and Bowen, 1989). Hence, the discussion of authenticity and standardisation as part of the product becomes now relevant within the context of promotion and pricing, because the type of service delivered will have an impact on the type of relationship developed with the customer. For example, standardised spa services offerings will assume utilitarian relationships, while more authentic and personalised spa service offerings can encourage more hedonic, co-creative relationships. For instance, a day spa in a city centre that targets a busy work force, can assume utilitarian relationships when the loyal clientele requires standardised treatments for quick frequent relief from shoulder tension. On the other hand, spa offerings that are tailor-made to customers' needs may assume a hedonic status as the input from the user is essential to co-create the experience (e.g. http://bespoke-you.co.uk/) Understanding the type of services and the type of relationships is important in order to determine their value.

The concept of value has been discussed with regards to value-in-exchange, value-in-use and value-in-context perspectives. Value-in-exchange follows the S-D logic, whereby value resides within a product or service and is delivered through an exchange process (Bagozzi, 1975; Whittaker *et al.*, 2007). The caveat of this conceptualisation is that it ignores the interaction between actors and the potential of value creation either through the interaction, or from the interaction itself. In contrast, value-in-use, assumes that value is the outcome of the interaction and is evaluated by the customer once consumed (Macdonald *et al.*, 2011; Sandstrom *et al.*, 2008; Vargo and Lusch, 2004; Woodall, 2003). The concern with this conceptualisation is that value is positioned within the consumer domain. Value-in-context, however, directly links value to the interaction as part of experience creation (Vargo *et al.*, 2010). Hence, with interaction being the prerequisite for experience creation, value is placed on the interaction *and* the experience as the outcome of the interaction (Ballantyne, *et al.*, 2011; Chen and Chen, 2010; Ramaswamy, 2010). In this sense, value derives from the consumption of the co-created experience, underlining the relational approach to value (Vargo *et al.*, 2008). Value is therefore, notionally, not restricted in the producer-consumer relationship, but assumes all actors creating value for themselves and others. The value-in-context conceptualisation, however, is also susceptible to the fact that the judgment of value is based on individuals' interpretations and dependent on the integration of other resources and elements within the specific context (Minkiewicz *et al.*, 2014; Vargo *et al.*, 2010). This can be particularly applicable to spas, considering the particular distinctions made in the product section, and the contextual implications of the spa servicescape.

From a solely economic standpoint, the perceived value of standardised utilitarian services is often judged by customers in terms of price and quality (Grönroos and Ravald, 2011). When such services are perceived as necessity services (Ng *et al.*, 2007), or when customers are serviced by the same company but different staff, as is typical in high staff turnover industries (Hess *et al.*, 2007), customer involvement is marginalised; therefore, standardised determinants such as price and quality are central to that judgement (Grönroos, 2008). On the other hand, participative, co-creative services, more hedonic in nature, entail value intrinsic to the interaction itself (Larsson and Bowen, 1989). Customer engagement has been seen as a driver for competitive advantage, increased business performance, and sales growth and profitability (Brodie *et al.*, 2013). Customers engaged in the co-production of a product or service, have higher evaluations of the end result (Mochon *et al.*, 2012; Troye and Magne, 2012). Additionally, the overall cost of production is reduced, as part of it is undertaken by the customer through their participation in the co-production process. So companies can reward customers for their efforts, by providing products and services in lower prices (Haumann *et al.*, 2015).

The discussion on value and price become more complex when contextualised within the spa setting. Decisions about standardisation – personalisation, and utilitarian-hedonic dichotomies or spectrums, have considerable implications on the production and consumption of value and the price tag that goes with it. It would be convenient to simplify pricing strategies assuming that differentiated products and services attract a premium and standardised services compete on price (Patterson *et al.*, 2008). However, differentiated co-produced services also compete on price (Mochon *et al.*, 2012; Troye and Magne, 2012), albeit the spa servicescape with underpinnings of luxury and pampering may not necessarily be comparable to IKEA-like coproduction savings model. Participative pricing has additional implications because technology enables consumers to further determine the value and price of services through interactive platforms. Customers now have options to use Name-Your-Own-Price (Hinz *et al.*, 2011; Scott and Seung Hwan, 2015; Voigt and Hinz, 2014) and Pay-What-You-Want platforms (Tudón, 2015; Weisstein *et al.*, 2016) and participate in classic auctions or reverse auctions (Chandran and Morwitz, 2005; Fugger *et al.*, 2016; Kim *et al.*, 2009). Kim *et al.* (2009: 45), gives an overview of the most common participative strategies:

> *The most prominent examples of participative pricing mechanisms with horizontal interaction are (1) classic auctions, in which multiple buyers compete with their (increasing) bids to buy a product from a seller; (2) reverse auctions, in which multiple sellers compete with their (decreasing) bids to sell a product to a buyer; and (3) exchanges, in which multiple sellers and buyers compete on both sides of the market.*

Considering the third 'exchanges' option, it becomes clear that the responsibility of price determination does not lie solely on the seller any more. Examples of platforms using participative pricing include eBay, priceline.com, hotelbids. com, extendedstayer.com and spalotto.com. Hence, it becomes evident that price is negotiated with the customers. Customers will pay more if they find value in a product or service, and the way to increase value is not just by reducing price; rather, it is by engaging customers in the coproduction of experiences, so they treasure the experiences they helped create.

Conclusion

Marketing of spas is a multi-faceted and complex practice. In this chapter, the basic 4Ps model was used to attempt to explain the intricacies of marketing spa servicescapes. It became apparent that understanding the spa product, with its various overlapping definitions and conceptualisations, is a feat in itself. Then, wider considerations of place were elaborated, including discourses on authenticity and experiences. Further, promotion was viewed under the relationship marketing perspective and attention was paid on the different forms of relationships developed in conjunction to types of product and service offerings. Price was then discussed in terms of value perceptions and the available negotiating mechanisms between sellers and buyers. This chapter argues for a conceptual shift from marketing spas to marketing spa experiences. Some of the implications of this shift have been discussed under an updated view of the 4Ps framework applied within spa servicescapes. However, further research is needed to understand a) the changes in customer behaviour, b) the new rules in the wider environment where spa businesses and customers interact, and c) the developments integral to the spa industry networked systems.

References

AA. (2015) The AA Standards, retrieved 20 Jan 2016, from https://www.theaa.com/resources/Documents/pdf/business/hotel_services/aa_hotel_quality_standards.pdf

Bagozzi, R. P. (1975) Marketing as exchange, *Journal of Marketing,* **30**, 32-29.

Ballantyne, D., Williams, J. and Aitken, R. (2011) Introduction to Service-Dominant Logic: From propositions to practice, *Industrial Marketing Management,* **40**, 179-180.

Barker, R., Peacock, J. and Fetscherin, M. (2015) The power of brand love, *International Journal of Market Research,* **57**(5), 669-672.

Beck, J. T., Chapman, K. and Palmatier, R. W. (2015) Understanding relationship marketing and loyalty program effectiveness in global markets, *Journal of International Marketing,* **23**(3), 1-21.

Binkhorst, E. and Den Dekker, T. (2009) Agenda for co-creation tourism experience research, *Journal of Hospitality Marketing and Management,* **18**(2-3), 311-327.

Bitner, M. (1992) Servicescapes: The impact of physical surroundings on customers and employees, *Journal of Marketing,* **56**(2), 57-71.

Bove, L. L., Pervan, S. J., Beatty, S. E. and Shiu, E. (2009) Service worker role in encouraging customer organizational citizenship behaviors, *Journal of Business Research,* **62**(7), 698-705.

Bowden, J. L. H., Gabbott, M. and Naumann, K. (2015) Service relationships and the customer disengagement - engagement conundrum, *Journal of Marketing Management,* **31**(7-8), 774-806.

Brodie, R. J., Ilic, A., Juric, B. and Hollebeek, L. (2013) Consumer engagement in a virtual brand community: An exploratory analysis, *Journal of Business Research,* **66**(1), 105-114.

Buchmann, A., Moore, K. and Fisher, D. (2010) Experiencing film tourism: Authenticity and fellowship, *Annals of Tourism Research,* **37**(1), 229-248.

Chandran, S. and Morwitz, V. G. (2005) Effects of participative pricing on consumers' cognitions and actions: a goal theoretic perspective, *Journal of Consumer Research,* **32**(2), 249-259.

Chathoth, P., Altinay, L., Harrington, R. J., Okumus, F. and Chan, E. S. W. (2013) Coproduction versus co-creation: A process based continuum in the hotel service context, *International Journal of Hospitality Management,* **32**, 11-20.

Chen, C. F. and Chen, F. S. (2010) Experience quality, perceived value, satisfaction and behavioral intentions for heritage tourists, *Tourism Management,* **31**(1), 29-35.

Chhabra, D., Healy, R. and Sills, E. (2003) Staged authenticity and heritage tourism, *Annals of Tourism Research,* **30**(3), 702-719.

Daunt, K. L. and Harris, L. C. (2012) Exploring the forms of dysfunctional customer behaviour: A study of differences in servicescape and customer disaffection with service, *Journal of Marketing Management,* **28**(1/2), 129-153.

De Chernatony, L. and McDonald, M. (2006) *Creating Powerful Brands.* Oxford: Elsevier.

Durna, U., Dedeoglu, B. and Balikçioglu, S. (2015) The role of servicescape and image perceptions of customers on behavioral intentions in the hotel industry, *International Journal of Contemporary Hospitality Management,* **27**(7), 1728-1748.

10

Fitzsimons, G., Chartrand, T. and Fitzsimons, G. (2008) Automatic effects of brand exposure on motivated behavior: How Apple makes you 'think different', *Journal of Consumer Research,* **35,** 21-35.

Fugger, N., Katok, E. and Wambach, A. (2016) Collusion in dynamic buyer-determined reverse auctions, *Management Science,* **62**(2), 518-533.

Gay, R., Charlesworth, A. and Esen, R. (2007) *Online Marketing : A customer-led approach.* Oxford: Oxford University Press.

Gázquez-Abad, J. C. and Martínez-López, F. J. (2016) Increasing a brand's competitive clout: the role of market share, consumer preference and price sensitivity, *Journal of Marketing Management,* **32**(1/2), 71-99.

Gentile, C., Spiller, N. and Noci, G. (2007) How to sustain the customer experience: an overview of experience components that co-create value with the customer, *European Management Journal,* **25** (5), 395-410.

GWI (2015) The Global Wellness Tourism Economy Report 2013 and 2014, retrieved 23 Jan 2016, from www.globalwellnessinsitute.com

Grönroos, C. (2008) Service logic revisited: Who creates value? And who co-creates?, *European Business Review,* 20(4), 298-314.

Grönroos, C. and Ravald, A. (2011) Service as business logic: Implications for value creation and marketing, *Journal of Service Management,* **22**(1), 5-22.

Gustavo, N. S. (2010) A 21st-century approach to health tourism spas: the case of Portugal, *Journal of Hospitality and Tourism Management,* **17** (1), 127-135.

Harmeling, C. M., Palmatier, R. W., Houston, M. B., Arnold, M. J. and Samaha, S. A. (2015) Transformational relationship events, *Journal of Marketing,* **79**(5), 39-62.

Haumann, T., Güntürkün, P., Schons, L. M. and Wieseke, J. (2015) Engaging customers in coproduction processes: how value-enhancing and intensity-reducing communication strategies mitigate the negative effects of coproduction intensity, *Journal of Marketing,* **79**(6), 17-33.

Hess Jr, R. L., Ganesan, S. and Klein, N. M. (2007) Interactional service failures in a pseudorelationship: The role of organizational attributions, *Journal of Retailing,* **83**(1), 79-95.

Hinz, O., Hann, I.-H. and Spann, M. (2011) Price discrimination in e-commerse? An examination of dynamic pricing in name-your-own-price markets, *MIS Quarterly,* **35**(1), 81-A10.

Hooper, D., Coughlan, J. and Mullen, M. (2013) The servicescape as an antecedent to service quality and behavioral intentions, *Journal of Services Marketing,* **27**(4), 271-280.

Hoppner, J. J., Griffith, D. A. and White, R. C. (2015) Reciprocity in relationship marketing: a cross-cultural examination of the effects of equivalence and immediacy on relationship quality and satisfaction with performance, *Journal of International Marketing,* **23**(4), 64-83.

Jones, D. L. and Mccleary, K. W. (2007) Expectations of working relationships in international buyer-seller relationships: Development of a relationship continuum scale, *Asia Pacific Journal of Tourism Research,* **12**(3), 181-202.

Keller, K. L. (2013) *Strategic Brand Management,* New Jersey: Prentice-Hall.

Kim, J., Natter, M. and Spann, M. (2009) Pay what you want: a new participative pricing mechanism, *Journal of Marketing,* **73**(1), 44-58.

Kitchen, J. (2015) Authenticity is key for trailblazers of wellness tourism, retrieved 25 Jan 2016, from http://www.spabusiness.com/detail.cfm?pagetype=detailandsubject=newsandcodeID=319068

Knudsen, B. and Waade, A. (Eds.). (2010) *Re-investing Authenticity : Tourism, place and emotions.* Bristol: Channel View.

Konus, U., Verhoef, P. C. and Neslin, S. A. (2008) Multichannel shopper segments and their covariates, *Journal of Retailing,* **84** (4), 398-413.

Kotler, P. and Armstrong, G. (2011) *Principles of Marketing* (14th ed.), Boston: Pearson Prentice Hall.

Kwon, R., Kim, K., Kim, K., Hong, Y. and Kim, B. (2015) Evaluating servicescape designs using a VR-based laboratory experiment: A case of a duty-free shop, *Journal of Retailing and Consumer Services,* **26**, 32-40.

Larsson, R. and Bowen, D. E. (1989) Organization and customer: Managing design and coordination of services, *Academy of Management Review,* **14**(2), 213-233.

Law, R., Buhalis, D. and Cobanoglu, C. (2014) Progress on information and communication technologies in hospitality and tourism, *International Journal of Contemporary Hospitality Management,* **26**(5), 727-750

Lindberg, F., Hansen, A. H. and Eide, D. (2014) A multirelational approach for understanding consumer experiences within tourism, *Journal of Hospitality Marketing and Management,* **23**(5), 487-512.

Lu, L., Chi, C. G. and Liu, Y. (2015) Authenticity, involvement and image: Evaluating tourist experiencesat historic districts, *Tourism Management,* **50**, 85-96.

Macdonald, E., Wilson, H., Martinez, V. and Toosi, A. (2011) Assessing value-in-use: A conceptual framework and exploratory study, *Industrial Marketing Management,* **40**, 671-682.

Mak, A., Wong, K. and Chang, R. (2009) Health or self-indulgence? The motivations and characteristics of spa-goers, *International Journal of Tourism Research,* **11**(2), 185-199.

Maklan, S. and Klaus, P. (2011) Customer experience: are we measuring the right things?, *International Journal of Market Research,* **53** (6), 771-792.

Minkiewicz, J., Evans, J. and Bridson, K. (2014) How do consumers co-create their experiences? An exploration in the heritage sector, *Journal of Marketing Management,* **30**(1-2), 30-59.

Mochon, D., Norton, I. M. and Ariely, D. (2012) Bolstering and restoring feelings of competence via the IKEA effect, *International Journal of Research in Marketing,* **29**(4), 363-369.

Neslin, S. A., Grewal, D., Leghorn, R., Shankar, V., Teerling, M. L., Thomas, J. S. and Verhoef, P. C. (2006) Challenges and Opportunities in Multichannel Customer Management, *Journal of Service Research,* **9** (2), 95-112.

Ng, S., Russell-Bennett, R. and Dagger, T. (2007) A typology of mass services: The role of service delivery and consumption purpose in classifying service experiences, *Journal of Services Marketing,* **21**(7), 471-480.

Ofir, C. and Itamar, S. (2007) The effect of stating expectations on customer satisfaction and shopping experience, *Journal of Marketing Research,* **44**(February), 164-174.

Patterson, A., Hodgson, J. and Shi, J. (2008) Chronicles of customer experience: The downfall of Lewis's foretold, *Journal of Marketing Management,* **24**(1-2), 29-45.

Pels, J. (1999) Exchange relationships in consumer markets?, *European Journal of Marketing,* **33**(1/2), 19-37.

Pine II, B. J. and Gilmore, J. H. (1998) Welcome to the experience economy, *Harvard Business Review,* **76** (4), 97-105.

Ramaswamy, V. (2010) Competing through co-creation: Innovation at two companies, *Strategy and Leadership,* **38**(2), 22-29.

Robinson, R. and Clifford, C. (2012) Authenticity and festival foodservice experiences, *Annals of Tourism Research,* **39** (2), 571-600.

Samiee, S., Chabowski, B. R. and Hult, G. T. M. (2015) International relationship marketing: intellectual foundations and avenues for further research, *Journal of International Marketing,* **23**(4), 1-21.

Sandstrom, S., Edvardsson, B., Kristensson, P. and Magnusson, P. (2008) Value in use through service experience, *Managing Service Quality,* **18**(2), 112-126.

Scott, F. and Seung Hwan, L. S. (2015) The role of customer expectations in name-your-own-price markets, *Journal of Business Research,* **68**(3), 675-683.

Shepherd, R. (2015) Why Heidegger did not travel: Existential angst, authenticity and tourist experiences, *Annals of Tourism Research,* **52**, 60-71.

Silva, F. C., Camacho, M. R. and Vázquez, M. V. (2013) Heterogeneity of customers of personal image services: A segmentation based on value co-creation, *International Entrepreneurship and Management Journal,* **9**(4), 619-630.

Sims, R. (2009) Food, place and authenticity: local food and the sustainable tourism experience, *Journal of Sustainable Tourism,* **17**(3), 321-336.

Soudagar, R., Iyer, V. and Hildebrand, V. G. (2012) *The Customer Experience Edge – Technology And Techniques For Delivering An Enduring Profitable And Positive Experience To Your Customer,* New York: McGraw-Hill.

Spafinder Wellness 365. (2013) Readers Choice Awards' from http://www.spafinder.com/blog/blank/readers-choice-awards/year-2013/rca/

Steiner, C. and Reisinger, Y. (2006) Understanding existential authenticity, *Annals of Tourism Research,* **33** (2), 299-318.

Stephen, S. A., Beck, J. T. and Palmatier, R. W. (2014) The role of culture of international relationship marketing, *Journal of Marketing,* **78** (September), 78-98.

Taylor, J. (2001) Authenticity and sincerity in tourism, *Annals of Tourism Research,* **28**(1), 7-26.

Telegraph. (2016) Strange spa treatments, retrieved 23 January 2016, from http://www.telegraph.co.uk/travel/weird-wide-world/10181092/Strange-spa-treatments.html?frame=2618288

The Good Spa Guide. (2016) The Good Spa Guide, retrieved 20 Jan 2016, from https://goodspaguide.co.uk/

Troye, S. V. and Magne, S. (2012) Consumer participation in coproduction: 'I made it myself' effects on consumers' sensory perceptions and evaluations of outcome and input product, *Journal o f Marketing,* **76**(March), 33-46.

Tsai, H., Suh, E. and Fong, C. (2012) Understanding male hotel spa-goers in Hong Kong, *Journal of Hospitality Marketing and Management,* **21**(3), 247-269.

Tudón, M. J. F. (2015) Pay-what-you-want because I do not know how much to charge you, *Economics Letters,* **137**(December), 41-44.

Van Birgelen, M., Ad de, J. and Ko de, R. (2006) Multi-channel service retailing: The effects of channel performance satisfaction on behavioral intentions, *Journal of Retailing,* **82**(4), 367-377.

Vargo, S. L. and Lusch, R. F. (2004) Evolving to a new dominant logic for marketing, *Journal of Marketing,* **68**, 1-17

Vargo, S. L., Lusch, R. F., Akaka, M. A. and He, Y. (2010) Service-Dominant Logic: A review and assessment, in N. Malhotra (Ed.), *Review of Marketing Research* (Vol. 6, 125-167). Bingley: Emerald.

Vargo, S. L., Maglio, P. P. and Akaka, M. A. (2008) On value and value co-creation: A service systems and service logic perspective, *European Management Journal, 26*(3), 145-152.

Verhoef, P., Lemon, K., Parasuraman, A., Roggeveen, A., Tsiros, M. and Schlesinger, L. (2009) Customer experience creation: determinants, dynamics and management strategies, *Journal of Retailing,* **85**(1), 31-41.

VisitMexico. (2016) Spas and Sweat Lodges, retrieved 25 Jan 2016, from http://www.visitmexico.com/en/spa-in-riviera-maya

Voigt, S. and Hinz, O. (2014) Assessing strategic behavior in Name-Your-Own-Price markets, *International Journal of Electronic Commerce, 18*(3), 103-124.

Weisstein, F. L., Kukar-Kinney, M. and Monroe, K. B. (2016) Determinants of consumers' response to pay-what-you-want pricing strategy on the Internet, *Journal of Business Research, Available online - In press.* doi: http://dx.doi.org/10.1016/j.jbusres.2016.04.005

Whittaker, G., Ledden, L. and Kalafatis, S. P. (2007) A re-examination of the relationship between value, satisfaction and intention in business services, *Journal of Services Marketing,* **21**(5), 345 - 357.

Wirth, R. and Freestone, R. (2010) Tourism, heritage and authenticity: State-assisted cultural commodification in suburban Sydney, Australia, *Urban perspectives, No 3,* 1- 10.

Woodall, T. (2003) Conceptualising value for the customer: An attributional, structural and dispositional analysis, *Academy of Marketing Science Review,* **12**, 1-41.

Zhu, Y. (2012) Performing heritage: Rethinking authenticity in tourism, *Annals of Tourism Research,* **39**(3), 1495-1513.

10

11 Developing an Effective Human Resource Strategy in the Spa Industry

Angela Anthonisz, Tim Heap and Olivia Ramsbottom

Introduction

The spa industry is facing a number of challenges linked to globalization, changing consumer preferences, new technologies, innovation, competition and more. As in any industry there is a time lag between cause and effect from the factors, but in the spa industry the lag within human resource management strategies and operational fit has been made more difficult due to the shortage of human capital available to the industry. A recent International Spa Association snapshot survey on recruitment (International Spa Association, 2014) found that it was often more 'difficult' or 'very difficult' to recruit qualified spa managers (52% of cases) and to recruit qualified therapists (58% of cases). In 2012 the McKinsey Company had produced a report on the state of human capital around the world. In it they identified that if there was one word that could describe the management of human capital, that word might be 'paralysis'. This paralysis can be attributed to "too much uncertainty, too many factors to manage, too many unfamiliar operating environments, too little support and too many risks". The report also identified that by 2020 a significant number of countries around the world would be confronted with a serious shortage of skilled labour and that both destinations and organisations needed to be developing strategies that would allow them to manage their global talent pools (McKinsey and Co., 2012).

The need for effective HR management

As highlighted by the Global Spa and Wellness Summit (GSWS) in their report on Spa Management Workforce and Education in 2012, the workforce is increasingly the most important factor when it comes to dealing with competition, but skilled and talented workers are increasingly difficult to recruit and retain. This challenge seems to be particularly prevalent at management level where demand far outstrips supply. However, in spite of the increasing awareness associated with the need for talent, it is also documented that few spa companies invest adequate attention and resources into human resources development and training in order to support their staff to progress within the company (Hunter, 2012). The spa industry is therefore adding further to the 'talent gap' that currently exists and subsequently storing up problems for the future.

The very personal nature of the spa experience from the customer perspective places a strong emphasis on service quality and consumer understanding. It is the employee that bridges the gap between the customer and the business, and has a direct influence on the customer's perceptions of service quality performance (Paulin *et al.* in Dedeoglu and Demirer, 2015). This is highlighted in Chapter 7 where service quality is seen to be linked to emotion.

The GSWS suggested that managing the talent gap for the future will require a much more proactive and partnership orientated approach to how the workforces is recruited and managed. This approach is shown in Figure 11.1 and highlights the key stakeholders involved in managing the workforce, and the need for training, knowledge retention, communication and talent management. This approach is unsurprising given that human capital (employee knowledge, experience, ability, personality, skills, internal and external relationships, attitudes and behaviours) turns out to be essential in the creation of specific competitive advantage for companies.

This chapter briefly introduces the current situation within generic HRM theory. But more importantly it looks at a model that uses the manager as the pivotal person managing human resources and assumes that all managers in the spa industry will understand the basics of managing cultural capital. The role for HRM is, therefore a much more strategic one with spa managers supporting and addressing the underlying people problems that are facing the industry. The focus is much more inward looking, something that managers in the service industry often struggle with, or in some instances choose not to deal with given that the care of employees is passed across to the human resources department and often 'dropped' on the way. We introduce the concept of the Employee Experience Journey (EEJ) and identify four stages where HR need to address the touch-points and ensure that managers are trained to deal with the emotional contagion that can lead to high employee turnover.

11

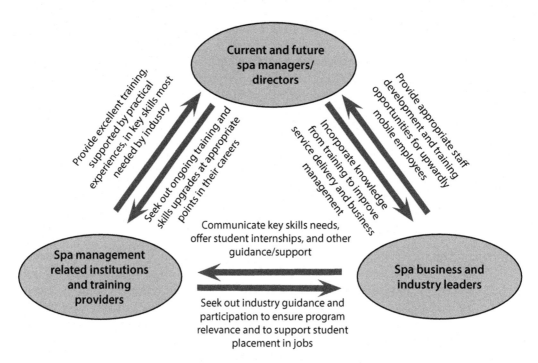

Figure 11.1: Stakeholder relationships in the management workforce system for the spa Industry. Source: Global Spa and Wellness Summit, Spa Management Workforce and Education: Addressing Market Gaps, prepared by SRI International, June 2012, pp iv

The role of HR management in spas

As services are intangible by nature, employees become part of the product, symbolizing the organization and helping to create and reinforce the company image (Bitner, 1990). Therefore employees, and the way in which they are managed, appear as determining factors for customer satisfaction, loyalty, service quality and performance (Tam, 2004; Saravan and Rao, 2007).

Human capital, according to Phillips and Phillips (2014) is the most critical part of an organization, yet the area often does not command proper respect and is considered administrative work in many organisations. HR's role and influence need to change relative to the environment, and for the spa industry change appears as a constant. The challenge of connecting important external changes to the human capital strategy is, therefore, made even more difficult. Unfortunately, the typical human capital strategy often has an operational focus on the administrative functions of acquiring, developing and managing talent in organisations. The changes facing the spa service sector requires a long term strategy and short term expediency, and a buy-in to both by managers in the organisation. If the HR function is relegated to purely an administrative role rather than a pro-active business role then the company will experience long term problems. Phillips and Phillips (2014) identified eight forces that will potentially impact on human capital and organisation success (see Figure 11.2).

Figure 11.2: Forces impacting on human capital. Source: Adapted from Phillips and Phillips (2014)

These forces include: technology and social media; shifting demographics; accountability and expectations; societal changes; energy and environment; globalization and the global economy; empowerment and engagement; and work/life balance. Each of these forces has the potential to impact individually and collectively on both sides of the spa product experience. This host-guest relationship, or service encounter, is the centre of that spa experience and for it to be successful it requires human capital, and regardless of size, needs a human capital strategy. These changes will create a change to the classic 'administrative' HR strategy and if not addressed properly they have the potential to impact on an organisation's success. If they are integrated into the strategy, Phillips and Phillips postulate that this will create a more powerful, successful, profitable organization.

HR management practices are recognized as resources that create competitive advantage and make a direct, economically significant contribution to organizational performance (Wang and Shyu, 2008). As the spa industry diversifies and becomes more complex there will be a requirement for highly skilled employees at all level of the spa operation. To provide that human capital will require an effective and integrated HR policy that considers both the internal and external operating environments to help set their spa (organisation) apart from the competition. This strategic HRM approach matches the human resources to the needs of the spa operation, but places less emphasis on the present skills required and more emphasis on the behaviours and values of those recruited. The question posed must be: "Do they share the ethos of the organisation, and are they prepared to develop themselves in line with the company's future requirements?" It is getting and using the *right* people.

Awareness of the future direction of the spa assists managers to be proactive rather than just reactive. This requires an understanding of the current progress of the business against staffing and financial targets. This is further explored within Chapter 14.

- Is there likely to be a need for more, fewer or different staff in future?
- Has the spa got expansion plans?
- Are there challenges created by seasonality?
- Will new technology or treatments require a new skills mix?
- Changing locations where the service will be offered
- Restructuring as a result of a downturn in business
- Key performance indicators (KPIs) require a different approach to business
- What are the succession plans?

This is then balanced with the current employee skills mix and triggers recruitment/selection, training and development needs. The success or failure of this strategic view depends entirely upon reliable data sets and a robust process for recording information on a continuous basis. This begins with a summary of each employee's education, experience, interests, skills, the duties performed in the organization and then a summary of training and development undertaken whilst at work. This information can be used for reviewing the current set-up of the organisation, succession planning for middle or senior management roles, and to identify gaps when people leave.

Successful HR relies on the individual manager taking responsibility for the employees within his/her department and focussing on them as a core resource. However, Miller *et al.* (2007) suggest that spa managers are often more concerned with filling a vacancy, in order that the therapist role can be performed, and have little regard as to who they employ to perform it.

■ Approaches to managing human capital in the spa industry

The complexity of the spa product, the extent to which the spa may be integrated into a larger business, and how service is delivered to the customer, means that there are a number of different management hierarchies and management roles, reflecting different products, markets and cultures. The spa industry has many different titles associated with the management role, from coordinator and supervisor to team leader and manager, with different titles used to attract people and differentiate job roles. The term 'manager' is used for the purpose of this chapter, but it is acknowledged that this means that they could be in any supervisory or management role, or have a 'leadership' title.

An individual manager's approach to dealing with their employees is influenced by their culture and the culture within the organisation and the wider community. The characteristics of the spa industry are that service is inseparable, heterogeneous, intangible and perishable (Brassington and Pettitt, 2013) and that the soft and pluralist approach to HRM, is more appropriate. The simultaneity or inseparability of a service (its delivery is at the same time as the consumption of the service or its immediacy), its heterogeneity (the risk of variability) and its intangibility (in many cases there is no product to touch or feel, but rather an experience to enjoy) places the importance of the service transaction on the supplier of that transaction. The member of staff needs to feel good, contented and looked after, in order to portray the calm and relaxed face of the business that the customer wants to see. This is more likely to be realised by the softer, pluralist approach according to the Hawthorne and Likert's Michigan studies (Cole, 2004) where production is related to recognition and when work was organised in a participative manner.

The intangibility element of the spa provision is often simultaneous with the 'hands on' of the therapy which needs strict adherence to training, therapeutic techniques and spa products, which are tangible and require control by the individual.

■ Challenges managing human capital in the spa industry

A number of key challenges have confronted the spa industry for several years and the fact that they are still prevalent suggests that the industry has not adopted more strategic responses to the problems. These challenges include high turnover (HABIA, 2012; Colliers International, 2015); a critical shortage of qualified staff especially at management level (International Spa Association, 2014); and problems with recruitment and retention, particularly at management level (GSWS, 2012; Colliers International, 2015). The reasons behind the skills shortages are complex, but unless HR examine and re-evaluate current working practices and retention policies in relation to management practices across all levels of the industry they are likely to continue. As the cost of replacing a staff member in the industry can reach £30,000+ (HR Review, 2014), including recruitment and lost productivity costs and dependent on the type of job and seniority, then it is necessary to ensure the recruitment, selection and staff development process is fit for purpose.

The traditional measure of turnover, and the one that is most commonly utilised, is one that uses an annual percentage:

$$\frac{\text{Total number of separations (involuntary staff turnover + voluntary staff turnover)}}{\text{Average number of employees during the surveyed period} \times 100}$$

More sophisticated models are more often used by individual businesses to ensure the metrics are useful in terms of strategic HR planning. These use monthly data (seasonality) and include sub units of involuntary (e.g. misconduct, seasonality or trading position) and voluntary (e.g. promotion, personal and internal transfer) data. (TFG White Paper, 2017)

The following section builds upon research undertaken by Hunter (2012) whose doctoral thesis identified that HR problems begin with the recruitment, treatment and lack of development of spa therapists. They are responsible for the touch-points with the clients that is at the center of the customer service journey, but their experiences in the industry do not suggest that it is a happy experience for many therapists. The section then explores the financial implications of the high turnover of staff and the requirements for HR to address those problems. The process is encapsulated in what we have called the Employee Experience Journey (EEJ), as shown in Figure 11.3.

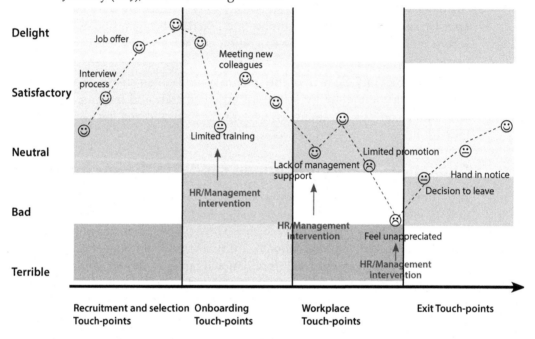

Figure 11.3: The Employee Experience Journey.

The four stages of EEJ have key touch-points in the horizontal journey similar to customer journey mapping (CJM), and the consumer decision journey (CDJ) (Chapter 7), but in this case the touch-points are the interaction (positive/negative) of employee with the employer (manager, colleague, HR). At each of these points there is a sequence of events where the employee will review their own employment experience (perhaps Personal Development Planning) and where management may review their progress/suitability (perhaps Development Performance Review) for the role. By understanding the nature of the employee employer touch-points means that HR can work with team members to manage and enhance their journey.

At each touch-point, there is (like CJM and CDJ) a vertical axis that includes the important emotional journey of the employee. The measurement of these emotions has been problematic (Lo *et al.*, 2015), but responsiveness by management was the most important in explaining positive emotions. This reinforces the need to develop a strategic approach to managing the experience, and as in CJM and CDJ, this emotional emphasis is what Tschimmel (2012) calls an empathy mapping exercise.

Developing a strategic approach to HR

The identification of the touch-points within the discourse relate to the four stages of the EEJ and may form part of a strategic HR review. This then could lead to responses in terms of management planning to include interventions such as further training or reviewing work life balance. The following questions are some that the spa industry are faced with in terms of developing a strategic approach to HR and could be linked to underperformance within the sector.

1 Why is turnover so high at all levels of staffing in the industry?'

Figure 11.4 outlines the key factors that Hunter (2012) identified as being at the centre of high turnover and links these to the potential effects upon business success and suggests that the answer to the problems lie within the remit of strategic HR responses.

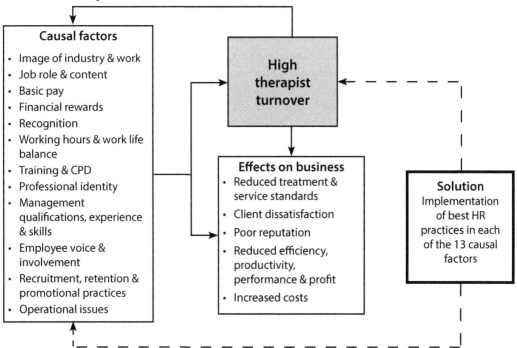

Figurre 11.4: Key factors in high turnover. Adapted from: Hunter (2012)

The EEJ (Figure 11.3) begins with expectations and the 'images of the industry and work' which are often positive, and designed to attract quality employees. The recruitment and selection touch-points are often seen as a marketing and sales exercise, especially as the International Spa Association state that it is more 'difficult' or 'very difficult' to recruit qualified spa managers and qualified assage therapists. In HR and management terms it is essential that the 'on boarding' touch-point stage is linked to the recruitment process. Initial training, for example, often fails to instill confidence within the therapists to perform treatments; the technical processes are taught, but not the fundamental relationship building with the clients that are necessary to provide consumption emotion, which is seen as an emotional reaction that an individual has in response to product consumption or service experience (Richins, 1997). These must be linked to the quality processes which in themselves create the spa experience.

Reasons for further emotional contagion include stressful working conditions, long (often unsocial) hours, low pay, unrealistic bonus payments, inequity in promotion opportunities, lack of support from management, operational issues, poor management processes, lack of recognition, no involvement in decision making processes and lack of professional identity. These are included in the onboarding and workplace touch-points and end up with the most important emotion of feeling unappreciated.

A further complication is added by the success of the industry in creating a global market for their products and staff. Expatriates, for example, form 87% of the total hospitality workforce in the United Arab Emirates (Dyes, 2009). The expectation is that international mobility will result in those employees wanting to either return to their home countries, or move on to other key international destinations. Family ties and issues are the second most common motivation for staff to leave.

It is not that all of the above are present in all of the spas all of the time, but that they have all been identified as being present for some of the time. As these are known (or given) it is difficult to understand the inertia on behalf of the industry and why they are not part of an HR strategy that includes management interventions.

2 What are the effects of turnover upon employees and the spa businesses?

This is important for the development of the HR strategy as the reasons given in question one lead to actions by the employees and responses by the consumers. The current action is invariably that the employee leaves the organisation, which in turn leads to a high industry turnover rate. This then becomes self-perpetuating and embedded within the culture of spa employment. The high turnover rate also leads to further dissatisfaction, de-motivation, and further stress is then placed upon the remaining employees. This can be in the form of teams being disrupted, increased workloads, time needed to train replacement employees and the time it takes internally to build relationships with a new member of staff. Nowak *et al.*

(2010) confirmed that turnover culture negatively affects the remaining workforce, which in turn causes further turnover as these workload issues are exacerbated.

These issues potentially affect the service provision, and results in client dissatisfaction with instant impacts as comments are immediately posted on social media. The loss of the employee knowledge, skills and ability, in turn reduces the spa's service capacity and capability, (Buchner *et al.,* 2008; Ton and Huckman, 2008).The loss of a senior therapist often leads to the loss of regular clients who may follow the therapist to a new spa. Arbore *et al.* (2009) confirmed that high turnover created perpetual recruitment and training costs, adding the caveat that junior therapists would go to senior therapists for advice. Hunter's (2012) research identified that in most cases they were seen as more approachable and knowledgeable than their managers. This highlights the loss of tacit knowledge that is gained through working longer with the organisation.

A high staff turnover rate can directly impact on levels of profitability due to the costs associated with recruitment, training and the time required for new employees to reach full productivity (Ton and Huckman, 2008). Added to this are the indirect costs to reputation, erosion of differentiation and competitive advantage, reduction of performance and productivity, and a loss of value to the service offering (Nowak *et al.,* 2010; Zakaria and Yusoff, 2011). Low levels of employee turnover can be beneficial to an organisation as refreshing the workforce can add a new dimension to the service provision, and provide new product offering.

Attempts to measure the financial implications of staff turnover have led to the development of increasingly sophisticated models within the service sector, but most are focussed upon the generic hospitality sector. An industry white paper by TFG Asset Management (2017), for example, uses a formula that assesses the contribution that each staff member generates towards revenue generation. The model then factors in how a given role influences their potential contribution to, and impacts upon, revenue streams if they leave. The negative impact upon delivery of service, for example, was 5% for a receptionist, 2% for a head chef and 5% for an FandB manager. An overall 30% turnover rate in the hotel led to the revenue per available room dropping by 22% and occupancy by 14%.

The lessons for HR strategy from the high staff turnover upon human capital and the spa companies can, therefore, be measured in financial terms. The assessment of the employee journey in terms of impacts will cover all four stages. It is interesting how few employers insist upon exit interviews, and if they do undertake them they ignore the outcomes. If the organisation focussed on the financial implications and cost benefit analysis, perhaps the motivation to create interventions within the journey would be more forthcoming.

3 How can retention be improved?

This must begin with the first stage of the EEJ, with Dewar (2016) confirming that having a fit-for-purpose recruitment strategy emphasising correct fit, ensures the correct choice of employee. The recruitment process must be open and ensure that both skills and personality are evaluated. How often in spa recruitment is the emphasis purely placed upon the practical skill set of the candidate when the reasons for high turnover are more often down to personality fit? The process must include situational questions within problem solving. The requirement to cross check references and the candidate's awareness of brand identity and their personal identification with that brand is essential not desirable. The candidate must be aware of the opportunities and challenges posed by the emergent digital economy. The final aspect, according to Dewar (2016), is to establish whether the candidate is open-minded, because change happens frequently in the spa sector.

For managerial appointments the mix is similar, but places the emphasis first on experience, then attitude/personality, fit with culture/brand, being open minded and the essential concept of leadership. Many companies today (e.g. Hilton Worldwide and Movenpick) also use the 'fit with culture/brand' to ensure the potential employee could figure in succession planning, and so identify career pathways to potential employees. Considering spas close links with the hospitality industry it seems logical that this should be considered by the spa industry.

This means that from the first stage of the EEJ journey, the employee has an identified route which can then be turned into a development plan with an emphasis upon the manager to ensure progress along that pathway. This is built into both the new employee's and manager's objectives. Though these are large global companies the concept is still possible within smaller privately owned spas, where it is important to outline if there is potential for career progression. If there is no possibility for progression the employer may still get an ambitious, committed individual, for a limited time period, but not one that feels frustrated by lack of career progression.

Stages 2 and 3 in the EEJ must follow up on the promises made in the first stage of the journey, otherwise the employee is likely to leave very quickly. This must include an early inclusion of learning and training programmes that support professional development. The reason often given for not doing this for early career employees is that there is no return on investment as they may choose to leave as soon as they are upskilled. The converse to this is that you will retain a growing number of employees whose skills have not been developed, with obvious negative impacts on service quality. Unless employees have access to training, their lack of understanding of the company values and branding, which in turn leads to standards, will then lead to inconsistency in service provision and the further lowering of service quality.

The customer service journey (Chapter 7) emphasises the emotional responses by the client at the touch-points within that journey. This requires training in communication, professionalism, brand consistency and handling complaints. This training for spa employees may take the form of placing them outside their comfort zone in order to identify talent and potential business leaders within the organisation. This exposure may be one of the criteria to identify employees for further promotion, which will help to strengthen the loyalty of excellent performers. The idea is to consolidate talent within all areas of the business, so to do this it may be that top graduates enter fast track programmes instead of the 'time served' model often used within the spa industry.

Learning and development programmes have often been perceived as too costly within the global spa industry. Current thinking by asset managers, however, is that the cost of reducing staff turnover outweighs the cost of the programmes especially as they are shown to increase productivity. This professionalisation of the industry also has the added bonus that the employees are identified as 'professionals'. One of the current issues in staff retention is that employees have found it difficult to identify with what professionalism looks like in the industry and that they feel undervalued.

4 What are the management issues that lead to high turnover?

The traditional model in the spa industry suggests a top down approach to management, and is perhaps where high turnover or a role culture is found. The issue is that this traditional approach has led to a culture of resistance to change. Management frequently ignores employee requests for change and improved working conditions, resulting in frustration and feelings of inequity leading to turnover. This culture is sustained by management through poor recruitment practices and disregard for professional identity, and simply recruiting the next therapist that will accept the minimum wage (role culture)

Hunter's research pointed to management being the highest cited reason for spa employee turnover as they identified being "unprepared from initial training and not having the confidence to perform treatments, adverse initial work experience, with stressful working conditions and lack of support from management" (Hunter, 2012: 261). The interface between the manager and the employee does seem to break down very often within the industry, which leads to a lack of trust from both sides. It would be too simplistic to say that bad management is the issue that leads to high turnover, as that would ignore the role of HR in the recruitment of, and lack of development of, those managers. Management and HRM need to take ownership of the causal factors within their spa businesses, and by mapping these on a generic EEJ they are more likely to identify trends and clusters. The spa manager, for example, must take responsibility for ensuring that recruitment is role specific and follow the parameters outlined in question 3.

It is also essential that spa businesses employ more accountability in their recruitment of spa managers, ensuring appropriate background, qualifications and ability.

5 What strategic responses are required by HR?

The first step is to define the role of HR management in the spa industry, which has traditionally been seen as purely administrative (Ulric, 1997). The role needs to be strategic in order to protect and market the brand through investment in the employees of the organisation. This requires the identification of talented employees through the recruitment process, devising talent management programmes

11

for learning and development, and ensuring that excellence is rewarded. They are the gatekeepers between the company and employees. Employers demand strategies that provide a return on investment in human capital that leads to sustainable growth. The employees require a transparent strategy for their EEJ which identifies cause and effect in terms of their employment within the organisation.

The EEJ is by necessity a partnership between company and employee which means that HRM needs to define certain parameters for the employee. For example: What does quality look like in terms of the customer experience journey in order to protect the brand? What is 'excellent' and 'unacceptable' within the service provision? How are these essential factors then communicated, through management to the employee? This addresses one of the key reasons for high staff turnover, which is not understanding roles and responsibilities, and not being trained to the level to achieve that level of excellence.

In many cases this will mean that HR are the agents of change, but by showing the strategic imperative behind the need to change means they are supporting the managers that have to effect change. Too often new practices and procedures are adopted by organisations (change often being unpopular) and it can leave the managers dealing with resistance from the employees. The employees blame the managers and then cite them as reasons for leaving the organisation. This is often the case in the adoption of new technology, where the manager is perceived as simply trying to lower costs. It is the HR department that must introduce and oversea the implementation of change.

The *Global Human Capital Trends 2016* report suggested that the HR department is responsible for motivating staff to see the benefits of change. They outlined five key areas that in spa industry's case could form the basis for an HR strategy in order to provide, develop and retain the right employees for the organisation.

1 **Organisational networks** – to analyse, build and develop the existing talent and expertise.

2 **Team-building and team-leader** – develop potential team leaders who can later develop people.

3 **Employee engagement and culture** – Understand, the current culture at the hotel and propose improvements to the workplace culture.

4 **Analytics and statistics** – HR professionals must be proactive in studying the market trends and embracing changes. HR must be proactive in benchmarking them with the market KPIs.

5 **Crafting experience** – HR professionals are the brand ambassadors. They need to find the most effective way to communicate brand value to current and potential employees.

(Deloitte, 2016)

The organisational structure necessary to provide for the HR strategy may need to be flatter than the traditional hierarchical structure found in the spa industry, and in most of the service sector. The calls for transferable skills and multi-tasking are questioning the traditional job specific role and responsibilities. This opens up more opportunities for employees to develop their careers and not to be 'stuck in the same old job'.

The HR strategy must have the ability to measure key performance indicators as associated with performance measures. These are increasingly including happiness, motivation and engagement (disengagement) as essential metrics. Increasingly the service sector (and recommended for the spa industry) use satisfaction surveys from interview, on day one and after the first month of the employee's experience journey. They finish the employee's journey with an exit interview which very often gives an honest appraisal of the current situation within the organisation. The data must inform both the strategic direction of the HR strategy and the day to day operation of the spa business. Early intervention is essential if there are problems with leadership styles. The fact that HR is seen to intervene and to respond to concerns leads to increased employee satisfaction and reduced turnover.

A recurring theme within the spa industry is that it is perceived as part of the low wage economy. This factor is important in both trying to attract and retain talent for the development of the business. The reward and remuneration strategy for the organisation must be associated with achieving excellence as defined by HR and compare favourably with similar levels within other service providers. The professionalisation of the industry is therefore an essential part of HR strategy to ensure that reward follows expertise, commitment and development of the employees.

Conclusion

The need for a review of the HR strategy for the spa industry seems fundamental, as the talent pool for employees is decreasing while the size of the service sector increases at an exponential rate. The chapter emphasises the need for the industry to adopt HR strategies for retaining, developing and rewarding existing employees. It suggests that management will provide the key role in implementing the strategy, but alongside HR and not separate from it. This duality of responsibility is seen as paramount for the continued development of the spa product and success of the industry.

The chapter introduces the concept of the Employee Experience Journey in an attempt to provide a link between the employee, manager and HR. The touchpoints on the model are simply suggestions as individuals will have different journeys, experiences and inputs. The contract between the three parties is seen as a way to help retain staff, increase profitability and increase professionalism within all areas of the industry. This branding, based upon professionalism and excellence in the overall spa provision, is seen as essential in taking the industry forward into an agenda that is increasingly turning to wellness and spa.

Questions

- What is the value of your workforce within your business?
- How do you manage your employees once they are in the company?
- To what extent do you invest in your employees' future?
- What do you need to focus on in order to train and retain employees?
- How can your employees enhance performance and productivity within the business?
- Produce a EEJ for yourself

References

Arbore, A., Geunzi, P. and Ordanini, A. (2009) Capability building,relationship trade-offs and key service employees; the case of the Radio DJ. *Journal of Service Management*, **20**(3), 317-341

Bitner, M. (1990), Evaluating service encounters: the effects of physical surroundings and employee responses, *Journal of Marketing*, **54**, 69-82.

Brassington, F. and Pettitt, S. (2013) *Essentials of Marketing* (3rd edn.). Harlow, England: Pearson Education

Buchner, D., Snelling, A. and Cohen, M. (2008) Spa related education and training, in Chen, M. and Bodeker, G., (Eds) *Understanding the Global Spa Industry Management* Oxford, Butterworth Heineman.

Cole, G. (2004) *Management Theory and Practice* (6th edn). London: Thomson

Colliers International (2015) *Dubai Spa Benchmark Report*, Full Year Review

Dedeoğlu, B. B. and Demirer, H. (2015). Differences in service quality perceptions of stakeholders in the hotel industry. *International Journal of Contemporary Hospitality Management*, **27**(1), 130-146

Deloitte, (2016) *Global Human Capital Trends 2016*, Deloitte University Press. Available from https://www2.deloitte.com/content/dam/Deloitte/global/Documents/HumanCapital/gx-dup-global-human-capital-trends-2016.pdf

Dewar, J. (2016). The key to reducing employee turnover is to begin during recruitment. Lever.co. Retrieved 21 July 2016, from http://www.lever.co/blog/the-key-to-reducing-employee-turnover-is-to-begin-during-recruitment

Dyes, R. (2009). Expats account for 87 per cent of UAE's workforce. Emirates 24|7. Retrieved 21 July 2016, from http://www.emirates247.com/eb247/economy/uae-economy/expats-account-for-87-per-cent-of-uae-s-workforce-2009-11-23-1.21107

Global Spa and Wellness Summit (2012) *Spa Management Workforce and Education: Addressing Market Gaps*, prepared by SRI International.

HABIA (2012) *HABIA Employer Skills Survey*. Available at: http://www.habia.org/.

HR Review (2014) It costs over £30K to replace a staff member. Available at: http://www.hrreview.co.uk/hr-news/recruitment/it-costs-over-30k-to-replace-a-staff-member/50677, accessed 16 July 2015

Hunter, G. (2012) *The causes and consequences of high value therapist turnover in day spas in the UK.* Thesis submitted in fulfilment of the Doctor of Philosophy, University of Derby.

International Spa Association (2014) *Snapshot Survey Results Report – Employee Recruitment – August 2014.* Available at: experienceispa.com, accessed 15 July 2015.

Lo, A. S., Wu, C. & Tsai, H., (2015). The impact of service quality on positive consumption emotions in resort and hotel spa experiences, *Journal of Hospitality Marketing & Management*, **24**(2), 155-179.

McKinsey and Company (2012) ' *The State of Human Capital – False Summit. Why the Human Capital Function Still Has Far to Go. Research Report R-1501-12-RR*

Miller, J. E., Walker, J. R. and Drummond, K. E. (2007), *Supervision in the Hospitality Industry; Applied Human Resources*, (5th ed.) New Jersey, John Wiley and Sons Ltd.

Phillips, J.J. and Phillips, P.P. (2014) Developing a human capital strategy in today's changing environment: eight forces shaping HC strategy. *Strategic HR Review*. **13** (3), 130-134

Richins, M. L., (1997). Measuring emotions in the consumption experience. *Journal of Consumer Research*. **24**, 127-146.

Saravanan, R. and Rao, K. S. P. (2007) Measurement of service quality from the customer's perspective – an empirical study, *Total Quality Management and Business Excellence*, **18**(4), 435-449

Tam, J.L.M. (2004) Customer satisfaction, service quality and perceived value: an integrative model, *Journal of Marketing Management*, **20**(7-8), 897-917

Ton, Z. and Huckman, R. S., 2008, Managing the impact of empoloyee turnover on performance; the role of process conformance, *Organisational Science*, 19(1), 56-68

TFG Asset Management (2017) *The Impact of Staff Turnover on the Hotel's Income Statement.* Hotel Industry White Paper

Tschimmel, K. (2012) Design thinking as an effective toolkit for innovation. Proceedings from the XXIII ISPIM Conference: Action for innovation: Innovating from experience, ISPIM, Manchester, UK.

Ulrich, D. (1997). *Human Resource Champions: The next agenda for adding value and delivering results.* Harvard Business School Press. Boston, MA

Wang, D. S. and Shyu, C.L. (2008), Will the strategic fit between business and HRM strategy influence HRM effectiveness and organizational performance?, *International Journal of Manpower*, **29**(2), 92 - 110

Zakaria, S. and Yusoff, W.F.W. (2011) Transforming human resources into human capital, *Information Management and Business Review* **2** (2), 48-54

11

12 Finance for the Spa Industry

Tony Loynes and Victoria Rosamond

Introduction

Many employees entering the spa industry, do so with a basic level of business knowledge and financial appreciation. As long ago as 2003, ISPA, in collaboration with the Association for Hospitality Financial and Technology Professionals, released the first edition of Uniform System of Financial Reporting for Spas. However, this is primarily focussed on accounting principles and the development of an internationally comparative accounting system. The current employment market reflects the spa industry's growing need for higher academic levels of business acumen which will enable the industry to fill the gaps in middle to upper management positions. The Global Spa and Wellness Summit report (2012) on addressing the market gaps on workforce and education, outlines the need for a mixture of soft and hard skills in future spa managers.

Financial appreciation is a key example of a hard skill that is rarely popular with potential employees, but always relevant for supervisory positions within the industry. Spa businesses range from independent day spas through to destination and resort spas. In some cases, they are separate business entities, while in others they are business units within a larger organisation and contribute to both the appeal and profitability of the overall business. Economic theory teaches that the purpose of business is maximising profit for the shareholders, a concept that was developed by economist Milton Friedman (1975) and despite more modern views on this matter adopting the corporate social responsibility concept, the profit maximisation requirement is rarely, if ever, lost completely.

This chapter examines the concept of profit maximisation within the spa context and identifies some of the basic tools available for its measurement and management.

Making and measuring profit

Businesses make profit by either selling something at a higher price than it was purchased or by providing a service for which a customer is willing to pay. The successful spa business does both of these, providing the service of spa treatments and offers retail products to spa guests. Assuming that prices for these services and products have been set appropriately, the business will make a profit for each treatment and sale made. In simple terms, *Profit equals Net Sales Revenue minus Costs of Goods Sold (COGS)*. So, if we sold a retail product for £20 (net sales revenue), that we paid £10 (COGS) to buy, we would make a £10 profit. Likewise, if a guest purchased a treatment for £45 (net sales revenue) with products used costing £7 (COGS), we would make a £38 profit. Profit calculated in this way is known as *Gross Profit* and it should be noted that these calculations are exclusive of any sales taxes, such as Value Added Tax (VAT) in the UK. Currently VAT is charged at 20% which would make the full retail price of the examples given above £24 and £54 respectively. Adding or subtracting sales tax is a relatively simple calculation. Using the current UK VAT rate, we can add sales tax using the following formula:

Price Excluding Tax × (1 + Tax Rate as a decimal) or £20 X (1. 2) = £24

To remove sales tax, again using the current UK rate, the formula is:

Price Including Tax ÷ (1 + Tax Rate as a decimal) or £24 ÷ (1. 2) = £20

Understanding *Gross Profit* is an important part of a manager's role as it allows them to understand what profit has been made over a given period, check this against what should have been made and compare potential profit scenarios using different products or volumes of sales. To do this, Gross Profit needs to be converted to a *Gross Profit Percentage* figure and the calculations for this are again very simple.

Gross Profit ÷ Net Revenue × 100 = Gross Profit Percentage

Using the treatment example above, we identified that the Gross Profit was £38. Therefore, the Gross Profit Percentage would be:

38 ÷ 45 × 100 = 84.4%

For the retail product example, it would be:

10 ÷ 20 × 100 = 50%

The percentage figures above are often referred to as *theoretical* figures as they are calculated using theoretical information. For example, if a therapist performed twelve of the treatments identified above, the *Total Net Revenue* would be 12 × £45 = £540, the *COGS* would be 12 × £7 = £84 and would result in a *theoretical Gross Profit* of £540 – £84 = £456. If, however, at the end of the therapist's shift the calculation of the *COGS (value of opening stock + any additional stock provided during the shift– value of closing stock)* revealed that there had been additional product used to the value of £1 per treatment, the COGS would now be 12 × £8 = £96, the *actual*

12

Gross Profit would be £540 − £96 = £444 and the actual Gross Profit percentage £444 ÷ £540 × 100 = 82.2%. The 2.2% difference between the theoretical and actual Gross Profit percentages might seem quite small but if we considered a longer period with a Total Net Revenue of £500,000, it would represent £11,000 of lost profit. Variances between theoretical and actual Gross Profit percentages should always be investigated. In the example above the therapist was using too much product, but the effect on the *actual Gross Profit percentage* would be the same if product was being wasted through mishandling or being stolen.

Gross Profit percentages are also useful for comparing different product offers. For example, this might be used to identify the better retail product offer from two competing brands. The brand giving the highest Gross Profit percentage is initially likely to be the better option. However, we can only be sure of this if we take into account *Sales Volumes* and *Price* as these will influence the *Total Gross Profit* achieved. To illustrate this, we can consider two products with different theoretical Gross Profit percentages; Product A (80%) and Product B (50%). If Sales Volumes and Price were the same, say £40, then Product A would be the best choice because it would generate greater a Gross Profit.

Product A: £40 × 80 ÷ 100 = £32 Gross Profit

Product B: £40 × 50 ÷ 100 = £20 Gross Profit

If we now, consider the impact of *Price* and now say Product B retails for a price of £65 at the same Gross Profit percentage, it now produces slightly more Gross Profit than Product A.

Product B: £65 × 50 ÷ 100 = £32.50

Finally, if we account for differing *Sales Volumes* and say that over a given period Product A at £40 would have a Sales Volume of 100, while over the same period Product B at £65 would have a Sales Volume of 95. Now the better option would be Product A because it would generate a greater Gross Profit.

Product A: 100 × £40 × 80 ÷ 100 = £3200 Gross Profit

Product B: 95 × £65 × 50 ÷ 100 = £3087.50 Gross Profit

Managing Gross Profit is, however, not the only financial concern associated with the operation of a successful spa and there are other costs that also need managing. Staff and energy costs are normally the biggest of these additional costs which are deducted from the Gross Profit to leave the *Net Profit*. Net Profit in accounting terms is the final or bottom line profit of the business, but in multi-site or multi-business unit operations, Gross Profit and Net Profit are reported at site or unit level to provide the specific information that managers need to enable them to control the business. The report used to provide this information is known as a *Trading Profit and Loss Report* which shows all of the net revenue and all of the expenditure associated with that revenue over a given period (see Figure 12.1). The report gives information on Net Sales Revenue over the period, the Cost of Goods Sold to generate that revenue and the Gross/Net Profit made by the business.

Trading Profit and Loss Report – Spa

For the month of April

		£
Net Sales Revenue		
	Treatments	72,500
	Retail	18,000
Total Sales Revenue		90,500
Cost of Goods Sold		
	Treatments	4,000
	Retail	11,250
Total Cost of Sales		15,250
Gross Profit		
	Treatments	68,500
	Retail	6,750
Total Gross Profit		75,250
Expenditure		
	Staff	35,000
	Energy	1,000
	Marketing	2,000
Total Expenditure		38,000
Net Profit		37,250

Figure 12.1 : Example Trading Profit and Loss Report

In this example, we can see Net Revenue and Gross Profit by activity and could use this to make decisions on what staff training or promotional activity is required but, if we add percentage figures as discussed earlier in the chapter and some historic data, it becomes a far more useful management tool (Figure 12.2).

We can now see that Net Sales Revenue has grown for both treatments and retail over the four months and as would be expected given this increase, the Cost of Goods Sold has also increased but when we look at the Gross Profit percentage figures, we see that for treatments this has fallen from 93.8% in January and February to 92.7% in April. Unless there has been an increase in the price of products used, this business is using more products per treatment in April than it was in January and February.

Also, by calculating the staff costs as a percentage of Total Sales revenue using the formula **Staff Costs ÷ Total Sales Revenue × 100** we can see that these have risen from 44.8% in January to 51.7% in April and are, therefore, increasing disproportionately to the increase in Total Sales Revenue.

It would be easy to say that the business is growing and making almost £9,000 more Net Profit in April than it was in January, so why does this matter? But the effect of these changes on Net Profit is considerable. Reducing Staff Costs to 44.8% and increasing the Gross Profit percentage for treatments to 93.8% would result in an additional £7,923 of Net Profit in the month of April alone.

Trading Profit and Loss Report – Spa

For the month of April

	£ - Jan		£ - Feb		£ - Mar		£ - Apr	
Net Sales Revenue								
Treatments	52,000		77,100		80,000		82,500	
Retail	15,000		16,000		18,000		18,000	
Total Sales Revenue	67,000		93,100		98,000		100,500	
Cost of Goods Sold								
Treatments	3,200		4,800		5,500		6,000	
Retail	10,250		11,250		11,250		11,250	
Total Cost of Sales	13,450		16,050		16,750		17,250	
Gross Profit								
Treatments	48,800	93.8%	72,300	93.8%	74,500	93.1%	76,500	92.7%
Retail	4,750	31.7%	4,750	29.7%	6,750	37.5%	6,750	37.5%
Total Gross Profit	53,550		77,050		81,250		83,250	
Expenditure								
Staff	30,000	44.8%	46,000	49.4%	50,000	51.0%	52,000	51.7%
Energy	1,000		1,000		1,000		1,000	
Marketing	2,000		2,000		2,000		1,000	
Total Expenditure	33,000		49,000		53,000		54,000	
Net Profit	20,550	30.7%	28,050	30.1%	28,250	28.8%	29,250	29.1%

Figure 12.2: Example Trading Profit and Loss Report with historic data and percentages

Budgeting and forecasting

Budgeting and forecasting are two of the most important financial functions for a business of any size and are often linked together, as they should be, but they are not the same. A budget is a detailed financial outline of what the business thinks will happen financially over a period of time (often a year). The budget will include details about revenues and expenses over the given time period and is often then broken down into successive budgets with shorter time periods, such as months, to allow for the seasonality many businesses experience.

Ideally, a budget is used as a management tool to run the business. Actual financial results are compared to budgeted amounts and variances are analysed. For example, if expenses in a certain area are higher than budget, investigation should be undertaken to identify why this has occurred. Reviewing the budget on a regular basis is a key tool in managing the business and normally takes place on a monthly basis. Quite often, performance against budget and the previous year is included in the monthly Profit and Loss report as both a monthly and cumulative figure, with these informing performance related bonuses.

Trading Profit and Loss Report – Spa

For the month of April

	£		+/- Budget		+/- LY	
Net Sales Revenue						
Treatment	82,500		-2000		1200	
Retail	18,000		-1000		2000	
Total Sales Revenue	100,500		-3000		3200	
Cost of Goods Sold						
Treatment	6,000		100		-1000	
Retail	11,250		-500		-600	
Total Cost of Sales	17,250		-400		-1600	
Gross Profit						
Treatment	76,500	92.7%	-1900	-0.1%	200	-1.1%
Retail	6,750	37.5%	-1500	-5.9%	1400	4.1%
Total Gross Profit	83,250		-3400		1600	
Expenditure						
Staff	52,000	51.7%	-2100	-0.5%	-100	-1.8%
Energy	1,000		0		0	
Marketing	1,000		0		0	
Total Expenditure	54,000		-2100		-100	
Net Profit	29,250	29.1%	-1300	-0.4%	1700	0.8%

Figure 12.3: Example of trading profit and loss in spa.

A forecast, on the other hand, is a projection of what will happen at a higher level, generally key revenue items and overall expenses. Forecasts can be done over long-term and short-term time horizons. A longer-term forecast might look out over several years and feed a longer-term strategic business plan. Shorter-term forecasts are generally done for operational reasons with revenue forecasts leading to adjustments in staffing levels and stock holdings to minimise waste. In essence, forecasting is used to both produce the budget and predict compliance with it.

Forecasts are not perfect but they are a necessary strategic management tool. A basic forecast is better than none as it provides market and customer knowledge to enable proactive management of staffing and stock levels. It can also identify periods of low demand that might be addressed through targeted marketing activity.

One of the most common approaches to forecasting is known as *Time Series Forecasting* which uses historic data to predict future demand. It generally is undertaken at an aggregate level, such as the number of treatments per month, rather than each individual treatment and a financial value can be applied to this using an average price per treatment. Clearly, statistical forecasting has its limits because, for example, it does not recognise any external factors such as the number of treatment rooms, but it does provide a basis on which managers can apply their expert judgement.

Increasing profitability

If we accept the basic premise at the beginning of this chapter, that the purpose of business is maximising profit for the shareholders, then it is clear that this profit maximisation is the responsibility of the managers, as the stewards of the business. Using the simple view that profit is a residue of revenue minus expenditure they can achieve this by identifying ways in which revenue can be increased without increased expenditure or ways in which revenue can be maintained with reduced expenditure. Both of these would result in increased profit and can be identified and measured through the Profit and Loss report. How this might be achieved is the focus of this part of the chapter.

In a spa context, simple approaches to profit maximisation are product management, increasing the customer base, increasing current customer visits and upselling. The benefits of good product management were mentioned earlier in the chapter but this can be an often overlooked area. Ensuring the right quantities of product are used for each treatment and other losses are kept to a minimum should be considered as part of the general housekeeping activities of the manager. Increasing the customer base is the option most spa managers consider when attempting to increase profits but whilst success in this area does provide increased gross profit, it is often outweighed by the additional promotion cost that have been employed in pursuit of this goal. Increasing current customer visits is a more cost effective approach to increasing profits and links nicely with loyalty bonus activities that are prevalent in the industry. Whist up-selling – selling a more profitable treatment or selling retail product to existing guests – has an immediate impact on profit and should be part of the staff development for all therapists and hosts.

The following ratios are commonly used to calculate the revenue made from treatments and treatment rooms, based on capacity and occupancy.

Average revenue per guest = total spa revenue/total number of guests in the spa

Revenue per available treatment room (RevPATR) = total spa revenue/number of treatment rooms

Average treatment rate = total treatment revenue/ total number of treatments performed

Treatment room utilisation = number of treatment room hours used/ number of available room hours (occupancy/capacity)

Average unit sale per guest = number of treatments or products sold/ number of guests

Capture rate = number of guests in a hotel or resort/ number of guests staying on the resort or hotel using the spa.

The last of these is particularly relevant with low percentages of hotel and resort spa guests making use of the spa facilities. Most spas would increase profitability dramatically if they attracted a great number of the customers who were literally on their doorstep.

The above ratios are essential for a spa business to recognise the efficiency and productivity of their facilities; and for the team, an understanding of the processes of calculating these, gives the employee an insight into the revenues and timing of revenues generated by the business.

Getting the basics right should never be overlooked, but to really maximise profits, more advanced techniques such as yield management and revenue management, already widely employed in the hotel industry, should be considered. Yield management is very much focused on maximising revenue by a combination of selling price and volume manipulation. Initial yield management techniques were more tactical than strategic and were focussed purely on driving revenue, without any consideration of other potential client spends or associated additional cost. Revenue management is seen as a development of yield management with a broader, more strategic, focus.

Revenue management can be described as selling the right product to the right guest at the right time and at the right price. It requires some forecasting of future demand in order to optimise product availability and maximise revenue growth. The purpose of revenue management is not selling a treatment today at a low price, so that you can sell it tomorrow at a higher price. It is about matching, at a micro level, demand and supply through the use of innovative price strategies. Revenue management seeks to make use of the economic theory of the relationship of price and demand which identifies that as price increases, demand falls and vice versa. Figure 12.4 clearly illustrates this, and at a high price (P1) demand is low (Q1), while at a lower price (P2) demand is higher (Q2). Although, because of something known as *elasticity of demand,* the relationship between price and demand is more curved than the linear relationship shown in Figure 12.4, the underlying principles of revenue management seek to exploit the demand at all points along the price/demand curve. This does of course mean sometimes selling a treatment at low price today, if you do not expect higher demand, as not doing this results in a loss of potential revenue and the associated profit.

12

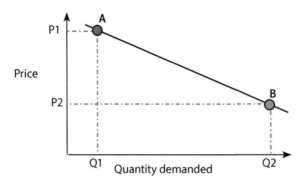

Figure 12.4: Example of relationship between price and demand.

Calculating a yield figure is relatively simple. It is a percentage figure that compares the revenue achieved with the maximum potential revenue available.

Actual Revenue ÷ Total Potential Revenue × 100 = Yield Management %

For example, on a specific day a spa has 100 treatments available at an average treatment price of £60. Therefore, the maximum potential revenue is 100 × £60 = £6000. If, however, only 60 treatments were sold at an average treatment price of £50, the achieved revenue is 60 × £50 = £3000. From this information we can calculate (3000 ÷ 6000 × 100 = 50%) that the Yield Management percentage is 50%. Given that most spas operate with a treatment room utilisation of between 35% - 40%, there is much to benefit from the adoption of yield management techniques.

To drive revenue management within a spa context, it is proposed that managers use a Revenue Per Available Treatment Hour calculation (RevPATH). This provides valuable information on the timing of revenue flow and could be compiled on a monthly, weekly or annual basis. It could also be broken down by therapist, if this deemed beneficial. This information might be compiled into a table like the one in Figure 12.5.

Average Hourly Revenue (£) per Available Treatment-Hour (RevPATH) for August							
	12:00 PM	1:00 PM	2:00 PM	3:00 PM	4:00 PM	5:00 PM	6:00 PM
Sunday	25	63	92	85	86	82	78
Monday	5	30	30	33	34	18	8
Tuesday	6	28	35	33	34	18	11
Wednesday	8	31	35	49	52	21	12
Thursday	10	28	35	34	36	20	10
Friday	8	15	20	28	44	58	50
Saturday	28	68	78	80	82	78	62

Figure 12.5: Example of revenue per available treatment hour calculation (RevPATH).

During periods of lower RevPATH, managers can implement marketing offers in an attempt to attract more guests or encourage therapists to spend additional time on upselling techniques to increase the average client spend. At times of high RevPATH, managers might consider reducing the amount of time between treatments or offering only premium treatments. What RevPATH analysis provides is the hard data necessary for managers to make informed decisions on how revenue can be increased and with it, the profitability of the spa.

Effective revenue management is, therefore, concerned with the efficient management of resources and expenses, treatments and retail as well as maximising productivity of areas and therapists. For example, when a treatment room is left empty we calculate the revenue lost for that period of time. It is easy to send a therapist home for the day if he or she is not busy and to reduce the capacity, but this is where the distinct difference between a proactive and reactive manager is highlighted. We need to change the thinking to where the first priority should be to fill the column before it has perished rather than reducing capacity for that day and taking the easy option of reducing labour costs. The notion of perishability is in 'time lost', which in the service sector cannot be replaced or sold again.

Conclusion

The spa industry is no different to any other when it comes to the need for making profit but some of those responsible for managing this, appear to be ill equipped. Understanding how profit is made, measured and maximised are key ingredients for successful business management in any context but are particularly important when products are perishable and sales shortfalls in one period cannot be recovered in another. The ability to quantify profit and control expenditure is vital for business survival and the knowledge and ability to maximise profit within the spa context will enable successful businesses and provide valued opportunities for career progression.

Discussion

- To what extent do you agree/disagree that spas exist purely to make profit?

- Managing Gross Profit is not the only financial concern associated with a spa operation. How might attempts at profit maximisation impact on the guest experience?

- Given the similarity of management activities related to profit maximisation, to what extent do you consider the roles of spa and hotel managers to be interchangeable?

References

Friedman, M. (1975) *Unemployment versus inflation?* London: Institute of Economic Affairs.

Global Spa and Wellness Summit (2012) *Spa Management Workforce and Education: Addressing Market Gaps*, SRI International.

13 Training and Development in the Spa Industry

Sarah Rawlinson

Introduction

This chapter outlines the importance of training and development to the success of a spa business. It provides evidence of how a well-supported training and development programme can improve profitability, staff loyalty and customer satisfaction. The human interaction between the spa consumer and the spa employee is a critical part of the customer experience, and a motivated and happy workforce is critical to the success of a spa business.

Training and development is one of many investment activities a spa business can use to improve its performance. However, investment in this area is often the first activity to be cut when budgets are tight. It is critical that training and development departments and spa managers can demonstrate that strategic investment in their staff has a high probability of success in helping to achieve organisational goals and contributing to improved business performance, if they are to be prioritised ahead of other investment activities. Robust quantifiable outputs are required that focus on the extent to which organisational objectives are achieved.

The importance of training and development

Successful learning organisations include how they plan to manage and develop their human capital in their corporate strategy. Training and development forms part of the strategic priorities of a successful learning organisation, with tools designed to measure the impact and demonstrate the ability of training and development to improve organisational performance and support business decisions. Businesses that link training to specific impacts are more likely to invest in their workforce because they focus learning opportunities on appropriate people and business critical activities where it will have most impact.

An innovative learning organisation requires investment in knowledge to generate and develop new services, products and processes (Figure 13.1). The outcome from that investment creates new knowledge, information and ideas which over time become obsolete and the whole process starts again. This cycle of investment and knowledge creation develops a learning culture within organisations. According to Casillas *et al.* (2010: 163) "Learning is the process of acquisition, integration and interpretation of new knowledge with the objective of later use". A spa business must have the ability to renew knowledge, create new ideas and be innovative. This requires a workforce with multiple skills, competences and problem solving abilities.

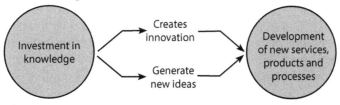

Fig 13.1: Learning culture

All organisations need to develop and change and they can only do that if their workforce develop and change with them. In a highly competitive environment such as the spa industry, new knowledge needs to be learnt and applied more quickly than its competitors. Many successful organisations are familiar with David Kolb's (1984) concept of learning as a continuous process of experience, reflection, conceptualisation and experimentation and embrace this as part of their training and development strategy

Training and development is one of the main ways in which organisations maintain and improve their intellectual capital. The quality of service, reputation and the ability to grow the business is highly dependent on the workforce. An untrained or poorly trained workforce costs an organisation more to support than a well-trained workforce. Therefore it should follow that investing in human capital makes good business sense. A research report for the American Society for Training and Development by Bassi *et al.* (2000) demonstrates a strong connection between workplace learning and financial measures, and that the quality of an organisation's training affects its value.

13

Businesses must be able to measure the impact of training and development to show how investment in organisational learning creates value for the organisation. Without impact measures, investment is unlikely to be forthcoming. According to Sonal Uberoi (n.d.), Director of Spa Business Consulting, spa businesses are reluctant to invest in training. Spa businesses do not want to take people out of their business for training unless it is going to make their business more successful. Global Spa and Wellness Summit report (GSWS, 2012: 84) suggest that spa businesses need "a proactive approach towards talent, leadership and human resource development" in order to address the management talent gap in the industry. They confirm that education, training and workforce development should be a key priority for the industry and that training and development requires quantifiable evidence on return on investment (ROI). This helps the business meet its strategic priorities, provides competitive advantage and increases profitability.

The creation of a learning culture in a spa organisation requires formal and informal learning opportunities as part of a strategic approach to training.

Formal learning opportunities include training courses and events away from the day-to-day activity of the workplace. This provides access to new information and concepts and brings people together to share ideas, collaborate on projects, solve problems, meet new people and build knowledge together. Formal learning opportunities are commonly used in the spa industry as they have the advantage of standardising a base of knowledge required by the business. For example, formal training programmes for product training, health and safety standards, policy and procedures etc. Structured formal education programmes, from NVQs to degree programmes, allow individuals to build on existing knowledge, develop new knowledge and skills and prepare them for promotion.

Organisations using formal learning as part of their training and development strategy would benefit from providing opportunities for staff to transfer their new knowledge to the workplace in a supportive environment in order to gain maximum benefit and ensure that training and development is not seen as separate from work. All too often investment in training is wasted because there are no mechanisms in place to support and monitor the transfer of new knowledge into the business.

Informal learning in the work place involves a combination of learning from others and learning from personal experience. At its simplest, informal learning can be implicit, unintended, opportunistic and unstructured. Providing structured opportunities for informal learning would include mentoring, action learning sets, communities of practice and, moving more towards the formal learning, would be coaching. According to Eraut (2011) the types of informal learning opportunities in the workplace is important because the learning opportunities exist in the challenge of work itself and learning from others. Eraut found that employees learned more through work than from formal organised learning events when the right conditions were put in place to enhance the learning opportunities. Eraut provides some examples of informal learning in the workplace.

Work processes with learning as a by-product	Learning activities located within these processes	Learning processes at or near the workplace
Participation in group processes	Asking questions	Being supervised
Working alongside others	Getting information	Being coached
Consultation	Locating resource people	Being mentored
Tackling challenging tasks and roles	Listening and observing	Shadowing
Problem solving	Reflecting	Visiting other sites
Trying things out	Learning from mistakes	Conferences
Considering, embedding and refining skills	Giving and receiving feedback	Short courses
Working with clients	Use of mediating artefacts	Working for a qualification
		Independent study

Table 13.1: A typology of early career learning processes and activities. Source: Eurat, M. (2011: 9)

Creating a culture where people can learn and share their ideas within an organisation requires team leaders and managers with the philosophy and ability to develop others and provide mentorship and coaching support to their teams. A learning culture encourages people to work together to identify challenges in the work system, solve problems and work together as a team and share knowledge.

Jennings (2013) supports an "adding, embedding and extracting model" for training and development which pulls together formal and informal learning. According to Jennings, adding learning to work can take the form of formal learning with learning activities designed to be integrated in the workplace that have the explicit purpose of assisting learning. Embedding learning in work provides informal learning opportunities where learning and work merge and knowledge is gained at the point of application, which develops problem solving skills. Extracting learning from work supports learning from day-to-day work activities that requires reflection to improve performance. Jennings (2013) suggests extracting learning from work is the most powerful aspect of workplace learning and can help drive engagement and performance. It can be achieved in a number of ways including: one-one coaching sessions or performance reviews that help people connect their contribution to the workplace with organisational priorities; team talks to develop a shared understanding of organisational purpose and focus; debriefs; and peer reviews.

The benefits of growing your workforce organically

The direct benefits of a well-developed training and development strategy relate directly to business performance, e.g. profitability, operating revenues, customer satisfaction, improvements in quality and processes, etc. as discussed above. There are however, a number of indirect benefits to an organisation, for example, employee retention, job satisfaction and improved reputation as an employer that invests in its workforce; an important factor when recruiting new staff. Many

people join organisations to develop a career not just for the job. The global reputation of the spa industry has a negative impact on recruitment as it does not have
well planned career opportunities and pathways. Opportunities for promotion
and advancement are essential to employee retention and performance.

The spa industry has identified that training and education and the lack of
well trained staff is one of the greatest challenges for spa businesses (GSWS,
2012). Spa businesses are facing a challenge to recruit enough people with the
right skills to fill management level positions. The GSWS report states that the
industry places little importance on educational qualifications when recruiting
managers, which is one of the key factors that contributes to the gap the industry
is experiencing in business skills. GSWS research found that most spa managers/
directors are deficient in at least one of the key skills areas, such as business, management or finance. The report (2012: viii) makes a number of recommendations
for improving the spa management workforce system that would be useful for
spa businesses to consider when planning their training and development. Whilst
these challenges are not unique to the spa industry, the report suggested that
few spa businesses adequately invest in human resource development and training to support their workforce as they move into management level positions.
The answer is a more proactive approach to succession planning, and developing career pathways within spa organisations, together with improvements in
the reputation of the industry and spa businesses as investors in training and
development. Training and development can help people understand how their
work fits into the organisation's mission, goals, structures and the contribution
they make to its achievements. People who are actively engaged with the organisation are motivated to learn more about their roles and understand that their
behaviours and performance matters to the organisation and its success. There
are many studies that directly relate to a motivated workforce, positive employee
engagement and work related happiness with organisational effectiveness (Amah
and Ahiauzu, 2013; Ankli and Palliam, 2012; Halm, 2011; Longenecker, 2011). A
motivated workforce can lead to better productivity, lower levels of absenteeism,
better levels of retention, improved quality and customer service.

Training and development can have a positive impact on individuals as well
as organisations. The commitment of an organisation to invest in an individual
has a positive effect on how an individual perceives their value and contribution
to the organisation and can build confidence. Individuals who are willing to learn
and manage their own professional development are an important asset to an
organisation. They continually update their skills and knowledge and cope positively with change. They also tend to be more reflective and are more productive
and efficient.

Table 13.2: Two pathways for hiring spa managers/directors: pros and cons. (GSWS, 2012: 26)

	Promotion within the spa	Hiring outside the spa
Pros	Have strong 'soft skills' and 'people skills' Have front-line and first-hand understanding of spa, spa modalities and guest relations Have demonstrated passion for spa Already know their spa's unique culture and operational style	Have strong 'hard skills' in technical business/management fields Have management experience and/or training Know how to run a business Can bring useful and fresh outside experiences and ideas to the job
Cons	Are weak on 'hard skills' in technical business management fields Usually have not had any business or management-related training May not have any management experience May lack an innate inclination toward management and 'left- brain' thinking	Are weak on 'soft skills' and 'people skills' Usually do not have any experience or training in spa modalities Often have not worked in a front-line spa position so lack empathy for these jobs May lack an innate inclination toward the holistic 'right-brain' thinking that permeates the spa world

Table 13.3: Spa managers/directors require a huge mix of both hard and soft skills (GSWS, 2012: 16)

Soft Skills	Mixed	Hard Sills
Passion for spa lifestyle Leadership Communications and interpersonal skills Cultural sensitivity Teamwork Dedication and hard work Confidence and self-esteem Flexibility and adaptability Understanding/awareness of spa modalities	Customer service and guest relations Strategic planning and thinking Problem solving PR and promotion	Management (financial, revenue, ops., facilities, etc.) Sales /Marketing / Retail Safety and Hygiene Legal and regulatory compliance IT skills Setting service sta ndards Program setting Foreign languages Training/experience in spa modalities

Measuring effectiveness and impact

It is important that organisations measure the impact of their investment. Training and development departments need to justify the costs of training if they are to compete with other investment demands within an organisation, and to demonstrate that investment in training and development is a business tool that can provide a return on investment (ROI). ROI is a form of cost-benefit analysis that measures the cost of investment verses the financial return on that investment. Measuring the ROI on training and development is complex. The lack of a structured approach and a learning strategy linked to business objectives will limit the importance of training and development and reduce training to a tick box exercise rather than a business improvement activity.

For any ROI measure to be meaningful it must include a description of all components of costs and benefits and how the values of these components are derived. Identifying what needs to be measured and ensuring the defined measures meet organisational priorities, are relevant and prioritised. There are no standard rules for calculating ROI so the selection of ROI costs and benefits are subjective and the results prone to scrutiny. It is crucial that all stakeholders are confident in the methodology and tools to be used to calculate ROI, and are clear about what is being measured and how the results will be communicated. When organisations are satisfied with the measurement tools they are more likely to have confidence in the results and justify the investment.

The Kirkpatrick (2006) model of training evaluation was first published in 1959 and is still widely used in many organisations. The model was updated in 1975 and 1994 when he published his best known work *Evaluating Training Programs*. Kirkpatrick's model has four levels of evaluation:

1 **Reaction.** Measuring the reaction of participants at the end of a training event. This is usually in the form of a survey.

2 **Learning**. Measuring the skills and knowledge gained by participants in pre-training and post-training tests

3 **Behaviour**. Measuring the application of skills and knowledge gained in training three months after the training event.

4 **Results**. Measuring the outcomes of training in terms of organisational objectives.

The Phillips (1991) model builds on the Kirkpatrick model adding ROI as a fifth level of evaluation. In order to measure the benefits of training against the cost the organisation needs to calculate the financial value of the training. For example, what financial value can be associated with improved customer satisfaction? It is important to consider both tangible and intangible benefits; the tangible benefits of increased sales are easier to quantify but the intangible benefits of increased job satisfaction are subjective and harder to evidence.

Once an organisation has measures for the direct and indirect costs of training they can calculate the ROI as follows:

ROI = (Financial benefit from training – total cost of training) / (Total cost of training) × 100%

One critic of the Kirkpatrick and Philips' evaluation model is Brinkerhoff (2005). Brinkerhoff's 'Success Case Method' suggests that the impact of a small number of successes normally justifies the investment of training and produces a positive return on investment. He argues that improved performance cannot be attributed to training alone. He suggests that some people will apply their learning and improve performance whilst some will not. Others will use some of their learning but there will not be a noticeable impact in performance. Brinkerhoff recommends that the evaluation of training should identify the differences between those applying learning and those who are not, rather than an evaluation of the training event. This approach would provide a focus on how effectively the organisation uses learning.

The four-stage CIRO (Context, Input, Reaction, Output) Model of Evaluation developed by Warr, Bird and Rackham (1970) is also a widely used training evaluation model. The model considers:

1 **Context**. Obtaining baseline information about the current situation to determine training needs and setting objectives.

2 **Input**. Evaluation of the design and delivery of the learning activity

3 **Reaction**. Evaluation of the training experience

4 **Outcome**. Evaluation of the effectiveness of the training

The Outcome stage of the CIRO model has three stages of evaluation which are similar to Kirkpatrick's second, third and fourth levels.

Kaufman *et al.* (1995) provide an alternative to Kirkpatrick's model which they suggest encourages a narrow focus on evaluating training. The core principle of Kaufman's model is based on the Kirkpatrick model with an additional fifth level evaluating the contribution an organisation makes to its clients and the good of society. It includes learning that is wider than training activities and allows organisations to evaluate interventions associated with strategic planning, organisational development, customer satisfaction, quality and societal contributions.

What these models have in common is the emphasis on the need for reliable measurement tools that provide effective evaluation in the workplace that can be shared with the relevant stakeholders. The Chartered Institute of Personal Development (CIPD) provide online practical tools for measuring the impact of training and development. A starting point for any organisation could be a comprehensive training needs analysis to identify the gaps in skills and knowledge.

The training needs analysis can be addressed at an individual or organisational level. At an individual level it should identify a gap between the individual's knowledge and the skills required to perform their current role effectively, a knowledge and skills gap that would enhance career progression, or where there is a gap in knowledge and skills to meet future objectives of the organisation. Training needs can also be concerned with individual attitudes and behaviours to improve team working, confidence and better customer service.

As an organisation they should identify the gaps between where they are now and the long term goals and provides development plans aligned to the future strategy. An organisation development needs analysis should also provide insights into succession planning and recruitment of new talent. Before an organisation begins to evaluate its training and development requirements it should consider the following questions:

1 What do we want to achieve?
2 What will success look like?
3 Is the training and development aligned to the organisation's mission, vision, goals and objectives?
4 Does it add value to the organisation by building capacity and talent?
5 Will it change people's actions in the future?
6 What evidence will be required to demonstrate impact? How will we collect it?
7 Are we measuring the right things?
8 What resources are available?

13

According to the Chartered Institute of Personal Development (2011) a forward looking training and development strategy would focus 75% effort on measuring strategic impact and less than 25% on measuring process efficiency. A strategic approach to evaluating leadership skills, innovation, gaps in talent or skills required for the future, rather than more process driven measures will help to build capacity and add value to an organisation.

Implementing training and development in a spa organisation

.A strategic approach to evaluating the leadership skills, innovation and gaps in the workforce and developing a forward looking training and development strategy will help to build capacity and develop spa managers with the right combination of skills the industry requires.

Stage 1: Getting started

When a spa organisation prepares its strategy and vision for the future it should include a workforce development strategy setting out how the organisation aspires to recruit, manage and retain an engaging and dynamic workforce who have the appropriate skills and knowledge to achieve its vision.

First, the organisation needs to establish what it wants to achieve. For the purpose of illustration, I am going to suggest four goals that can be applied to all spa businesses and will consider how the organisation can measure a return on its investment in training and development and link the impact to its business goals. The four goals are:

- Growth in revenue and profit
- Increase in productivity
- Improved customer service
- New market development

The second step is to agree what success will look like. For example, how much growth in revenue and profit is the spa required to make in order for it to meet the organisation's expectations. What does increased productivity look like? Does the organisation want to improve customer service feedback or will it focus on repeat business? What markets does the spa want to develop and will this require new products? These outcomes need to be agreed so everyone in the organisation knows what it wants to achieve.

Once an organisation is clear on what the strategic priorities are and what success will look like, it can align its workforce plan with its organisation strategy and consider the training and development needs.

This is where I will link the outcomes of the GSWS report with the goals I have identified for this illustration to establish the strategic HR drivers for a spa business. The strategic HR goals for a spa business may include:

- Creating innovative capacity within the organisation;
- Skills development that adds value;
- Improved productivity levels;
- Improved customer service levels.

Stage 2: What is being measured

Identifying what is being measured is crucial to the success of this process because the organisation cannot evaluate the impact of the training and development interventions without quantifiable data. The CIPD suggests three types of measures in their online practical tool: efficiency, effectiveness and impact.

Efficiency measures allow an organisation to ensure they are operating cost effectively. For a spa to achieve its goals these measures may include:

- Reduced staff absenteeism rates;
- Number of vacant positions filled;
- Improved staff turnover and retention rates;
- Improved qualification levels in the workforce;
- Increased training spend per employee.

Effectiveness measures reflect the outcome of training and development interventions. For a spa these may include measuring:

- Differences in performance between internal and external recruits;
- Strength of brand as an employer/ease of recruiting;
- Development of management skills in the workforce;
- Development of key skills and knowledge for current and future business priorities;
- Opportunities to share knowledge;
- Differences in staff engagement and motivation.

Impact measures the focus on the value of training and development to the organisation and demonstrates how the strategic HR drivers contribute to the achievement of the organisation's strategic goals. The department or person responsible for training and development within the spa needs to align the strategic HR measures with training and development initiatives and evaluate the impact of the initiatives in achieving the goals.

Stage 3: Measurement tools

There are a range of measurement tools that will provide an analysis of the impact of training and development. For example, if we consider the efficiency and effective measures for our spa outlined above, we would need to identify where in the organisation this information is held and what tools are used.

13

Efficiency measures	Examples of measurement tools	Commentary
Reduced staff absenteeism rates	The Bradford Factor	The Bradford Factor is a system used to calculate a score for each employee's absence. The higher the score, the more disruption the employee's absence is to the organisation. Bradford scores are a way of identifying individuals with serious absence and patterns of absence worthy of further investigation. The Bradford Factor is a simple formula that allows organisations to apply a relative weighting to employee unplanned absences (sickness, doctor's appointments, emergency childcare, etc). The Bradford Factor supports the principal that repeat absences have a greater operational impact than long term sickness.
Number of vacant positions filled	Recruitment/ vacancy monitoring spreadsheet	There are some key recruitment measures that spa organisations should monitor: how long it takes to recruit to key positions; what are the channels that attract the best candidates; how much does it cost to recruit; what is the retention rate; the number of vacancies the organisation has vs the number of vacancies that have been filled recently; the acceptance ratio. The information can be recorded on a simple spreadsheet and reviewed at regular intervals to measure the metrics.
Improved staff turnover and retention rates	Exit interviews and surveys	The organisation needs to decide what its optimum level of staff turnover is and benchmark this with similar spa organisations to decide whether it is acceptable, too high or too low. Exit interviews and surveys are good tools that can provide valuable information on why people are leaving and what changes would have encouraged them to stay.
Improved qualification levels in the workforce	Job evaluation Recruitment/ vacancy monitoring spreadsheet	Job evaluation is a systematic and objective process used by organisations to determine the relative value or worth of each job. The focus is on evaluating the job and not the people that perform the job. Criteria used in job evaluations can include factors such as education qualifications, skills needed, working conditions and job responsibilities. A well-qualified workforce is flexible, motivated, up-to-date and more able to respond to change. Accredited qualifications provide external validation for the quality of the spa's workforce.
Increased training spend per employee	Training-cost-per-employee spreadsheet	Most spa businesses are not investing in training and development activities for their managers (GSWS, 2012). Spa businesses tend to invest in training in areas such as product knowledge, retailing and health and safety but do not invest in development of their employees. This lack of investment in development means that therapist wanting to progress into a management position typically receives little or no support. Tracking the training-cost-per-employee helps determine the investment in training at an individual level and can identify when a well-trained therapist is ready for the development stage of her career.

Effectiveness measures	Examples of measurement tools	Commentary
Differences in performance between internal and external recruits	Monitoring of individuals against key business performance indicators	The GSWS identify a number of pros and cons for recruiting spa managers either externally or internally. (See Table 13.2.) Reviewing the difference in performance between internal and external recruits using key performance indicators will help the spa organisation identify skills gap to inform training and development programmes and help to establish career pathways for talented staff progress into management.
Strength of brand as an employer/ ease of recruiting	Recruitment/ vacancy monitoring spreadsheet	The spa industry is competing with many other service sector industries for talented people. Persuading young people to select a career in the spa industry is difficult to sell because the industry has a reputation for long unsocial hours, physically demanding work, poor rewards, poor training and no clear career pathways. Having a training and development strategy will enhance a spa organisation's reputation as an employer According to Lockhart-Meyer (n.d.), the salon marketing and business specialists, a strong brand and reputation attracts talent. A spa organisation that offers training and development and a clear career pathway is an attractive benefit to ambitious people and will help spa organisations attract the best recruits.
Development of management skills in the workforce	Skills gap analysis	The GSWS research identified the key job responsibilities and skills of a spa manager/director identified in Table 13.3. The spa industry leaders (GSWS, 2012) identified six top skills deficiencies among spa managers/directors: business savvy/management skills; strategic thinking; leadership; IT skills; communications and interpersonal skills; flexibility/adaptability. A skills gap analysis will allow the spa organisation to systematically review the skills held by their potential managers and compare them to the skills required to carry out their new role.
Development of priority skills and knowledge for current and future business priorities	Training needs analysis	The next step to consider is whether the spa organisation has the talent, innovation, skills and knowledge required to achieve its goals and how can training and development contribute. This process identifies the training and development needs of people so that they can carry out their job effectively and efficiently and also to continue to grow and develop their careers. This involves an analysis of job roles to include the skills and knowledge required for future business priorities.
Opportunities to share knowledge	Knowledge sharing platforms	The GSWS recommend that spa organisations provide employees with access to information about the organisation's knowledge base, operations, performance and other information tools and also have platforms through which they can communicate and share information.

13

Differences in staff engagement with the organisation	Staff engagement surveys	Staff engagement is important to the spa business because the service delivery to customers is fundamentally about the human interaction and the power of the human touch. The workforce is a spa's greatest asset and critical to its success. Therefore the aims of the spa business cannot be achieved without its workforce. Staff engagement surveys measure a lot more than whether employees are happy or their levels of satisfaction. The hierarchical reporting lets managers drill down into the data allowing them to compare departments, regions and teams. They can quickly identify where there is high or low engagement.

Stage 4: Baseline data

The next step is to collect the baseline data from within the spa organisation. If the data is not available then you will need to collect it before you implement your training initiatives using the measurement tools identified above. This will give you a baseline to compare the effectiveness of any training and development.

Stage 5: Learning opportunities

There are two ways of providing formal qualifications to the spa workforce: before they enter the industry though colleges and universities, or training programmes whilst in work. There are approximately 64 spa management-related degree programmes and 41 providers of spa management continuing education around the world (GSWS, 2012). There are also numerous colleges offering skills-based qualifications at the therapist level.

Most spa organisations believe that on-the-job learning and mentoring are the most important ways for spa managers to gain skills. However, spa businesses are not investing sufficient resources and effort into training and development with most training taking place when someone joins the organisation. Structured opportunities for informal learning can be effective but need to extend beyond an occasional offering to a coordinated and proactive approach to talent, leadership and human resource development.

The GSWS suggest that continuing education, mentoring, professional development pathways and succession planning are critical for all levels of spa employees. They recommend a mix of both formal and informal learning that allows employees to share knowledge with each other and to bring new knowledge into the organisation.

A mix of both formal and informal learning training and development initiatives are included in Table 13.4.

Table 13.4: Impact measures

Strategic HR drivers	Training and Development initiatives	Information required to evaluate the impact	Measures to develop organisational insights
Creating innovation capacity to develop new products, new services, new processes and new ways of doing business	Develop an internship programme and graduate training scheme to attract new talent. Identify management competencies required and provide management training Establish career pathways Skills gap analysis Establish a mentoring and work shadowing programme to share knowledge	Individual's performance data against key business performance indicators Improvements in recruitment/vacancy data Reduction in the skills gap Evaluation measurements for training and development Evaluation measurements for training and development to include new initiatives	Differences in performance between internal and external recruits Number of vacant positions filled Strength of brand as an employer/ ease of recruiting Development of management skills in the workforce New market development Growth in revenue and profit
Skills development that add value	Develop knowledge sharing platforms Establish a mentoring and work shadowing programme to share knowledge Training Needs Analysis is mapped to a learning and development strategy	Evaluation measurements for training and development Data on usage of knowledge sharing platforms Exit interviews and surveys The Bradford Factor data Improvements in job evaluation data Increase in training-cost-per-employee data	Development of priority skills and knowledge for current and future business priorities Opportunities to share knowledge Improved staff turnover and retention rates Reduced staff absenteeism rates Improved qualification levels in the workforce Increased training spend per employee
Increase productivity levels	Develop knowledge sharing platforms Establish a mentoring and work shadowing programme to share knowledge	Evaluation measurements for training and development Data on knowledge sharing platforms usage Improvement in staff engagement survey data Productivity KPIs at business unit level	Development of priority skills and knowledge for current and future business priorities Opportunities to share knowledge Differences in staff engagement with the organisation Increase in productivity
Improve customer service levels	On-the-job training programme	Evaluation measurements for training and development Improvement in staff engagement survey data Customer feedback data	Development of key skills and knowledge for current/ future business priorities Opportunities to share knowledge Improved customer service

13

Stage 6: Evaluation of data

Evaluating the impact of training and development extends beyond the course evaluation forms or 'happy sheets' that check how highly the learner rates the training and whether the conditions for learning were appropriate. Evaluating the impact of training is about measuring the effectiveness of training. Questionnaires can be effective if well designed, but focus groups and semi-structured interviews can be more effective. However, in order to measure the effectiveness of training, assessments or witness statements provide an objective view, as these will provide evidence of how the learner is implementing and using their new skills and knowledge, and how the training and development is meeting business objectives. Whilst this can be time consuming it is valuable information if you want to know that your training and development activities are improving the spa's performance.

Table 13.4 provides an example of how to map the strategic HR objectives developed earlier in this illustration with the training and development initiatives that will help to achieve the objective. The information required to evaluate the impact is drawn from the measurement tools identified at implementation stage 3. The measures and metrics are drawn from the efficiency and effectiveness measures identified at implementation stage 2. These will also allow you to demonstrate how the strategic HR drivers have direct impact on the spa organisation's ability to meet its strategic aims, identified at implementation stage 1.

Stage 7: Communicating impact

Once you have completed your evaluation, how do you communicate your success and encourage your spa organisation to invest in further training and development initiatives? Communicating the results of training and development needs to be in the form that is easily accessible, for managers and trainers to take ownership of the findings. The results have impact if there is buy-in at all levels of the organisation, so a communication strategy needs to be developed to target a number of stakeholders. The communications will vary according to the audience and address the key messages and at the time relevant to them. The messages need to be clear and concise to provide the information they require to make decisions. They should create a picture and tell a story that illustrates what has been achieved. They should be goal orientated with a specific outcome in mind, for example further investment in the training and development budget, and should be of sufficient interest that your audience wants to know more. The key messages should be about how training and development initiatives have had a positive impact on business performance and has helped to resolve some of the important issues facing your spa organisation. This can only be achieved if the data collection processes are transparent and the outcomes reliable and valid. Success is judged by how much the evaluation and findings are used and lead to business improvements

Conclusion

The GSWS report (2012) highlights the importance of investing in human resource development activities to address the spa management skills gap. Investment in human resource development creates opportunities for individuals to bring new knowledge to their job role and develops a culture of continuous learning, innovation and intellectual growth in an organisation. The spa industry is beginning to recognise the added value of a learning culture and sees well trained individuals as assets to their organisation. The GSWS recommend spa businesses clearly define and prioritise the management and leadership skills they require and align them with organisation's overall business strategy. They also recommend active engagement with colleges and universities to find new talent and provide internship and work placement opportunities so students can gain knowledge and experience of the industry. Spa organisations need to encourage, capture, use and grow learning for its own benefit.

Case study

Introduction

Mosaic Spas and Health Clubs (MSHC) operate over 30 facilities across the UK and employ over 350 staff. Their portfolio has grown from one spa in 2007 to 18 spas in 2016, including Imagine Spas, which are located throughout the UK in a variety of settings. Their spa ethos of 'time not treatments' is based on the length of time booked with the therapist and not the treatment. The therapists are trained not only to give great treatments but to help the guest choose the most appropriate treatment; and to ensure that each treatment is tailor made to the outcome the guest seeks. MSHC believe that their product is the people they employ. Investment in training is important to MSHC. They believe in investing in their employees, who have grown with the business, and their core value is to attract the best people and promote from within the organisation. They offer well planned career pathways and opportunities for promotion using formal and informal training methods. The age old argument of what happens if you train staff and they leave isn't one that concerns them. They are more concerned about what happens if you don't train staff and they stay.

Mosaic Spa and Health Clubs' career pathway for therapists

MSHC have a four stage career path for their therapists.

At the induction stage the focus is to ensure the consistency of the treatments as well as an understanding of the core values of the business, policies, procedures and systems used in the spa. The induction training supports the business ethos that all the therapists must be able to do all of the treatments all of the time to a high standard. As the business

13

grows this can be a challenge with new therapists starting all the time. The solution is an online training programme that breaks down all the core components of all treatments and provides online video demonstrations of the treatment being delivered. The therapists can download materials and learn the treatments to the required standard.

A Bronze, Silver and Gold therapist programme was shaped by MSHC spa managers, who have ownership of the programme and its implementation across the spas. There is an expectation that a therapist will complete the Bronze award within their first 12 months with the company.

The Bronze therapist award requires the therapist to demonstrate a good knowledge of the core values of the organisation and all the treatments offered. This is assessed through a series of online questions. The therapist is also assessed on a pre-treatment consultation and the treatment they perform on a mystery customer, usually from the product company. The pass mark is 85%, and 95% of therapists pass first time.

The Silver therapist award requires the therapist to demonstrate a good knowledge of spa products and to be able to recommend products for particular treatments or required outcomes stated by the customer. The therapist is also assessed on a pre-treatment consultation and the performance of a different treatment to the one performed to achieve their Bronze award. The therapist is also required to demonstrate a set level of retailing performance, averaged over a three month period and revenue generation per week.

The Gold therapist award requires the therapist to demonstrate higher revenue performance targets than those at the Silver award stage. Achievement of the Gold award results in a guaranteed pay increase.

Mosaic Spa and Health Clubs' Development Programme

The Mosaic Spa Academy was launched to provide training and development to support those staff interested in moving into management level positions. The proactive approach to developing a management career pathway has directly supported the expansion plans of the company by training their own spa managers with the skills set and commerciality required to manage a new business or turn around the prospects of a failing business. MSHC regional managers identify talented people in the organisation who demonstrate the company core values, and the business acumen to succeed in a management role. The Mosaic Spa Academy provides training in management supervision, human resource management, finance and revenue management, sales and marketing and key performance indicators. The Academy provides a formal learning situation and an opportunity for staff to share their experiences and learn from each other.

MSHC have seen a positive effect of investment in management training on their staff. The staff have developed their own learning culture to continually improve their performance. For example, they have formed informal groups to share ideas, developed a mystery shopping system to provide feedback to other managers, and they tend to be more reflective, productive and efficient.

MSHC support the transfer of knowledge back into the workplace through their regional managers. Fortnightly meetings with regional managers allow spa managers to discuss new ideas and to implement their learning in new contexts in a supported way. MSHC also provide mentors to support staff with a development need. Mentees are matched with a mentor with strengths in the area where skills gaps have been identified.

Return on Investment in training

MSHC measure the direct benefits of their training and development through their operating revenues and customer feedback. They can measure a direct correlation between the operating revenues of a spa and the number of Bronze, Silver and Gold therapists operating in the spa. They also use indirect benefits to the measure the impact of their training. MSHC have a high employee retention rate of 72%, low absenteeism rates and good employee engagement and satisfaction results.

MSHC are confident that their training programme provides them with the quality team they need to move their business forward.

References

Amah, E and Ahiauzu, A (2013), Employee involvement and organizational effectiveness, *Journal of Management Development*, **32** (7) 661-674

Ankli, R. E. and Palliam, R. (2012) Enabling a motivated workforce: Exploring the sources of motivation. *Development and Learning Organisations* **26** (2) 7-10

Bassi, L., Ludwig, J., McMurrer, D.P. and Van Buren, M. (2000) Profiting from learning: Do firms' investment in training pay off? Research White Paper, American Society for Training and Development. In *Handbook for Workplace Learning* (2010) Malloch, M. Cairns, L. Evans, K. available at: www.astd.org (Accessed Jun 15 2015)

Brinkerhoff, R. O. (2005) The Success Case Method: A strategic evaluation approach to increasing the value and effect of training. *Advances in Developing Human Resources.* **7**(1)

Casillas, J.C, Acedo F. J. and Barbero J.L. (2010) Learning, unlearning and internationalisation: Evidence from the pre-export phase *International Journal of Information* **30**(2) 162-173.

Chartered Institute of Personal Development (2011) Shaping the Future: Using HR metrics for maximum impact. *A CIPD online practical tool.* www.**cipd**.co.uk/.../using-hr-metrics-for-maximum-**impact**_2011.pdf (Accessed Jun 15 2015)

Eurat, M. (2011) Informal learning in the workplace: evidence on the real value of work-based learning (WBL). *Development and Learning Organisation. An International Journal.* **25** (5) 8-12

GSWS(2012) Spa Management Workforce and Education: Addressing the Market Gaps Accessed 09.01.16, from http://www.globalspaandwellnesssummit.org/images/stories/pdf/gsws.2012.research.spa.management.workforce.education.revised.june.2012.pdf

Halm, B. J. (2011) A Workforce Design Model: providing energy to organisations in transition. *International Journal of Training and Development.* **15** (1) 3-19

Jennings, C. (2013), The 70:20:10 Framework explained, www.702010forum.com (Accessed Jun 15 2015)

Kaufman, R., Keller, J. and Watkins, R. (1995). What works and what doesn't: Evaluation beyond Kirkpatrick. *Performance and Instruction,* **35**(2) 8-12. http://home.gwu.edu/~rwatkins/articles/whatwork.PDF (Accessed Jun 15 2015)

Kirkpatrick, D.L. and Kirkpatrick, J.D. (2006). *Evaluating Training Programs* 3rd edition Berrett-Koehler.

Kolb, D.A. (1984). *Experiential learning: Experience as the source of learning and development.* Englewood Cliffs, NJ: Prentice-Hall.

Lockhart–Meyer (n.d.) www.lockhart-meyer.co.uk/how-to-recruit-the-best-salon-team-for-less/ (Accessed Jan 16 2016)

Longenecker, C. O. (2011) How the BEST motivate workers. *Industrial Management.* **53**(1) 8-13

Phillips, J. J. (1991). *Handbook of Training Evaluation and Measurement Methods* (2nd ed.). Boston: Butterworth-Heinemann.

Sonal Uberoi, Director of Spa Business Consulting, http://www.spaopportunities.com (Accessed Jun 15 2015)

Warr, P., Bird, M.W. and Rackham, N. (1970) Evaluation of management training, In *Kirkpatrick and Beyond: A review of models of training evaluation.* Tamil, P. Yarnall, J. and Kerrin, M. Institute of Employment Studies (2002) Report 392

14 Strategic Management in the Spa Industry

Tim Heap and Angela Anthonisz

Introduction

The spa industry globally has entered a more mature growth phase in which increasing competition and economic uncertainty in many countries present managers with a number of external environmental challenges. The spa business is, by definition, a very operations based industry and almost entirely focussed upon service encounters. This means that the time required to respond to dynamic market forces presents managers with dilemmas; not the least of which is developing their own skill set whilst continuing to provide service excellence. Quite simply, thinking strategically within a results driven service business environment is difficult.

The chapter, therefore, considers the implications for spa businesses of the skills gaps that can arise (at management level) from the traditional target driven strategies that are associated with customer throughput. Is it possible to manage a spa from a strategic perspective at the operational level? One of the main issues in addressing the problems of developing strong management responses, is the lack of clearly defined strategic parameters from the industry perspective. There are many generic business strategy models, paradigms and philosophies, but what is important is how to apply philosophy and theoretically constructed models into live business operations. The process is particularly challenging in an industry that continues to utilise traditional theories and approaches to management that are, perhaps dated and based upon models that were developed in areas such as manufacturing and economics.

We present the view that in today's turbulent business environment, managers need to do more than 'roll out' a plan they have used before, or just focus on what might give them some type of short term competitive advantage. We also consider the limitations to strategy that may be linked to the size and scale of the spa operation and the extent to which it may be integrated within another business (brand) that supersedes the requirement for individual spa strategies.

Strategy is often considered to be a complex process and in academic terms the models and theories have perhaps reflected that sense of complexity as a pre-requisite for effective strategic thinking. Current thinking, however provides a more pragmatic approach to strategy, with scenario planning based upon a set of metrics that enable service sector businesses to adapt to changes quickly and more efficiently. In other words, decision making is simpler and this needs to be reflected in the recruitment of managers that are able to accept the speed of change and to make change happen.

In order to provide a clear framework for the reader, discussions revolve around a commonly cited academic model by Johnson *et al.* (2013) which considers strategy to be present at three levels within the organisation. Each level of strategy reflects the level of management within the organisation and subsequently presents the manager with a different set of tasks and responsibilities that will ultimately inform on the success of the business. This model has also been used as a foundation for the development of the typology of spas created in Chapter 2 of this book. The typology has been built around the size and scale of the spa business, and subsequently the discussions on strategic management follow that rubric.

The spa business environment

The business environment in which a spa operates can be used to define the potential criteria for success or failure of the business. The interpretation of the environmental data and the scenarios that are then presented, often set the strategic directions for the company. The turbulent nature of today's external environment is being driven by a globalisation agenda that is even more difficult to predict, especially as it is set alongside the neoliberal agenda that is at odds with that globalisation. Today a business leader is president of the largest economy in the world, the British have rejected the European Union's moves towards federalism and the growth of extremism restricts the flow of capital necessary for investment in the service sector. These are just three reasons why the fundamentals of strategic planning are even more important today in the spa industry.

Future success can depend on such diverse aspects as national and/or local market conditions, level of government support for the leisure industry, pace of change and cost of setting up and/or maintaining the business operations. These trading conditions may vary geographically within a country, region or location.

As with all other sectors of the leisure industry, spas now operate in an extremely competitive and dynamic business environment. The extent to which managers are able to anticipate and deal with change, including new entrants to the market, can often determine the level of success for the new spa entrants, who are often encouraged by favourable environmental conditions, which can often be manifest in the success of the existing spa provision.

In the more traditional sense, spa facilities were developed as attractions that made up part of a destinations' tourism offering, or added to existing hotel amenities as a means of attracting guests and providing a point of differentiation from the competition. In this context the spa was a means of adding value to the customer or tourist experience and so long as the outcome was an increase in visitor numbers or occupancy, the spa may only have been expected to break even. However, as exponential growth of the spa industry in recent years has completely changed the competitive landscape in which they operate, it is no longer sufficient to just add value to the consumer experience. Madangolu and Brezina (2008) point out that spas have transformed from use as a marketing vehicle to becoming independent profit centres, particularly where they are developed as part of a resort or hotel facility. Spas are big business, whether they operate as small SMEs, independent chains or as 'add ons' to the existing operations of resorts and luxury hotels and within a global spa market forecast to grow at a CAGR of 8.7% between 2016 and 2020 (Research and Markets, 2016). The emphasis placed on how spas are managed will increasingly be called into question by owners and investors who are looking for a return on their often costly investment.

Internal challenges to the spa industry

A number of more recent industry publications have observed that as the spa industry continues to grow and evolve, the need for fully trained and capable spa managers will continue to escalate more quickly than the supply of candidates (Hunter, 2012). This gap is particularly problematic when it comes to leadership that is capable of thinking strategically. Research conducted by Forbes in 2010 identified that strategic leadership does not come easily in any context, with most organisations showing that fewer than 10% of leaders exhibit strategic skills. This would indicate that as a priority the spa industry needs to develop strategic thinkers and leaders, a view confirmed by a recent article in *The Caterer* which identified that "in an extremely competitive market place there are a lot of beautiful but empty spas out there, mainly because they lack a co-ordinated strategy and plan" (Whittle, 2012). This situation was identified by Hunter (2012) whose research confirmed that the basis of the spa experience was provided by the therapists, but that the lack of experienced managers was fundamental to the poor retention levels of those therapists.

While a supply of suitable candidates for spa leadership may be an issue, it has also been identified that existing managers are failing to capitalise on their

14

business. This may be an outcome of coming from a hotel background, where short term gain and immediate wins often overshadow the need to think strategically. Many managers appear to adopt the 'copy & paste' approach to strategy rather than thinking about how they can set themselves apart from the competition and provide added value to the consumer. Research on health and fitness clubs in the UK identified that the managers of many facilities have looked at new entrants in the market (often offering limited facilities and low cost) and then fundamentally changed their strategy without fully realising the implications (Cassop-Thompson, 2014). Adopting a low cost strategy, for example, may serve only to bring in the 'wrong sort of clientele' and drive away existing clients whose motivations were based upon high price, high quality. Developing competitive advantage must support the customers' true value seeking and should be built on strategic capabilities that are difficult for the competition to duplicate and for which there are no obvious or easy substitutes.

As the spa industry continues to evolve and diversify (see Chapter 2), the need to think strategically becomes even more critical in terms of developing a competitive advantage. The move to a wellness brand, for example, is more complex than a simple name change and requires a fundamental strategic repositioning. What is true is that shiny new spa facilities are being developed everywhere and the consumer has more choice than ever. While it is expected that 5 star hotels and resorts will contain a spa, 3 and 4 star hotels are now providing spa facilities. Diversification of the industry now includes 'Integrated Health Spas' that focus on wellness and lifestyle and 'Cosmetic Medical Spas' where treatments such as chemical peels and micro-derm abrasion can be obtained. The 'Beyond Spa' concept at Harvey Nichols is a good example of how a cosmetic spa can be introduced into a business as a self-contained unit (Favaro, 2015).

Strategic management

As identified, for the spa manager the need to develop a suitable strategy for the business has never been more important. As the industry enters a more mature growth phase, increasing levels of specialisation and differentiation are required in order to stand out from the crowd and meet with increasingly diverse customer expectations. Developing a suitable strategy is not without its challenges and, as Evans (2015) highlights, many managers are hindered by short-termism, concentrating on the most pressing tasks, rather than looking ahead and taking a more holistic, long term view of the business. While this is understandable, based on the spa business environment mentioned earlier and the pressure of meeting both consumer and investor expectations, it is not necessarily the best way to manage.

As a starting point, it is perhaps worth considering what is meant by the term strategy, particularly given that individuals often have different views on what the concept includes and the number of terms that are used interchangeably in the academic literature. As highlighted in a recent article in the *Harvard Business*

Review there are important distinctions to be made between strategy, its implementation and its execution, that can be helpful in running a successful business, but in practice these distinctions can be blurred, incorrect or ignored, which creates poor decision making and limited action at all levels of the business (Favaro, 2015).

This chapter has adopted a similar view to Favaro (2015) and Johnson *et al.*, (2013) and considers strategy from two perspectives: t. The strategy that exists at the operational unit level (the independent day spa) and the strategy that is created at corporate level (the spa chain or the hotel chain in which the spa operates).

Strategy at the operational, single unit level relies on the strong leadership of the manager, or owner of the business and should focus on how the business can differentiate itself from the competition. Based on the characteristics of the single unit identified in Chapter 2, this process should involve asking a number of key questions. Who are our target market(s)? What should our value proposition be? What capabilities do we need to deliver that value proposition to the customer? (Adapted from Favaro, 2015). These decisions can be quite straightforward when it comes to operating a single unit or business and it is likely that the manager will be able to identify the answers fairly quickly. However, the operational aspects of the business can often overshadow the need to think a little more long term and subsequently the business focus may be lost.

Strategy at corporate level is a more complex process in which CEOs and senior executives consider the overall purpose and scope of the business (Johnson *et al.*, 2013) and is usually defined by the brand. Strategy at this level is focused on the capabilities that distinguish the company from its competition and what comparative advantage can be used to add value within its SBUs (strategic business units). The availability of resources at this level of strategy is less likely to be an obstacle to the introduction of new products and services and as such the strategy developed at corporate level is often used to frame and guide the decisions taken by managers responsible for the various functions of the business. The spa manager in this instance is responsible for implementing the decisions of others in addition to making decisions about how his/her own business unit should operate successfully.

Overall strategy is likely to be the outcome of a number of factors which are determined by the spa manager to be important in terms of developing the business, and is likely to be based on a common set of variables such as level of competition, location, resources, size and scope of the operation etc. According to Johnson *et al.*, (2013) the decisions taken to inform the choice of strategy will vary at every level within the business and will vary in terms of focus, complexity, time horizon and level of uncertainty (See Figure 14.1)

14

Figure 14.1: The three levels of organisational strategy. Adapted from Johnson *et al.* (2013)

The three levels of strategy shown in Figure 14.1 consider the implications this has for strategic decision making in terms of a common set of characteristics which involve:

- The **long term** direction of the organisation
- The **scope** of an organisation;s activities
- Developing competitive **advantage**
- Managing **change** in the business environment
- Building on what you do best (**capabilities**)
- Balancing the **values and expectations** of stakeholders

Considering strategy in this more traditional way can be a useful starting point for thinking about how strategy is integrated within a business. It does provide a clear set of boundaries and levels within the organisation that help us to understand the types of decision that can be made and what the implications of these decisions are.

If we consider the application of the model in Figure 14.1 to the management of a spa then we need to consider the type of spa and the extent to which the spa manager has control over the strategic decision making process.

For example, in a small independent day spa the owner will generally determine the strategy of the business and will be responsible for making all decisions pertaining to aspects such as staffing, marketing, investment etc. The model of strategic decision making would therefore lack the definition identified by Johnson *et al.* (2013) as the need for a corporate strategy is unnecessary (see Figure 14.2). Subsequently the need to implement strategy at middle management level is no longer required and as such the management approach is likely to be characterised by focusing on more short term aspects of the business and the challenges that arise on a day to day basis. The larger single unit operation such as the Golden Door Spa and Resort, identified in Chapter 2 is likely to have a more balanced approach to strategy in that it is large enough and diversified enough to have an international appeal. While this does not imply a need to think at corporate level, there are definite elements of more formal business planning that would be required in order to plan and manage the business. Elements such as finance and marketing would become more distinct areas that require the creation of a business hierarchy, albeit a fairly flat hierarchy.

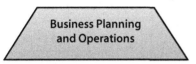

Running the business
Involves numerous short and medium term tasks linked to staffing, finance and marketing but emphasis would be on day to day operations

Fig 14.2: – Strategy in a day spa operation

This may be positive in that decision making may be faster and knowledge of the local area could aid in marketing decisions and developing positive relationships with the client base. However, the owner would still need to have a clear business plan and be able to develop effective systems for running the spa on a daily basis.

The bulk of the spa industry in many locations around the world, particularly in developing countries, is made up of spas that operate as part of a much larger organisation such as a hotel or resort, which may in turn be part of a larger chain operating on an international basis. In this instance the levels of the organisation highlighted in Figure 14.1 would definitely be present, with the implication being that the spa manager, as a departmental head or senior manager would need to be involved with strategic decision making at a higher level. Decisions would be much more orientated towards securing the long term competitive advantage of the total operation rather than just considering the day to day operations of the spa. Spa processes and procedures therefore need to be thought of as part of a system in which they can be managed at a strategic unit level and at a functional level. The systems thinking body of knowledge recognises that organisations can only be efficient and effective if they are able to develop as units that are integrated either within their own value system of buyers and suppliers, or they can effectively contribute to the cohesion of a whole organisation (Senge, 2014).

The manager of a spa in this instance is likely to be confronted with numerous challenges when it comes to making strategic decisions. As highlighted earlier, strategy within larger operations is developed at corporate level and as such the spa will often be a function of a larger operation. The spa manager will therefore need to consider strategy from a number of perspectives. This includes the need to think outside of their own operation to consider the synergies that could be developed with other functions such as food and beverage, health and fitness, marketing and finance. The spa manager will need to consider how corporate strategy can be implemented within their department and will need to develop a strategy that allows the unit to perform in terms of meeting not only customer, but also corporate, expectations and justify revenue spent in terms of maintaining or developing the spa in terms of the competition. The implications of this are represented below in Figure 14.3.

14

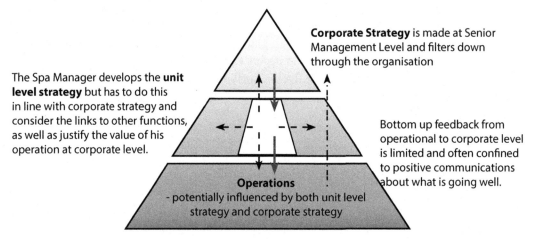

The Spa Manager develops the **unit level strategy** but has to do this in line with corporate strategy and consider the links to other functions, as well as justify the value of his operation at corporate level.

Corporate Strategy is made at Senior Management Level and filters down through the organisation

Bottom up feedback from operational to corporate level is limited and often confined to positive communications about what is going well.

Operations
- potentially influenced by both unit level strategy and corporate strategy

Fig. 14.3: Strategy in an international spa operation. Adapted from Johnson *et al.*, (2013)

As shown in Figure 14.3, the challenges for the spa manager in terms of developing an effective strategy become rather more complex and the fact that the spa exists within a much larger operation creates serious implications for the creation of a disconnect between corporate and unit level thinking and between unit level thinking and operations. Effective strategy is often reliant on effective communications and while the size of the business creates significant resources on which to draw, the lack of synergy may mean that these are not utilised to achieve maximum impact. If you combine this situation with the fact that today's international business environment is highly competitive and unstable, then developing a strategy is anything but straightforward. Many managers however, still focus on a strategy that revolves around developing competitive advantage, and to a certain extent that competitiveness can extend to competing with the other functions within the business, rather than working with them. Today's international business environment, particularly in the emerging markets of the world, does not really allow for this approach which is more synonymous with stable environments. Grant (2016), for example, highlights that strategy has moved beyond the simple quest for competitive advantage. Strategy and strategic thinking need to embrace the need to adapt to turbulence, which requires a number of approaches including:

- Adapting to and exploiting digital technology
- The quest for flexibility and strategic innovation
- The creation of strategic alliance
- The demand for social and environmental responsibility (Grant, 2016: 15)

The typology of spas presented in Chapter 2 may be useful here in focusing on the characteristics of the business in a way that influences strategy. It is well documented in the academic literature that the larger an organisation becomes, the taller the hierarchy and the more bureaucratic the systems. The international hotel chains are no exception to this rule and as such the spa manager needs to balance the need for innovation and focus on the spa experience, with the need to operate within the system/organisation.

This requires strong leadership capable of clear strategic and perhaps innovative thinking, as response times are often short for implementing strategic change. Rath and Conchie (2008) identify this particular skill as one of the four domains of leadership. Leaders with strategic thinking strengths are supposedly those individuals who are constantly seeking new information and looking around corners, but, as we have already identified, these skills are hard to find. One of the reasons for this may be the tendency of managers to continue to utilise traditional strategies such as Porter's 5 Forces (1980) or Porter's generic strategies (1985). A recent review of the strategic literature conducted by Harrington *et al.* (2014) identified that this pattern of adopting established models of strategy has been a main reference point in tourism and hospitality for the last 40 years. The shortcomings of these approaches are increasingly being exposed in terms of their application in an increasingly diversifying and volatile environment. This view is affirmed by Navarro (2014) in a recent study of how innovation has shaped the spa industry, which points out that it is the nature of innovation within the context of spas that has contributed to the levels of competitiveness and growth that currently exist, and that the generic models of business cannot therefore be fully applied to the business environment of spas.

Bowman (2008) identifies a number of questions in terms of whether the adoption of generic strategies are just a substitute for strategic thinking and considers that these strategies are adopted because they make the job of developing strategy easier, but not necessarily effective. As a leader in the spa industry have you actually considered what influences your strategic choices? What do you really know about strategic planning? Are you utilising approaches that worked in your last company and if so, are they really applicable to your current situation? Are the strategic choices you make sufficient to cope with the competitive environment in which you operate?

Conclusion

The spa industry is at an important point of its development cycle and the emergence of academic debate surrounding the industry is adding to the discussions on the future of the industry. The demand for a more strategic approach to that future direction is industry led, as is the demand for spa sector strategies as opposed to the generic models of the past. The lack of suitably qualified spa managers and managers with the ability to think strategically is a key challenge going forward. This chapter, coupled with the earlier discussions in Chapter 2 are an attempt to provide a framework for bridging that gap and for practitioners and students to ask the above questions in order to help populate the framework. Today's spa industry is characterised by competitiveness, growth and high levels of innovation and effective strategy is not about taking a 'copy & paste' approach.

14

The industry is in danger of being led by the tourism or hospitality sector and in doing so may lose some of its identity alongside the growth of the globalisation strategies of corporations and destination management organisations.

References

Bowman, C. (2008). Generic strategies: a substitute for thinking? *The Ashridge Journal*, Spring. 1-6.

Cassop Thompson, M. (2014) Strategic Thinking, *Health Club Management* (March)

Evans, N. (2015) *Strategic Management for Tourism, Hospitality and Events*. 2nd Ed. Routledge: London

Favaro, K. (2015) Defining strategy, implementation and execution, *Harvard Business Review* Online. Available from: https://hbr.org/2015/03/defining-strategy-implementation-and-execution Accessed [21/11/2016]

Research and Markets (2016) *Global Spa Market Report 2016-2020*. Available from: http://www.researchandmarkets.com Accessed [04/09/2016]

Grant, R.M. (2016) *Contemporary Strategy Analysis: Text and Cases*. 9th Edition. John Wiley and Sons Inc: UK

Harrington, R.J. Chathoth, P.K. Ottenbacjer, M. and Altinay, L. (2014) Strategic management research in hospitality and tourism; past, present and future, *International Journal of Contemporary Hospitality Management*, **26** (5), 778-808

Hunter, G. (2012) *The causes and consequences of high value therapist turnover in day spas in the UK*. Thesis submitted in fulfilment of the Doctor of Philosophy, University of Derby.

Johnson, G. Scholes, K. and Whittington, R. (2013) *Exploring Corporate Strategy. Texts and Cases*. 7th Edition. Pearson Education Limited, England.

Madangolu, M. and Brezina, S. (2008) Resort spas: how are they massaging hotel revenues? *International Journal of Contemporary Hospitality Management* **20**(1), 60-66

Navarro, J.V. (2014) How innovation shapes the spa industry and determines its evolution. *Global Journal of Management and Business Research: Real Estate Event and Tourism Management*, 124 (2) pp. 7-22

Porter, M.E. (1980) *Competitive Strategy*, Free Press, New York.

Porter, M.E. (1985) *Competitive Advantage*, Free Press, New York, 1985.

Rath, T. and Conchie, B. (2008) *Strengths Based Leadership: Great leaders, teams and why people follow*. Gallup Press, New York

Senge, P (2014) "Systems Thinking for a Better World" at the 30th Anniversary Seminar of the Systems Analysis Laboratory "Being Better in the World of Systems" at Aalto University, 20 November. Available from http://yutub.live/watch/QDBRdFFxWjZRNS1v/peter-senge-systems-thinking-for-a-better-world-aalto-systems-forum-2014.html [Accessed 05/09/2016]

Whittle, C. (2012) Make your spa the star. Available from: https://www.thecaterer.com/articles/342206/make-your-spa-the-star [22/09/2015]

15 Future Directions

Tim Heap

Introduction

Business growth and profitability worldwide in spa continues to outstrip other areas of the service sector, with more people using spas year on year. This exponential growth has not been affected by the global economic turndown, the real and perceived threat of terrorism or the instability in the Middle East. The growth does, however, mask some of the fundamental changes that are happening within the industry and which have been introduced in the chapters of this book. These include the increase in wellness/health tourism spa brands, spa destinations that reflect the changing consumer needs, and the on-going search for qualified staff. The complexity of the product mix, and difficulty of defining the brand identity would seem to be an attempt by the industry to attain competitive advantage and get away from the heritage and history of spas. What it seems to be doing is merging tourism with hospitality, and creating the sense of an event or series of events in a chosen 'unique' location. The description of 'spa' is no longer the key selling point, but by defining the product/brand as hedonistic addresses all the features of the postmodern client. How do we define spa in 2017 and how do we identify our clients?

The current environment

This chapter considers the potential future directions of the spa industry largely through the lens of the recent growth in Dubai, a city with a reputation for luxury that is currently going through a period of exponential growth. The conclusions drawn here serve only to reaffirm many of the views presented across the chapters in this book and which are considered reflective of an industry which, according to the Global Wellness Institute, grew by 25% across Europe and Asia between 2013 and 2015, with an additional 16,000 new spa locations worldwide (now 121,595 spas) during the same time period (Global Wellness Institute, 2014).

Examples, from around the world:

- A quote from a customer at an exclusive spa in the Duoro Valley, Portugal indicates how diverse this client base has become. "A good bottle of Portuguese red, plus a day by the pool and a bit of yoga, equals my kind of spa".

- An exclusive wellness clinic in Spain describes itself as a "medi-spa destination", and brands itself as exclusive and as using "natural therapies alongside preventative and aesthetic medicine". It offers Shamadi menus that draw upon "expertise in macrobiotics and Mediterranean cuisine" and that offer a "unique Bio-Light concept in nutrition" and "gastronomic and healthy". The emphasis is on medical and wellness expertise, with "cognitive development programmes and neuro-feedback" and finally it uses products that are anti-aging and based upon "internal medicine".

- An exclusive spa in Bodrum emphasises the most important feature as being its location and "the attractiveness of the property", with the product offer being a mix of contemporary wellness experiences from the "Art Noveau to traditional Latvian pirts sauna rituals", but alongside Turkish Hammam rituals and therapies.

- A resort and spa on Lake Garda emphasises the views, natural sustainable design, wooded hillsides and that it is eco-friendly. It supplies a modern Mediterranean diet, with locally sourced products, but is not focused on losing weight. The offer is rooted in the principles of Classical Chinese Medicine, but offers "an intriguing selection of international spa modalities and complementary disciplines". These use "locally sourced herbs" and their own olive oil, grown in the region. There is no Botox, but face-lifting treatments based upon acupuncture and massage, "designed to stimulate energy points and reduce the signs of ageing". They have a large range of medically supervised complementary disciplines including naturopathy, thalassotherapy, acupuncture, moxibustion, osteopathy, physiotherapy and medical check-ups, to evaluate stress and dietary intolerance.

These exclusive spas/destinations/resorts/wellness centres seem to emphasise, the panoramic views before treatments, wellness before therapies, gastronomy before medicines, and all note the fusion of East/West or traditional/contemporary and are holistic and sustainable.

In this complex and dynamic environment, we have attempted to address a number of critical concerns that will potentially impact on the successful management of spa facilities in the future. These are best considered in terms of the following questions:

- What does the workforce look like for these evolving and fusion driven businesses, and how are they different to the majority of day spas worldwide?

- Can we consider these scenarios to reflect a view of the future or will this simply remain as a model for the 'exclusive spa'?

- Is it time to re-evaluate the strategic direction of the whole industry?

The descriptions are all gathered from the high end business sector of the spa industry, but the fact that they are re-defining product, location and consumer, and are ultimately providing brand identity for an industry in flux, would seem to reflect the strong trading position of this part of the service sector. The position is, however, not without its challenges, as exampled by a number of excerpts taken from a spa benchmark report published by Colliers (2016) for one of the top global resorts (Dubai), synonymous with luxury experiences. The report provides an example of the operational side of the spa industry today, its profitability, current growth path and changing nature of the host guest exchange.

- Capture rate of guests within hotels was up 20% from 2014;
- 70% of spa managers expected similar growth rates of 9% for 2016;
- Number of walk in guests rose to 43%;
- Staff pay increased at a quicker rate than the average costs of treatment.

The challenges

The challenges (the researchers of this book do not see them as threats) facing the spa industry in Dubai were ranked by Colliers (2016) report are shown in Figure 15.1. Each of these challenges are fully covered within one or more chapters within this book.

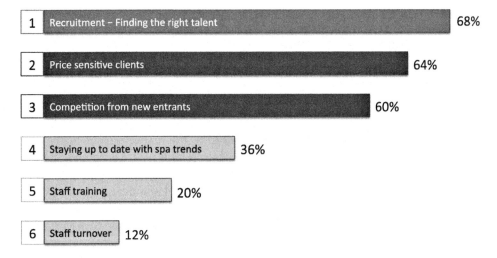

1	Recruitment – Finding the right talent	68%
2	Price sensitive clients	64%
3	Competition from new entrants	60%
4	Staying up to date with spa trends	36%
5	Staff training	20%
6	Staff turnover	12%

Figure 15.1: Top Challenges Faced in 2015

■ Recruitment of suitable staff

Recruitment of staff is a perennial problem in the industry and is fully explored in Chapter 11. The industry requires both individual spa HRM strategies, but also training and development strategies for the industry to include the professionalisation of the workforce. There is a requirement for an international framework of qualifications similar to the UK Institute of Hospitality, with both benchmarking and introduction of professional values. The examples of the first BSc. and MSc. in International Spa Management and the first ever Doctorate in Spa Management at the University of Derby are examples of internationally accepted benchmarks and professionalisation of the individual. The introduction of the Employee Experience Journey model in Chapter 11 also could provide a framework for both assessing progression and for increasing workforce retention (ranked number 6 of the Dubai challenges).

These top graded spas are now identifying suitable staff upon 'attitude' and not on the traditional rubric of experience. The individuality of the product and/or brand requires extensive training and so willingness to adapt to new challenges is more important than carrying existing 'baggage' (these are referred to later as the "can don'ts"). These organisations are likely to attract top employees which in turn means that the rest of the industry will either have to mirror the continuous training model or to settle for second best.

The spa industry also faces a further challenge as global industries continue to recruit more women within junior and senior management positions. In many countries positive discrimination and targets for numbers of women in senior positions are used as strategies for recruitment. The spa industry has traditionally been one that recruits more female than male employees (90%+ in most areas); in the future this will mean there are even fewer women willing to put up with low wages, long hours and no career pathway.

■ Price sensitive clients

This is perhaps due to the success of the industry (especially in a destination like Dubai) where the availability of product increases the bargaining power of the client. The industry in its continuous drive for competitive advantage introduces new products on a regular basis, which if successful, are then copied by competitors, refined and re-introduced to the market very quickly. With the increase in walk-in guests reaching 40%+ in Dubai there is an inevitability that price comparison will form part of buying process. To continue to attract these clients may require the development of more package deals that are price sensitive, but essentially include 'free product' within that package. This means that to ensure the revenue streams are maintained, up-selling must form an even more important part of the customer sales journey. This in turn increases the amount of time taken by therapists to deal with each client (as evidenced in the research) and therefore increases costs for the organisation. The industry has traditionally paid bonuses based upon the numbers of treatments per employee or team, but it now becomes impossible for those employees to achieve the targets in order to gain the bonuses. This is probably one of the reasons why wages per employee were seen to rise during 2015. The effect of not paying those increases by other spas will then leads to lower staff retention levels.

The spas above identify uniqueness, exclusivity and differentiation to maintain their pricing strategies, and often use a 'glocal' branding strategy to help provide that differentiation. This fusion of local and global appears in all their product offers and also is their pricing strategy which is linked to the exclusivity. In other words they are saying if you need to bargain for prices you are not likely to be one of our clients.

■ Competition from new entrants

Again this is down to the drive for growth in the service sector in Dubai (and globally), where the hotel industry has grown exponentially in recent years, a trend set to continue as the number of hotel rooms increases from 64,200 in 2014 to 91,200 by the end of 2019 (STR Global, 2015). The majority of 4 and 5 star properties, which make up about 80% of the growth, use spa facilities as a point of differentiation in this highly competitive environment.

Competition, in theory, should drive quality up and the philosophy behind Uber, the on-demand mobile service, is suggested to be the "poster child for the future economy" (Walker Smith, 2016: 383). Zeel as a company, for example, identified the growing interest in wellness, and used the increased engagement of online platforms (Spafinder, 2016) to enter the spa market. Product was then allied to the potential market of those customers looking to maintain well-being by providing increased accessibility at the right price in the right place at the right time. The success of this model is based upon access to a wider demographic, as the target includes all genders and age groups with the only dependent variable being that they all have access to the internet.

■ Keeping up with trends

Today's clients are often well-travelled, wellness aware, spa savvy consumers who demand more than just pampering. Introducing the concept of wellness (in its many guises) has perhaps been a response by the industry to the large percentage of the population who want to stay healthier longer and to increase life expectancy. We are continuously being faced by media coverage of health epidemics such as depression and obesity, which alongside declining confidence in current healthcare provision have led us to look for alternative products. The problems for the industry are that the demand for new product, required to fulfil expectations, is elastic and so phenomenal complexity theory requires an almost continuous conveyor belt of new product to satisfy the current whims of the consumer.

Added to this is that the market demographics are changing, with more men and the younger consumers entering the market. In the case of the Dubai research, the ratio has reach 60/40 female to male clients. If we add the cultural dimension in the increased demand for Muslim-focused products with, among other factors, male/female segregation, then the industry has to be in a state of continuous change.

15

The alternative answer, which was introduced in Germany as a response to the increased demand for new treatments, was embedded within the reform of the health care system in 1990 (Hurst, 1991). The reform considered increased efficiency, quality and higher individual financial contributions to the system and placed a greater emphasis on prevention and personal responsibility of the individual. This concept of avoidance of illness, as well as curative properties, led to considerable growth in what is known as the "second healthcare market" (Pforr and Locher, 2014). This includes wellness products and services such as spas as holistic therapies and products. It is still possible to be prescribed a medical cure at a registered spa town through German medical insurance companies. It must be prescribed by a doctor (confirmed by science) and the treatment should minimise or delay the development of a potential condition or treat a chronic condition (curative). Once approved the patient is sent to a certified spa for a holistic experience of exercise, nutrition, relaxation and motivation designed by the medical team. The focus is to provide a natural and relaxing environment to prevent the further development of the illness.

This means that the spa industry has a framework in which to work to re-design and create new product which in turn leads to re-branding. This structured approach does seem far removed from the walk-in demand experienced for spa products in Dubai and it would be interesting to see how far this concept would be accepted within the postmodern hedonistic environment of the wider global market.

Staff training

The continuous requirement for product development reflecting global trends, often social media-led, and ethereal short lived manifestations of existing product mean that training must be a continuous process. This increases staffing costs, but is positive in terms of staff turnover as the change of work practises are seen as relieving the boredom that can come from repetition, which in turn leads to greater customer satisfaction. Staff training and development, once seen as an expensive luxury by the industry, are now seen as essential contributors to increasing revenues and retaining client base, as outlined in Chapter 13. One of the exclusive spas mentioned earlier was prepared to provide over 5000 hours of individual training, which would assume they were getting a good return on that investment, by increasing loyalty, and providing career pathways with commensurate salaries.

Staff turnover

The process of lowering staff turnover begins with the recruitment process as outlined in Chapter 11. The industry has traditionally recruited staff based upon experience and practical skill sets. Current thinking focusses more on the concept of attitude, as this leads to employees that 'can do' and that the return on investment of training those employee is positive. Too many potential employees arrive with what I call the *can don't* attitude. These are individuals who have the ability and 'can do' the job, but for some reason 'don't' want to do the job. It may be interesting to estimate how many *can do's* and *can dont's* you have in your spas. Lowering the levels of staff turnover is, therefore, an essential financial consideration for the business as currently the percentages are higher than in other comparable service sector industry. Chapter 11 indicates ways of including a turnover strategy within an organisation, as it focusses upon interventions into the employee experience journey.

Conclusion

This chapter is not an attempt to second guess the direction the spa and wellness industry will take in the future, and it cannot predict the size, shape and mix of that industry. Rather it is an attempt to look at strengths and opportunities inherent within the industry that will enable it to continue to grow exponentially. For too many years we have lived by the concept of fearing your enemy, perhaps it is time to *ignore* your enemies. The industry is a 'can do' industry as evidenced by the exponential growth that continues to challenge individual companies as they try to keep up with the constant change necessary to maintain market share. This competition has led to a forward thinking industry with innovation and with continuous drive to provide even higher customer satisfaction levels.

It is not an industry for the faint hearted, and it does need to provide professional qualification very quickly as the move to more clinical treatments and more complex fusion products requires taking the clients along with you. They will need to be re-assured that those undertaking these treatments have the backing (recognition) of an 'official' organisation.

References

Colliers International (2016) Dubai Spa Benchmark Report, 2015 Full Year Review. Available from: http://www.colliers.com/-/media/files/emea/uae/case%20studies/2016-overview/dubai-spa-benchmark-2015-review-en.pdf?la=en-gb

Hurst, J. W. (1991). Reform of health care in Germany. *Health Care Financing Review*, **12**(3), 73–86.

Pforr, C. and Locher, C. (2014) Health tourism in the context of demographic and psychographic change, *The Business of Health Tourism Symposium*, Curtin University, Perth, 13 February

Global Wellness Institute (2014) *The Global Spa and Wellness Monitor*, SRI International, Available at http://www.globalwellnessinstitute.org/press-room/statistics-and-facts/

15

Index

4Ps
  place 119–121
  product 114–118
  promotion and price 122–124

authenticity 29, 77, 119

balneology, definition 25
balneotherapy
  definition 25
  return to popularity in Renaissance 27
bathing 23–35
  in Roman world 26
brands
  ambassadors 105
  and consumers' perceptions 115
  and products 117
  and spa's philosophy 105
  identity 115
  image 41–42
budgeting 150–152
building design
  costs and savings of sustainability 40
business environment 176–177
Buxton water 9
buyer behaviour. 69

career learning processes, typology 159
case studies
  Anantara Hotels, Resorts and Spas 44
  Banyan Tree Hotels and Resorts 44

Champneys Health Spa 10
Ishga 109–111
Mosaic Spas and Health Clubs 171–172
mother and daughter at Centre Parks spa
    71
Six Senses Hotels & Resorts 43
challenges for spa industry 187–189
Champneys Health Spa 10
changing market, as a challenge 189
characteristics of spa business 19–20
climatotherapy, definition 25
company value
  and customer perception 77
complementary and alternative medicine
    53
competition from new entrants, as a
    challenge 189
consumer decision making stages 65
consumer behaviour 60–72
  models 68–70
  principles 65–67
consumer decision model 70
consumer demand
  and service design 91–92
control systems 87–88
Costs of Goods Sold 147
customer experience 118
customer journey
  rules for success 79
customer orientation and sales 107
customer service touch-points 75

definitions of terms 24–25
demand
  continuum 63
  regional patterns 61–62
  typologies 63–64
determinants 65, 67

EarthCheck 42
eco-labels 42
eco-spas 36–48
  defined 39
effectiveness measures for training 165
efficacy of spa therapies 32–33
efficiency measures for training 165
emotional content of spa experience 78
emotional labour 78
Employee Experience Journey 136
existential authenticity concept 29

finance 146–155
forecasting 150–152

globalisation
  as an enabling force 62
Global Reporting Initiative 42
global spa therapies 3–4
global wellness economy 15–16
goods logic
  and service logic 115
Greco-Roman spas 26
Green Spa Network 42
greenwashing 42
Gross Profit 147
Gross Profit Percentage 147
guest experience 74–76
guest experiences
  designing to meet demand 92
guest journey 73–82

health demand continuum 63
health tourism 5
hedonism, definitions 50
history of spa 1–13

HR, developing strategic approach 137–143
HR management
  and competitive advantage 133–134
  role in spas 132–136
human capital
  definition 131
  forces impacting on 133
  managing 134–136
  training and development 157–174
Human Resources 130–145
hydrotherapy 2
  definition 25

innovation, key factor in spa industry
    development 21
International Medical Spa Association 42
International Spa Association 42

Kellogg's 9
key performance objectives 90
Kneipp 2, 9, 28

learning opportunities 158, 168–169
learning organisation 157
link selling, defined 103
luxury consumption 54

marketing 114–129
market segmentation 63–64
Maslow's hierarchy of needs 66
massage 3
medical evidence for efficacy of therapies
    32–33
medical tourism 5
medical wellness components 57
medicinal spas 4–5
motivators 65, 67
multi-national businesses 8–9

naturopathy 2–3
Net Profit 148
Net Revenue 147
Net Sales Revenue 147

operational planning 90
operational procedures, standardisation 93
operational strategy 88
operations management 83–98
  basic principles 95–96
organisational strategy, three levels 180
origins of spas 25–28

pampering 54
pelotherapy, definition 25
performance improvement 94
place in marketing 119–121
planning processes and performance
      objectives 90
price and demand relationship 153
price sensitivity as a challenge 188
Priessnitz 2, 28
procurement 92
product and service design 91–93
products, marketing promises 115
profit
  measuring 147–149
  maximisation 146–155
promotion and price in marketing 122–124

retailing 99–113
  and visual merchandising 108–109
  defined 103
retail layout 108
return on investment (ROI) 161
revenue management 153
Revenue Per Available Treatment Hour 154

sales
  maximising 105–109
  price and profits 148
sanatorium 2
self-care components 56
selling
  approaches 99–100
  barriers 101–102
  benefits 100–101
  training 106–107

servicescape model
  in marketing 114–115
services standards 94
spa, origin of term 24
spa business characteristics 19–20
spa industry
  diversification 178
  challenges for future 187–189
  internal challenges 177–178
  size and shape 15–17
spa markets, globally 16
spa operations
  input element 85
  output element 87
  transformation element 86
spa operations, information management
      elements 87
spa operations management
  basic principles 95–96
spa product
  diversity 17–21
  marketing 114–129
spa resorts in 18th & 19th centuries 28
spa services standards 94
  variability 117
spa towns 6–7
springs 23–35
  hot and cold 27
staff motivation, key areas 142
staff recruitment as a challenge 187
staff turnover
  as a challenge 190
  effects of 138–139
  management issues 141
  retention 139–140
  strategic responses needed 141–142
  why so high? 137–138
standardisation
  and uniqueness of experience 121
stff turnover
  measuring 135
strategic management 175–184
  developing a suitable strategy 178–180

I

strategic objectives 89–90
strategy
  in a day spa operation 181
  in an international spa operation 182
sustainability 36–48
  business benefits 41–42
  champions of the spa industry 43–45
  in spa design 39–41
  integral to spa experience 37
Swedish massage 3
systems analysis thinking perspective 84

taking the waters, definition 25
talent gap 131
thalassotherapy 3
  definition 25
thermal and mineral spas 23–35
thermal and mineral springs
  size and shape of industry 30–31
  types of establishments 29
Time Series Forecasting 152
touch-points
  for sales 103–104
  in the guest experience 74
Trading Profit and Loss Report 148–149
training 156–174
  benefit of 159–160
  evaluation model 162
  link to business goals 164
  measures of success 165–166
  measuring effectiveness 161–163
  ROI calculation 162

training and development
  evaluating impact 170
  implementing 164–171
triple bottom line 38–39
typologies of spa product 18–21
up-selling
  defined 103
  impact on profit 152

Value Added Tax (VAT)
  calculations 147
Vichy water 9
visual merchandising 108–109

water 23–35
  in purification rituals 25–26
wellness
  and mental health 51
  definitions 52
wellness and medical products
  blurred boundaries 56
wellness industry 49–59
  and levels of luxury 55–57
wellness services
  why do people choose? 50–51
wellness tourism 6–7
wellness tourists 50
  characteristics 8
work-life balance 51
workplace wellness 5

yield management 153

Printed in the United States
By Bookmasters